Merry Christmas - 1973

Lorne & Bonnie

FAST COMPANY

FAST COMPANY

THE MEN AND MACHINES OF AMERICAN AUTO RACING

Jerry Miller

Follett Publishing Company

Chicago

Acknowledgments

Special thanks are given to the following persons for their assistance and cooperation in the publication of this book:

Al Bloemker, Director of Public Relations, Indianapolis Motor Speedway Corporation; Donald Davidson, Official Historian, United States Auto Club; Lynn Justis, Photographer, National Association for Stock Car Auto Racing.

PHOTO CREDITS

All photographs by Jerry Miller with the following exceptions:
Edward E. Breen—85, 91; Bill Broderick (Union 76)—8; Robert F. Burke, Jr.—159, 277; John E. Chambers—31, 86, 143, 227, 230, 254; Daytona International Speedway—28, 29, 45, 46, 49, 114, 144, 148, 218, 259; Jeff DeWolf—58; Geoffrey S. George—33; D. Lynn Justis—276; Dick Martin—239, 282, 283; NASCAR Photo—1, 3, 41, 219, 233; Professionals In Motion, Inc.—129; Wide World Photos—178.

Manufactured in the United States of America.

First Printing

Library of Congress Catalog Card Number: 72-3520

ISBN: 0-695-80327-1 cloth

CONTENTS

Introduction

THE PICTURE is still clear: a young boy of 10 or 11 squeezed into the cockpit of the high-tailed race car, his brown hair swirling like a spinning haystack, his eyes wide open and glazed, his bony hand gripping the side of the cockpit, the wind full in his face.

Beside him sits his father, a tall sturdy man with thick yellow hair combed back in waves from the borders of his pale, firm face. His hands hold the steering wheel loosely, one hand at the 11 o'clock position, the other at 1 o'clock. The hand at 11 o'clock also holds a cigarette, a column of gray ash slowly building.

There is no sound save the rumbling thunder of the car's engine. The yellow-haired man leans slightly forward, relaxed, his eyes fixed on the road ahead. The boy, pressed against the side of the upholstered cockpit, sits flush against the back of the seat, his wind-blown face frozen with a mixture of fear and joy.

The little white car rattles between stands of tall elms as it moves westward from Hagerstown, Indiana, on Highway 38. The spindly-wheeled machine sweeps through the hyperbolic curve in front of the Hoosier Pete gas station, darts through the railroad underpass, and shoots up the hill to the turnoff beside the whitewashed nursing home. The car makes a slow, wide arc at the turnoff, its tires crackling in a patch of loose gravel. Pulling to a stop, the man at the wheel glances down at the small boy stuffed into the seat beside him.

"How we doin'?" he asks, smiling, raising his voice above the uneven rumble of the engine.

"Okay," the boy answers shakily, nodding, still suspended in an uncertain balance of ecstasy and terror.

Rolling back onto the highway the car plunges down the hill toward the underpass, a puff of bluish smoke spitting out the fat tailpipe as it picks up speed.

The townspeople had smirked quietly, curiously, to themselves when his father bought the midget racer. A childish whim and a damned nuisance, they probably thought when he hung a license plate from its tail and drove it noisily through the streets of Hagerstown.

It was left to a young boy of ten or eleven, lashed and nearly blinded by the wind as the little car whipped down the hill that summer day to understand, though only vaguely then, what was happening.

The growl of that engine, the blurring world flashing past, the tight contented smile on his father's face—all etched themselves on the mind of that boy, who suddenly found he had surpassed the exhilirations of riding in the rumble seat of his grandfather's old '37 Chevrolet coupe or rolling down a hill in a crude wooden soapbox racer. This was something clearly different, something more than a mere physical or emotional elation. It had a metaphysical edge to it, this brief submersion in the backwater baptism, the spiritual orgasm of speed, racing cars, and sturdy men with firm faces. And it was to take that same young boy some twenty years to figure it all out, see it clearly, and finally put it in writing.

This book started there, twenty years ago, on Highway 38 just west of Hagerstown, Indiana. It has been a great many miles, a great many days and nights, since that green afternoon when a boy and his father raced up the hill in front of the nursing home, but that is surely where it all started.

That summer, and the ones to follow, that same boy went with his father to dirty little race tracks in places like Alexandria and Columbus, Indiana, the white midget car swaying gently on a clumsy trailer behind the station wagon. He watched with a young boy's enthusiasm as that car, and flocks of others, buzzed around those grimy tracks.

Most of those scenes are fairly hazy now, but some still remain crystal-clear. There was the day at one of those broken-down speedways when the exhaust pipe on the little white car broke loose and fell onto the track, a short distance from the track's rim, where the small boy pressed his face against the rusting fence. His father, hands smeared with black grease, walked slowly to the spot where the exhaust pipe had dropped. The still-hot piece of pipe burned his hand when he tried to pick it up. He muttered something under his breath, took a rag from his hip pocket, and, wrapping it around the middle of the pipe, gingerly lifted it up and started back toward the pit area.

The little boy, his eyes never leaving the grim-faced man in the white workclothes, waved his hand frantically in the air from the time his father first approached until he was halfway back to the pits with the broken exhaust pipe. But his father, unsmiling and unswerving, never saw him.

Later, the same day at the same track, after the races were over for the day, the boy saw his father smile as he drank a can of beer and joked with the other men who had brought cars to race. And, with only a little childish urging, his father wiped his greasy hands on the back of his trousers and led him over to a shiny yellow race car. Briskly, he lifted the boy into the padded cockpit.

The boy sat in that car, which had won the race that day, for a long time, looking at each little dial on the dashboard and cautiously touching all the silvery toggle switches. As he became restless, he twisted around in the soft seat and his elbow dropped down onto the hot exhaust pipe. He drew his arm back instinctively as he felt the sharp burning pain on his elbow. A red welt grew on his arm; his face was swept with concern and consternation as he looked at it. He wanted to cry. But, with his father and the other car owners and drivers nearby, he didn't.

There was also the day at the track in Salem, Indiana, a bigger one with steep asphalt banks, when the boy wanted to go across the track with the other men after two of the roaring cars sailed over the wall and crashed with a thunderous jolt. His father stopped him.

Everybody else was running across the track and climbing over the wall. The young boy wanted to go too but his father wouldn't let him, and he couldn't understand why. But, when the other men came stumbling back and reported the two men in the cars were dead, torn to shreds in their mangled machines, he understood and never again tried to join the swarm of people that always rushes to the scene of a racing wreck.

A few summers later, the white race car was replaced by a cleaner, sleeker, richer-sounding white car with red trim. It roared louder than the other car, went faster, and took the boy and his father to even more dusty race tracks.

And, as time went along, the young boy came to know the men who drove his father's race car. There was a burly man named Bud who constantly chewed on the butt of a fat brown cigar and always had to borrow money to pay his light bill or buy groceries for his wife and kids. Then there was Shorty, a muscular little man with deep-set eyes who used a phony name whenever he drove so that his boss wouldn't know he was racing.

It became a common sight for the boy to see the two men, in his own house or theirs or at the houses of other drivers around eastern Indiana, drivers like Tom Cherry, Kenny Eaton, and Dick Frazier. On Saturday afternoons before the races or Sunday nights after the races, the boy would sit, fascinated, as his father and the other men talked of racing.

But, summers and adolescence being temporary things, those times faded away. The sleek white car and the little boy grew older, and eventually both departed from Hagerstown. It would be some years before he finally drifted back to those noisy little race tracks as anything more than a casual spectator. He did not return to that fast company until he was ready and able to put his thoughts and reactions to it all on paper as a permanent record.

But come back to racing he did. Back among the men who, like his father, pressed flesh to metal to find their own magic. Back to the rumbling sounds, the blurring machines, the pungent smells, the moments of triumph and tragedy, the dusty tracks, the hot dogs and beer, the women, the kids with autograph books clutched in their hands, the cheering crowds.

Each time he walked through a pit gate into the midst of racing men and their cars, he felt that old nervous joy he had experienced some twenty years before. By the time he walked out through the gate again, his mind was set on committing to writing what he had seen, what he had heard, what he had felt.

And as he sat at a typewriter putting the words onto paper, things came full circle. He returned to Highway 38 and that afternoon twenty years ago. He was back in that little white race car with his father.

His hair was swirling like a haystack. His eyes were wide-open and glazed. His hand gripped the side of the cockpit. The wind was full in his face.

JERRY MILLER

Prologue

MARION, INDIANA, is not really a racing town. It is a factory town of some 40,000 people situated about sixty miles northeast of Indianapolis. Many of the 40,000 inhabitants are racing fans, but they have to leave the county to find any races.

There are no race tracks in or around Marion now. The only track there—it was called a driving park then—was erased from the landscape thirty-five years ago to make way for a state highway.

Yet for one day many decades ago, Marion, Indiana, was the very center of the racing world. For one afternoon, this rather ordinary town and its primitive driving park served as one of the spawning grounds for the roaring spectacle that would become the multimillion-dollar sport of auto racing.

The day was July 10, the year 1903. Almost 10,000 of the 21,000 who then lived in Marion crowded their way into the old driving park to see a strange new machine intriguingly called a "race car."

They streamed into the driving park grounds to get a close look at these four-wheeled whirlwinds and two amazing men who would eventually become legends in the history of racing—Barney Oldfield, the greatest of all pioneer racing drivers, who was on his way to a national championship when he appeared in Marion, and Earl Cooper, a then young and unknown daredevil who would later become a three-time national champion.

The two speed aces were brought to Marion for a special match race, not by anything as sophisticated as today's USAC, SCCA, or NASCAR, but by the Marion Elks Lodge, which saw the spectacular attraction as a natural for enriching its coffers for various lodge projects.

And though the Oldfield-Cooper match race didn't come off, the Elks and the thousands in attendance that afternoon still got their money's worth.

The local newspaper recorded the excitement and magic of that historic day in a news story which appeared at the top of the front page:

PEOPLE GET WORTH
OF THEIR MONEY
Exhibition Given by Barney Oldfield at
Driving Park Yesterday Very Excit-
ing—Elks Clear About $1,000

The automobile races given at the driving park yesterday afternoon was (*sic*) the occasion for the largest gathering of people that ever congregated within the park. The grandstand was filled to its fullest capacity, and all available standing room about the track was occupied. Barney Oldfield was the star attraction. He succeeded in lowering the world's record for one mile on a half mile track, held by Winton, which was 1:26.

Oldfield clipped nine and three fifths seconds off the record, establishing a new record of 1:16 2-5. The performance given by Oldfield was worth the price of admission and the crowd seemed to be satisfied, but the event of the day, a match race between Oldfield and Cooper for five miles, was declared off on account of the illness of Cooper. Edgar Apperson, of Kokomo, kindly consented to enter the race and was given a handicap of a quarter of a mile and drove a nice race. Oldfield passed him two different times in the five miles which demonstrated the terrific speed at which Oldfield was traveling.

In the five mile race Oldfield made the first mile in 1:27 1-2; two miles, 2:54; three miles, 4:22; four miles, 5:46 1-2; five miles, 7:18 1-2.

Oldfield then attempted to lower the world's one-mile record on a half-mile track. He made the first mile in 1:16 2-5, the second mile in 1:18 1-5. He made the second attempt to lower that record, but was unable to do so, but succeeded in making the mile again in 1:16 2-5, smashing Winton's record.

The performance given by Oldfield was one of the most exciting events ever witnessed in Marion and one which has never been seen in a city outside Marion. Oldfield has driven a mile in faster time on mile tracks in cities, but the mile made here was the greatest performance he has ever given as it was attended with greater danger on account of the sharp curves of a half mile course. Oldfield has made a study of how to attain the greatest speed on a track and the manner in which he makes the circuit shows superior judgment. He clings to the outside of the stretch until near the turn, when he sent the machine near the pole fence and then to the outside of the back stretch. The great speed at which the machine was going caused the rear end to veer around on the curves, sending up a cloud of dirt and dust that resembled a cyclone. The speed was so great that Oldfield would overtake the cloud of dust left behind him and when he made the last half mile of the two mile trial when he broke the record, he was in a cloud of dust the entire distance.

In the race for 2,000-pound machines, in which three Apperson machines, of Kokomo, were entered, a nice exhibition was given. The race between three local machines was a tame affair, but gave the spectators an idea of the great speed made by Oldfield.

The Elks' lodge treasury is at least $1,000 richer than it was yesterday morning as the result of the great outpouring of people to witness the races.

A little simple division shows that the great speed attained by Oldfield that day was about forty-seven miles per hour, a rather meager speed by today's standards. But in 1903, it was an unheard of feat, equal in emotional impact to today's 200-miles-per-hour-plus speeds.

There in 1903 at that now-extinct race track in Marion, Indiana, the townsfolk saw not just an auto race but a glimpse into the future as well. The undoubtedly electrifying display by pioneer auto racer Barney Oldfield was a chapter in the infancy of both the automobile and the sport of auto racing, and even today's super-powerful racing machines can not match the thrills of those who saw Oldfield whip his flimsy high-wheeled machine around that old dirt track.

It was, in short, the birth of a sport, the seeds of a legend, and a promise of things to come.

Driving car number 30, Walt Ballard crashes at the Daytona 500, February 20, 1972.

I THE SPORT

1. For Love and Money

AUTOMOBILE racing is not really a sport. It is hand-to-hand combat, a bar-room brawl, a bare-fisted free-for-all in a dark alley.
It is no game; it has none of the sporting niceties of a Davis Cup
match or the U. S. Open. It is a primitive, violent, uncompromis-
ing struggle for survival. Chances are, most hot-stuff sports stars
wouldn't last five minutes in a race car; they'd loose their cool
going into the first turn at Indianapolis. Driving a race car is
like taking on Dick Butkus without shoulder pads, stepping up to
home plate blindfolded, or boxing Muhammed Ali with one foot
nailed to the floor. A cockfight, a tightrope act, a tug-of-war, a
cavalry charge, a kamikaze raid—maybe. But a sport? No way.

Talk all you want about the aggressiveness of football, the raw
courage of slamming linemen and slashing halfbacks. Just try
sticking the nose of a 1,400-pound race car underneath another
one going into the turn at Indy at 160 miles an hour.

Talk about the violence of football or ice hockey if you wish.
Racing people do it all the time, trying to peddle the idea that
racing is no more violent than those sports. But nobody ever
burned to death on a football gridiron. And no one ever had his
arm or leg or head slashed off in a hockey match.

Talk about the muscle control of a baseball slugger or the
shooting eye of a basketball hot-shot if that's your thing. Then
try your hand at keeping a spidery fuel dragster heading in a
straight line at two hundred miles an hour or squeezing a four-
foot-wide sprint car through a four-and-a-half-foot opening between two other sliding sprinters. Talk about the strength and endurance of a choice thoroughbred if you're still in a mood to
talk. Then see if you can put together an engine that will turn
9,000 revolutions per minute for twenty-four hours straight without breaking stride. The comparisons almost always fail. Racing just doesn't fit the traditional American sports mold.

In a country that cherishes a delicate and incongruous balance
of teamwork and individual brilliance, auto racing is an absurd

anomaly. It has more than its share of "teams," to be sure, but one member of the team always gets all the glory—the racing driver, who can blow the rest of the team's competence in a split-second but rarely overcome its silly mistakes—is the one who collects the trophy, the kiss from the race queen, and the biggest slice of the paycheck.

To make matters worse, all the teams compete at once. It's a little like tossing all twenty-six NFL teams into the Super Bowl at the same time.

Racing also resists the long-time sports tradition of meticulously cataloguing its performers to show their relative merits. In the realm of batting averages, earned-run averages, shooting percentages, and yards-per-carry figures, racing defies all such numerical analyses.

Al Unser may sweep the Indy-car circuit, Richard Petty may

Walt Ballard walking away from his wrecked car at the 1972 Daytona 500.

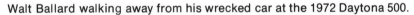

knock down a passel of Grand National victories, and Denny Hulme may win all the Can-Am races, but there is no common denominator to weigh one's success against that of the other two. Unser only occasionally runs a stock car race and almost never tries a Can-Am; Petty wouldn't be caught dead in anything but his faithful blue Plymouth; Hulme only leaves the Grand-Prix circuit long enough to run the Can-Ams and a few Indy-car contests.

It's comparing oranges and apples, like trying to determine if Juan Marichal is as good at throwing fast balls as Hank Aaron is at hitting them. Even the most-diligent baseball statisticians haven't been able to unravel that one.

It's racing's diversity that makes it so totally unfathomable. While football is always played on a clearly-defined field with a ball of fixed size and shape, a race can use anything from a go-kart to a Ford Torino and be run anywhere from the floor of the Astrodome to the side of Pike's Peak. On any Saturday night or Sunday afternoon of the year, in any state of the Union, somebody will be running a race. The cars will be one of at least a dozen varieties; the tracks can assume some six or seven different forms; the formats of the events will have as many variations as the human imagination is capable of devising.

Men will race so-called "stock cars" on any size track you care to find. The machines may have been stock when they rolled off the Detroit assembly lines, but by the time those cars reach the race track, with their beefed-up chassis, stripped cockpits, and souped-up engines, they are race cars, pure and simple. They are raced until they fall apart. When new, the cars are late models or Grand Nationals. After outliving their usefulness, they become late-model sportsmans, hardtops, modifieds, hobby stocks, or just plain jalopies. They end up as clay pigeons in such pseudo-racing shooting galleries as figure-eight races and demolition derbies.

Others race nimble little buzz-bombs called sprint cars and midgets. These are hump-backed open-cockpit machines with whining powerplants and churning wheels, which are too fast for their size and run too close together for their own good.

Another breed of race cars is the lean rear-engined missiles with fat tires known as championship or Indianapolis cars.

Everything about these rockets is exotic—their high-winding Offenhauser or Ford engines, their delicate suspension systems, their methanol fuel, their ability to threaten a man's life against a concrete retaining wall.

Also raced are growling full-fendered sports cars, the shiniest of which get labeled as Can-Am cars. Just sitting silently at track-side, they exude raw power, with their sleek bodies and wide airfoils. Then there are the clumsy little Trans-Am sedans. Called "pony cars" because Mustangs poured onto the market before Barracudas, Camaros, Javelins, Cougars, and Firebirds, they are no more stock than their big-iron Grand National counterparts.

Some people also like to race fire-breathing dragsters with tractor-size tires at the back and tricycle wheels at the front. Little more than engines suspended between two rails of metal, they are so headstrong, they need parachutes in order to stop.

And the sub-species of those basic breeds are almost endless.

Midget cars come in a complete range of sizes—full midgets, three-quarter midgets, half-midgets, micro-midgets, and quarter-midgets. A slightly less-expensive sprint car or one with a home-made body is a supermodified, and one with a giant wing mounted atop its roll-cage becomes a "super-sprint."

Slip a stock-block Chevrolet or Ford engine—again, the stock label is only a courtesy to Detroit—into an Indianapolis style chassis and you have a Formula 5000, Formula Ford, Formula A, Formula B, and so on down the alphabet.

The sports-car category can, and does, encompass everything from the proud Can-Am machines to the Corvettes college kids slap a little tape on and drive to the nearest track on weekends.

The cars at a dragstrip range all the way from the smoking dragsters to 1937 coupes with Cadillac engines crammed under their hoods.

That is not the end of it, either. Just about anything can be raced, provided two or more can be found—motorcycles, go-karts, dune buggies, garden tractors, snowmobiles, pickup trucks, or motorized pogo sticks. And they are raced anywhere the wheels can touch ground.

Most often in America men race their mechanical menageries around oval-shaped tracks of widely-differing size and quality.

The ovals can be as small as a quarter-mile or as large as 2½ miles, they can be asphalt or dirt, they can be as flat as Kansas or as steep as the price of butter.

The physical configuration doesn't change the basic pattern: a burst of full speed down a straightaway, the nervous negotiation of two turns with the rear wheels protesting all the way, another shot of straight-out speed, another wheel-whipping struggle through two turns, and back down the original straightaway to do it all over again.

Paved ovals hold out the promise of blazing speed; the dirt ovals offer the ulcer-forming spectacle of cars powersliding sideways through the turns. Both put a premium on physical compactness, keeping the race where all the spectators can see it.

Road courses sacrifice the viewability to throw a stiffer test at the competitors. Twisting up and down hills, into tight blind corners, through forests, around lakes or farmhouses, a road course is racing's version of a labyrinth. The speeds are less spectacular but the drivers are busier, shifting gears frantically and varying speeds delicately.

The relative worth of the ovals versus the road courses is the subject of an unending debate between the fanciers of each. The oval trackers worship the awesome speed and courage of their bullrings; the road-racing buffs point to the demands their tracks put on the fiber of their contestants. Both are probably right in their own ways. But if emotion were left out of it, one tends to think oval races and road races are often fairly dreary affairs, turning into monotonous parades of cars—some have all the competitive action of a carnival merry-go-round.

All track races are inclined to get dull in direct proportion to their size and the size of their machinery. A championship race around the 2½-mile Indianapolis Speedway is considerably more uninteresting than a midget-car race on a quarter-mile dirt bowl, and a pony-car event around the four-mile Elkhart Lake roadway won't come close to the slam-bang excitement of a modified race on a half-miler. The distance and the time cancel out the competitive potential. The best car can stretch its lead by several yards on a long and difficult course; on a short oval, its advantage will be measured in inches. Not all the competitive cars in a 500-

miler will last the distance, but most of them will go all the way in a 25-mile sprint.

The truth of that racing axiom is stamped most indelibly on the numbed senses of those unfortunates who sit through the handful of endurance races that invade the U. S. racing season each year. Twenty-four hours at Daytona, twelve hours at Sebring, or six hours at Wakins Glen, it all amounts to the same thing: the winner is so incredibly far in front, as much as 200 miles in some cases, nobody really cares if it is a Porsche or a Ferrari.

The idea, of course, is to demonstrate the durability and reliability of machines and men, but it is difficult to see through eyes reddened by gasoline fumes and lack of sleep.

Drag races aren't much better. The strip is only a quarter-mile long, true. But it's all in one direction and only two cars try it at the same time—that is, if one of them doesn't get disqualified for jumping the gun or destroy its engine on blast-off.

The somewhat sad state of the competitive art has led to some of the far-out racing concepts that keep springing up. It probably explains why the race up the side of Pike's Peak has always existed, why figure-eight "races" are even tolerated by good honest racing fans, why snowmobile racing is catching on so rapidly, and why something called "off-road racing" could even get rooted in the land of freeways and one-way streets.

Off-road racing is an insane piece of business, patterned roughly after the "rallies" which are infrequently run through the wilderness of East Africa or from London, England to Sydney, Australia. Motorcycles, dune buggies, pickup trucks, passenger cars—everything but Sherman tanks—are turned loose at the edge of a roadless desert and told to get to the other side in the shortest time possible.

The cure for unexciting racing actually is worse than the disease. No one, absolutely no one, can watch an off-road race. It just is not possible to take in all of the Baja peninsula in one sitting. And even if it was, you couldn't tell what was going on, because the entries start off at measured intervals and race the clock, not each other.

But everybody who drives in it, including Parnelli Jones, the

Fuel man Buddy Parrot refueling the Dodge
stock car racer of Bobby Isaac.

Unser brothers, and actor Jim Garner, seem to think it's a barrel of fun. Everyone's entitled to his own opinion. It seems that, if nothing else, off-road racing may prove that the more orthodox forms of the art aren't so bad after all.

Races do have their moments, those spine-tingling episodes when two cars lock up in a wheel-to-wheel dogfight right down to the fall of the checkered flag. And the fans keep pouring into the crowded and crumbling grandstands at tracks across the country, anticipating the particular kind of magic that comes when two of the leading cars swing onto a straight stretch of race track together. The trailing car darts abruptly to one side and edges up slowly beside the lead car. When the challenging car pulls even with the other racer, the stage is set for the most decisive of moments in auto racing. As the two cars hurtle full-blast down the straightaway, a curve looms in the distance. Each of the dueling drivers knows the score—only one of them can get into that curve first. The battle becomes a high-speed game of Chicken. One driver must lift his foot from the accelerator first, however reluctantly. Neither does until the very last second. When one finally does, the other jumps ahead as if he had suddenly turned on more juice. He can then safely lift his foot too; he has won the joust, and his victim must concede and give him room to slant into the approaching turn.

It is this moment of direct confrontation the fans come to see. In theory, every race should have scores of such thrilling duels, but they seldom do. Too often, the cars simply string out in the order they qualified earlier in the day and maintain their places like a line of horse cavalry. Narrow or poorly-groomed tracks sometimes are at fault, but the absence of enough good race cars to go around is the greater factor.

Almost always, the fans see a race where at least half the field can't keep up with the truly competitive cars and drivers. They see a race between the dozen or less frontrunners for the top prizes and another between the rest for what's left over. This doesn't necessarily bother them, though. For the hard-core racing fan, there is always some good to be found in everything.

Pot-bellied, beer-breathed, coarse-talking though he may be, the real racing fan takes on a unique sophistication when he comes to the race track. He knows about racing and race cars, and he knows what he likes. He is quite capable of channeling his enthusiastic support in the direction of some poor driver whose car couldn't even win a race through an automatic car wash. If he's really high on a struggling tailender who finishes 13th in a 24-car field, the die-hard racing fan has no difficulty noting: "He drove one helluva race. If he'd had a good car, he woulda blown those hot-dogs right off the track."

The drivers, however, cannot extract that kind of obtuse satisfaction from a 13th place performance. They are that peculiar breed of men whose desire for winning, for being the very best, is more fanatical than that found in any sport.

Racing drivers are not athletes. They are broken-knuckled street fighters, brawling roughnecks who drive their cars as if they were billy clubs.

To each of them, his race car is a weapon, a bludgeon to hammer home his belief that he is the best goddamned race driver there is. Occasionally he also uses it to hammer into an opponent who wants to argue the point and, if that doesn't settle the argument, he'll meet the guy in the infield later and settle it with a short right to the mouth.

They are a short, wiry breed with thick, hard shoulders and arms. Their hair is usually thinning on top, their manner cocksure and intense, their language rough and to the point.

Some of them never bothered to finish high school once they found out they could drive cars very fast. They are single-minded and have a reputation for being lazy in the traditional sense. Any job they might have on the side is only going to get enough attention to keep their racing ambitions solvent.

They drive their cars with ruthless precision, as if there were no tomorrow. They are convinced that each race, the one they are driving in at any particular moment, is the one that will prove that they are ready to move up to a better, richer circuit. Yet they are practical enough to know they might not do as well as they hoped in the race and can adeptly reconcile themselves to the idea that the next race will be the one to send them on their way to racing fame and fortune.

The drivers rattle around the dim little tracks where all the next races are run, always striving to impress the yet-faceless car owner who can take them to race on the big tracks at Indianapolis or Daytona. Some find that man and move on; countless numbers never leave the inglorious backwoods speedways.

They also have an amazing capacity for accepting their defeats. They acknowledge early in their racing lives that they will always lose more races than win, and they quickly learn to bury the inherent frustrations. Not that they accept their lot, they merely recognize its existence and anticipate it.

They are proficient at making excuses for their racing failures. They blame poor performances on their cars—one suspects there just can't be that many ill-handling cars in the world—and wrecks on the other guy. There have been numerous landmark cases where the legal question of who caused a particular tangle has been adjudicated by the party of the first part and the party of the second part directly behind the judges' stand.

It seems that race drivers also have a penchant for aging quite a bit slower than nature intended. Youth is a valuable commodity for a race driver on the rise. Car owners take it into account when they're in the market for a new driver, so drivers often accommodate them by neatly shaving three or four years from their ages. It all becomes rather ludicrous when a driver who has trimmed years away gets to the point where he is much too paunchy and much too balding to be believed any longer. But that won't stop him. Even when pressed, he will dispel any suggestion that he is "over the hill."

"All I'll admit to is 29," Chuck Weyant will tell you, his swarthy face threatening to smile. It is a matter of record that Weyant drove his first race over thirty years ago and was racing at Indianapolis in 1952.

Team McLaren crew discuss a problem during practice runs at Indianapolis.

"Let's just say that the age in the (USAC) yearbook isn't the right one," grinning Don White will offer. He has been racing stock cars for at least twenty years and the yearbook last listed him as 45.

When they're not racing, race drivers are a free-wheeling, fun-loving bunch, prone to partying, boisterous jokes and pranks. They have an enormous capacity for beer, the adoration of pretty girls and children, and the smell of success.

They also have a history of harvesting quite a bit more than admiration from the pretty girls who flock around them at the race tracks. Their reputations for promiscuity may have been exaggerated considerably through the years, but it is not totally without foundation. There have been enough documented cases of sexual indiscretions to keep racing's divorce rate at a healthy all-American level.

The occasional infidelities are race-track diversions; the girls are there for the taking, and the drivers who want them take them. Away from the track, they fill their roles as family men with equal ease. At home, they escape the uncertainties of racing in the security of a stable family life. They are generally the casual, stay-at-home types, preferring a quiet night in their sanctuary to an evening on the night-club circuit.

They particularly cherish their sons, and spend the bulk of their leisure time rollicking with them in go-karts, snowmobiles, and other mini-mobiles. They claim they don't encourage their offspring to follow their paths, but racing is historically an avocation where the sons generally do, usually with hopes of equaling the parent's success.

The closest racing drivers come to organized recreation is hunting and fishing or golf. Usually, they spend their free time racing along the countryside with their sons or friends on motorcycles, dune buggies, or snowmobiles. Such excursions are usually punctuated with the same reckless high-jinks race drivers practice at trackside.

When it comes time again to race, however, the horseplay and hanky-panky suddenly cease. Driving a racing machine is serious business and the men who do it pour all the strength and concentration at their command into it.

They know they may be tempting death. But they accept the

Dick Smothers' scoring crew at Elkhart Lake's Road America
course during the running of the 1970 Formula A Continental.

risk readily, bolstered by a belief in a benevolent God and in their
own ability to handle any situation that might develop. They
simply love what they are doing too much to worry about the
consequences.

The passion for the speed, the competition, the glory, even
the risk, is so overpowering it can outweigh the monetary considerations involved. Big-name drivers like A. J. Foyt or Mario
Andretti or one of the Unser brothers freely admit they would
race for nothing if they had to. Even the most successful of them
will occasionally compete in a small-money race if the competition is formidable and a good car is available.

And the purses paid at the race tracks rely on that insatiable lust for winning. The racing payrolls are small and top-heavy; the winner frequently takes home twice what the runnerup does, and everyone else gets chicken-feed.

The risks hold their own strange attraction, too. It is almost as if the threat of injury or death underscores their manhood and separates the men from the boys, as the saying goes. Astoundingly enough, there have even been loud protests when obvious safety improvements came along.

When cage-style rollbars filtered into the sprint car and midget circuits with their promise of greater protection for the driver in a crash, there were those who were leary of the new contraptions. Gary Bettenhausen, hard-nosed son of a tough old racing great, Tony Bettenhausen—who died in a crash at Indianapolis—was one of the first to express displeasure with the roll-cages. So was the late Bob Tattersall. "I just don't like 'em," said the ex-paratrooper and veteran of over 20 years of midget racing, "Hell, when I first started racing, we didn't have rollbars or shoulder harnesses or anything."

The roll-cages stayed though, as did the rubber fuel bladders and on-board fire extinguishers, and everybody lived with them. Still, even today you can hear grumblings in certain corners about how the current racing machines "just don't look like race cars anymore."

If they have occasionally distrusted safety gadgets in their own bailiwicks, they have had even less regard for anything or anybody in a branch of racing foreign to them. For many years, there existed a deep line of demarcation between the worlds of oval-track racing and road-course racing.

Sports car drivers from the road-racing circuits were inclined to sneer smugly at the oval racers, calling them "roundy-rounders" and equating their driving skills with those of truck drivers. The oval-track set, on the other hand, viewed the "sporty car" drivers as some kind of long-haired pansies who would be scared silly if they ever got close to an Offy.

The distance between the two groups has somewhat narrowed in recent years, as drivers like Andretti, Mark Donohue, Parnelli Jones, and Peter Revson have demonstrated they could hack it on either side of the fence.

A group with a long background of feuding with drivers of

all persuasions has been the army of mechanics who build and groom the complex equipment the drivers wheel around the track. The histories of American racing circuits, large or small, have been punctuated with the hot emotions and violent words exchanged by drivers and mechanics.

Mechanics and drivers get on rather nicely when things are going their way and they are winning races. When their racing luck turns sour, they increasingly get on each other's nerves. In such situations, the driver begins to suspect his mechanic isn't doing his job properly. The mechanic tends to figure his driver has lost his touch or his nerve, or both. The inevitable conclusion of such thoughts is an explosive blowup, and that is what happens with considerable regularity on any circuit you can name.

Such outbursts are inherent in the common racing situation where the mechanic does all of what he considers the hard work and the driver receives the bulk of the praise and reward. The spotlight always falls on the driver of the car, not its mechanic. And the fact that the driver collects four or five times more money for his effort than the mechanic does heightens the apparent inequity. These indignities cannot sit well with men who put together the intricate chassis and engines of racing cars with the precision of a surgeon.

The craft of a racing mechanic is one built on long years of tinkering with automobiles. He probably worked over his first car as a teenager and never found anything he liked better. He got into racing when one of his buddies wanted to try his hand at piloting a racing car and needed someone to fix up his car for him. The race-driving buddy probably went on to be a very good used car salesman in Santa Monica. Or, if that buddy became a very good car salesman, or something else that made him independently wealthy, he may have graduated to the fairly exclusive ranks of racing's car owners.

The men who own racing machinery are mostly successful businessmen fascinated with the speed and spectacle of racing or one-time race drivers who never got it completely out of their systems. The only thing required from them is money, and usually lots of it.

They are men like Andy Granatelli, the rotund Italian who flopped as an aspiring race driver but turned a little-known oil additive called STP into a multimillion-dollar success. Granatelli operates one of the most expensive racing stables going and has had some of the most expensive drivers like Mario Andretti, Joe Leonard, and Richard Petty.

On the top circuits, the Indy-car, Grand National, or Can-Am series, it takes between $100,000 and $500,000 to field a top-notch team, with at least one primary car, a backup car, the necessary spare engines and parts, a good engine man, a good chassis man, two or three husky handymen, and maybe a part-time scorer or two.

For the less well-heeled, a car can be scrounged up for as little as maybe $25,000, but its only function will be to fill out the field and give the flagmen something to wave their flags at when the leaders start lapping it.

Even down on the lower levels, where the smaller cars run

The cars line up for the start of the Indianapolis 500.

the smaller tracks, a first-line machine can put a car owner's expenses into the five-figure bracket without much trouble. It is possible, however, to invest a few thousand dollars in a solid midget, sprint car, or modified and have a decent chance of competing.

Of course, the lower a car owner goes on the ladder, the smaller the race purses. Not that it makes much difference for the owner. The only financial reward for the great majority of them is the satisfaction they get from writing it off their income tax as a business loss.

When the paychecks are divided up, the owner doesn't get to keep very much. The biggest chunk comes off the top for the driver, forty percent in most cases and fifty percent for a choice chauffeur. The next slice, about ten percent, goes to the chief mechanic. What's left over pays the rest of the crew and the team's expenses; more often than not, the car owner ends up digging into his own pocket to pay the hotel bills. On the small circuits, corners are cut pretty easily. Often the car owner is also the chief mechanic and recruits his sons and brothers to be his crew. In some cases, he is also the driver and pockets the whole paycheck, but he puts in a lot of hours for that privilege.

Up on the top levels, it becomes impractical to trim a team's manpower. To win the big races, it takes a full staff of crewmen, coordinated into an efficient unit that can manicure the equipment flawlessly and perform lightning-fast pit stops almost instinctively.

It all costs money, but the car owner does have an opportunity to at least lighten the financial load. The acquisition of a sponsor for his car can relieve a car owner of $50,000 to $100,-000 of his operation's expenses.

Other monies can flow into a top team, but the funnel generally goes directly into the driver's pocket. The Detroit automakers, the tire companies, the automotive accessory firms, have diverted millions of their dollars into racing operations over the years.

At the height of the money rush, the supporting companies accounted for a luxurious degree of affluence throughout racing's upper strata. In the very good years, racing stables could easily operate with a profit margin, and the most sought-after drivers—already drawing a salary from their car owner plus

their cut of the prize money—could pull down as much as $500,-
000 a year from all their revenue sources.

Surely the most flamboyant of the racing spenders were the
two tire companies, Firestone and Goodyear, who persistently
battled each other for the advertising treasure generated by big
race wins.

The two tire mills handed out contracts to almost every driver
they could find. The big-name drivers were encouraged to post a
few victories with checks of up to $250,000; obscure also-rans
were slipped $5,000 checks, just in case they ever finished high
enough for somebody to notice what kind of tires they used.

The tire war became so feverish that Firestone and Goodyear
even owned a number of racing engines and chassis to pass out
to their favored clients when necessary to improve their chances
of putting their tires in Victory Lane.

The investments of the rubber empires were so gigantic and
far-reaching that a man close enough to the racing scene to know
looked through the cafeteria window across from Indy's Gasoline Alley one afternoon and moaned, "You know, it wouldn't
surprise me one bit to find out that Firestone and Goodyear own
every last piece of equipment in there."

Smaller accessory firms, the producers of spark plugs, piston
rings, oil filters, crankcase additives, and the like, added to the
kitty with contingency prizes for top finishers who used their
merchandise. Like the tire companies, they eagerly supplied their
products to anyone who would use them, free-of-charge.

But when the nation's economy went into a long slump, so did
racing's. The Detroit auto factories were the first to pull out,
leaving their tangible collateral in just two Grand National garages and a single Trans-Am stable.

The tire companies followed. Firestone pulled out of Grand
National racing completely, and joined Goodyear in announcing
an end to the innumerable and extravagant contracts with
drivers. The withdrawal announcements were not completely accurate, as it turned out. Each of the tiremakers has managed to
keep its very best accounts on the payroll to maintain what it
felt was its own strategic advantage. The best educated guesses
envision Firestone's cash still trickling down to Indianapolis
winners Al Unser and Mario Andretti, perennial Indy favorite

Lloyd Ruby, the Can-Am Chaparral operation of Jim Hall, and Bud Moore's Trans-Am Mustangs.

Goodyear's funds are perhaps still to be seen making their way into the hope-chests of 1968 Indy winner Bobby Unser, the Plymouth-backed Grand National tandem of Richard Petty and Buddy Baker, the championship car efforts of the ever-popular A. J. Foyt, the unconquerable Can-Am campaign and promising Indianapolis venture of the Team McLaren combine, and the Javelin-supported Trans-Am endeavor of owner Roger Penske and driver Mark Donohue.

The total effect of the new arrangement is that the rich stay rich and the poor at least get to buy their tires at a discount, about $60 apiece.

Other faces in racing's financial picture are those of its sanctioning bodies, the organizational alphabet soup that tries to hold the whole thing together. Their own corporate structures anchored with the fees collected from their members, race participants. promoters, and those companies seeking official approval of their products, the sanctioners have found at least a stopgap solution to the empty feeling left by the withdrawal of the auto and tire companies. When the money wells dried up, America's three top sanctioning bodies—USAC (United States Auto Club), NASCAR (National Association of Stock Car Auto Racing), and SCCA (Sports Car Club of America)—made a straight player deal with the television industry.

Cigarette makers, exiled from the tube at the end of 1970, suddenly had thousands of advertising dollars they didn't know what to do with. Racing held out its hand, and the barons of tobacco row came across. USAC signed Marlboro to sweeten the pot for its prime attraction, the Indy-car circuit with its trinity of 500-milers at Indianapolis, Pocono, Pennsylvania, and Ontario, California. NASCAR landed the Winston marquee to raise the ante for its caravan of Grand National speedfests on the high-banked superspeedways of the South. SCCA persuaded L&M to throw its chips into the club's struggling Formula A/5000 Continental road-racing series.

Meanwhile, as the cigarette accounts shuffled from television to auto racing, racing opened its own account with television. USAC, NASCAR, and SCCA all ushered their products onto the

USAC champion Joe Leonard is swamped with requests for autographs.

television screen through contracts with ABC, CBS, and independent sports networks.

The networks finally bought the idea of televising auto races, though the price they were willing to pay was much more modest than what they shelled out for football and baseball. The television money still was a nice addition to racing's financial holdings and the national exposure it afforded was expected to pull more cash customers through race track turnstiles. However, the early telecasts probably drove viewers back to the tracks like rats fleeing a sinking ship. The first race broadcasts were total disasters, characterized by inept camera work, inane and inaccurate commentary, and shoddy technical direction.

Broadcasts gradually got better, but they retained hints of the long-standing inability of the mass media to grasp the nuances of auto racing.

For most of its history, auto racing had been mistrusted, maligned, and ignored by the press. It had only sporadic success in attracting newspaper sports editors and sportscasters who maintained that anything that wasn't played with some kind of a ball by clean-cut young athletes was outside their sphere of responsibility. Sports-page space and radio and television air time were filled with the exploits of the footballers, baseballers, basketballers, and the rest. Racing simply didn't meet the criteria.

Sports editors tended to flinch whenever the word "racing" was mentioned, visualizing speed-hungry young maniacs ripping down a dark country road two abreast or leather-jacketed motorcycle hoodlums flailing old ladies with tire chains. The only time they became enthusiastic about the subject was when they gleefully slapped a photograph of a gory racing crash into a prominent position on the sports page.

Only in the cities that owed something to racing, like Indianapolis and Daytona Beach, was racing brought out of the freakshow tent and into the spotlight of semi-respectability with periodic stories and results on the sports pages and in radio and television newscasts.

With network television's acceptance of auto racing as a marketable commodity, the picture slowly began to change, but the old guard in the newspapers and broadcast stations gave ground grudgingly. The bedrock racing fans, whether the beer-loving Mr. and Mrs. mid-America at the USAC and NASCAR ovals or the mop-haired college kids at the SCCA road courses, still had to rely heavily on a handful of national racing papers and magazines for news of their "sport." For most, Chris Economaki's *National Speed Sport News*—an artistic disaster but astonishingly comprehensive in its coverage—quenched their thirst best.

Television stole the ball away from the recalcitrant newspaper editors, much to the delight of the men heading the sanctioning bodies. The sanctioners never had been very happy with their treatment from the press, which generally consisted of newspaper men continually pestering them for free passes to the races and then publishing little or nothing about what they saw.

They welcomed television coverage with the ecstatic disbelief of a "Queen for a Day" winner.

Television was exactly what was needed, the racing executives assured themselves. What better place to get racing before the public and gain equal footing with the traditional American sports.

The advent of televised racing set the wheels of the sanctioners' polishing machines into motion. The rough, prickly flaws were to be ground smooth to aid the digestion of mass-media audience consumption.

The safety features, already steamrollered past the few quixotic protests, would help relieve the fears of queasy sports fans who might shy away from being parties to the violent destruction of men.

The next step would be to initiate a campaign to isolate its star properties from the gawking public. For years, racing fans had been allowed to fraternize with the drivers, mechanics, car owners, and officials, freely roaming into the pits or garage area at the conclusion of a race program. It was like letting the Riverfront Stadium crowd parade through the dressing rooms to rub

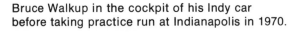

Bruce Walkup in the cockpit of his Indy car
before taking practice run at Indianapolis in 1970.

shoulders with Johnny Bench, Tony Perez, and their teammates as they headed for the showers. It would have to stop.

Fences already have cropped up around the garage areas of shiny new speedways to keep the spectators out. More and more garages at places like Indianapolis have closed their doors and declared themselves off-limits to fans, reporters, and distant relatives. Thus segregated, racing's big attractions, particularly its drivers, could be lifted to the same pedestal from which stars of other sports receive their praise and adulation. Carefully groomed and pre-packaged, racing drivers could be like the articulate athletes who speak at sports banquets, get invited to appear on television shows, and maybe enter politics.

Yes, yes, the brain trusts of racing thought to themselves, we can be the sport baseball is, the sport football is, the sport basketball is. And they probably can. They have already started. No doubt, if they keep their races sanitary and transform their drivers into glib dandies, it will happen. Racing will someday truly be a sport.

The frightening thing about it, though, is that it may no longer be *racing*.

2. The Powers That Be

AUTO RACES do not run themselves. That is one of the cold, hard facts of life.

They are run not by the grace of God, but by the grace of sanctioning bodies—the monolithic, self-ordained defenders of everything that is good and pure and wholesome and decent for auto racing. Good, pure, wholesome, decent things like money and the status quo, to name but two.

In the early days, running auto races in America was a pretty haphazard affair. Individual tracks would stage race programs, drawing drivers and cars primarily from the immediate vicinity.

There were no organized sets of drivers and cars that would show up at a particular race; whoever wanted to race on a given day could.

There were few rules for those early races, fewer safety requirements for either the cars or the tracks, and very little cash reward for the participants.

With the major exception of the American Automobile Association, which had sanctioned Indianapolis car racing since 1909, there were only loosely-knit groups of racing people on a highly localized basis who produced the bulk of American auto racing prior to World War II. Most racing circuits, if they could be called that, were run on a track-by-track arrangement, almost always on the track owner's take-it-or-leave-it terms.

Some neighboring tracks eventually were linked together to form something resembling a championship series of races, but these still were generally restricted to a narrow geographical region. From those casual confederations sprang, in the Thirties and early Forties, a number of regional racing bodies that attempted to organize and police the racing activities of their members.

Some of these early sanctioning bodies, through mismanagement or internal discord, went under. But many of them gradually jelled into stable entities that were able to slowly upgrade the quality of competition, the safety standards of equipment and racing venues, and the purses.

Still, when racing came back to life after its wartime hiatus, the AAA was the only national racing organizer of any real stature. Some of the old regional outfits resumed their operations after the war, but American auto racing retained much of its provincial flavor. Even AAA, which ultimately expanded its racing domain to include divisions for midget cars, sprint cars, and stock cars, tended to promote its races with the coarse sensationalism left over from the barnstorming days when small bands of drivers traveled from track to track, staging races that were more theatrical than honestly competitive.

As the Forties moved along, however, a handful of men involved with auto racing to one degree or another began to recognize the long-range possibilities of organizing racing on a national scale. Two groups of such men, one in the South and the other

Supermodifieds racing at Kokomo (Indiana) Speedway.

in the East, started building the frameworks of two racing structures that could develop and exploit the potential of auto racing into a nationwide phenomenon.

The eastern group actually was formed in 1944 as the Sports Car Club of America, but mainly for the restoration and preservation of vintage sports cars. As time went along, the club became more and more involved with the conduct of amateur competition in a wide-ranging variety of sports cars and production car classes.

The club, which had but seven members at its birth, grew steadily into a vast network of regional sports car clubs, overseeing sports car races and rallies in scattered road-race layouts and makeshift race courses projected onto abandoned airport runways. For the first 22 years of its existence, SCCA would confine its racing enterprises mainly to amateur racing, offering only trophies and glory to its army of enthusiastic part-time competitors.

In 1948, the southern group became the National Association of Stock Car Auto Racing and immediately entered the marketplace of professional auto racing. Dedicated to the proposition that stock car racing was the type race fans could identify with most readily, NASCAR began organizing stock car events throughout the South.

Committed to a single brand of racing and cultivating its own stars, NASCAR gradually broke AAA's monopoly on top-line racing programs, eventually routing the northern organization from most of its southern encampments.

Even with the NASCAR incursion, AAA still was safely set as the leading sanctioning body in the country. It ran its four divisions at the best tracks in the East and Midwest, with its Indianapolis show-stopper unchallenged as racing's premier event. The only would-be challenger to AAA was its long-time shadow, the International Motor Contest Association, which had tried to match AAA's success with Indy-cars, sprints, midgets, and stock cars in the Midwest since 1915, but never could quite pull it off.

But it was not AAA that, with NASCAR and SCCA, entered racing's golden era as the powerful triumverate of sanctioning bodies in whose hands the destiny of American auto racing rested. The year 1955 was a black one for racing in general, and AAA in particular. Racing's public image was dealt a near-fatal blow in June 1955 during the 24-hour sports car marathon race at LeMans, France. A sleek gray Mercedes driven by Frenchman Pierre Levegh slashed into a crowd of spectators, killing some 80 persons including Levegh. Instantly, in Europe and North America, there were screams of horror and disgust, followed by cries that auto racing be abolished.

The effect of the LeMans slaughter on the American public was particularly sharp. Less than two weeks before, Americans had seen popular Indianapolis winner Bill Vukovich killed in a horrifying crash during the running of the 500 and they were quick to lend their voices to the protests against the racing carnage.

The controversy placed AAA squarely in the middle of an embarrassing dilemma. For years, the association had decried the wholesale killing of Americans on U. S. highways and pleaded for greater safety on the nation's roadways. The incidents of 1955 put AAA in the perplexing position of trying to justify that philosophy with its involvement in a sport that had wiped out over 80 lives in a 12-day span.

Ultimately, it could not unravel that Gordian knot. In August 1955, AAA disbanded its competition board and turned its back on auto racing forever.

The sudden withdrawal of AAA left its hundreds of racing participants dumbfounded. But after the initial shock, they began to close ranks to salvage what they could from the remnants of the once-mighty AAA empire. The car owners, race promoters, drivers, and mechanics formed a new organization, the United States Auto Club, in September of 1955 to perpetuate their racing activities.

The desperate reorganization, shaky at first, somehow managed to hold the fragments together. USAC survived and maintained AAA's traditional stature as racing's pre-eminent sanctioning body.

The advent of the Seventies found USAC, NASCAR, and SCCA standing as a powerful trinity, holding the reins of America's fastest growing sport. The three bodies controlled all the major track racing across the country, and they no longer were simply sanctioning bodies—their sphere of influence spread far beyond merely lending their names to competitive events and providing the necessary fields of entrants for the same.

They were now involved with negotiating race purses with track owners, drawing up and enforcing complex sets of rules for their races, dickering with radio and television networks over broadcast rights to their events, enticing giant manufacturers to pour more of their advertising budgets into racing endeavors, and selling their programs and policies to the general public through high-powered public relations campaigns.

They had come a long way from the romantic days when sanctioning bodies served mainly to protect the interests of drivers, mechanics, and car owners against the not-always-altruistic motives of race promoters and track owners, and to give racing some semblance of order. The rough edges polished away, they had become slick, quasi-political wheeler-dealers by the Seventies, closer in appearance to Madison Avenue ad agencies than racing sanctioners.

They handled advertising accounts, constructed their own public images, sold their products to industry and the public. They laid down rules for their members, told them to shave their

Racing on the beach at Daytona in the early years of auto racing.

beards or shorten their hair if necessary, and justified it all by wrangling larger purses for their races.

Somewhere in that transition, the original concern for the welfare of race participants became subjugated by another, over-powering consideration. The top sanctioning bodies came to cater not to the wishes of the drivers, mechanics, and car owners, or of the spectators who paid to see their races, but to the wills of the automotive manufacturers who produced the components and assorted hardware of which race cars were fabricated.

The Detroit automakers, along with the smaller companies that manufactured the assortment of accessories used in or on racing machinery, pumped great quantities of cash, equipment, and personnel into racing as they tried to impress the buying public with their prowess as racing performers. The car makers —Ford, Chrysler, Chevrolet (though they constantly refused to admit it), and American Motors—put in the most money and machinery, and got the most gut-level advertising appeal in return.

The accessory firms put in, and got out, their share, too. Though they could not take the kind of direct credit the auto-makers did when their cars and engines were victorious, the accessory makers inflated the use of their products in winning cars into spectacular, near-ludicrous sales spiels. "Unser Wins

Lee Petty crosses the finish line at the original Daytona beach course.

Indianapolis 500 Using Fram Oil Filter" and "Mallory Ignition-Equipped Cars Came In 1st and 2nd at Indianapolis" were typical of the ad pitches they made as they held their merchandise up to the reflected glory of racing.

The races-to-riches tactic reached all the way down to such obscure items as oil additives, crash helmets, driving gloves, and mechanic's tools, whose real contributions to the success of a race car were, at best, borderline. But the companies that made them boldly implied in their ads that they made a difference and did it with such bravado one almost believed the kind of wrench a mechanic used could determine the outcome of a race.

The investments of the automotive companies became the foundation upon which racing anchored itself and provided the sanctioning bodies with the collateral necessary to build a multimillion-dollar nationwide racing emporium. In the view of the sanctioners, it was imperative to protect those investments —and those of the non-automotive companies who sponsored cars or races—at all costs. The conclusion committed the sanctioning bodies irrevocably to a strategy of enforcing the status quo, shielding the supportive companies from deviations that could endanger their positions in racing.

Any innovations were scrutinized for possible threats to the established order—the more radical the innovation, the less likely it would be accepted. Even the developments of the automotive companies were checked closely to insure the delicate balance of power would not be shifted drastically. If one auto company came up with something that seemed to give it an edge over its competitors, the other auto companies screamed and the sanctioning bodies quietly wrote up new revisions for their rulebooks.

In the late Sixties and early Seventies, a rash of spectacular racing experiments put the inflexible philosophies of the nation's racing sanctioners squarely in focus. The rapid-fire series of revolutionary concepts in the areas of powerplants and traction devices forced the sanctioning bodies to either make their immovable stance public or let the gates down forever.

They chose the former. Propped up by the entrenched racing investors, they stood, backs bristling and mouths firm and smug, the realities of the age striding irresistibly toward them.

The most infamous of the confrontations was USAC's turbine ordeal of 1967 and 1968. USAC had permitted experimental turbine-powered cars to test at Indianapolis, but in 1967 colorful and controversial car owner Andy Granatelli brought a turbine car to Indy which definitely was not experimental. It was competitive, so competitive, in fact, that it ran away with the race until a gearbox failure stopped it four laps from the finish.

The sudden emergence of a raceable turbine car presented USAC with a crisis of the first magnitude. Turbines, used in airplanes and certain industrial processes, utilize the blades of a turbine wheel to develop horsepower rather than pistons and crankshafts as conventional engines do. They have fewer moving parts than piston engines and run on kerosene, not gasoline.

The ramifications of a wholesale takeover of Indianapolis racing by turbine power were painfully clear. The prime engine makers, like Ford and Offenhauser, would be deflated; the makers of piston rings, valve seals, radiators, distributors, and all the other things a turbine doesn't need, would be wiped out; the

Lining up for time trials at Indy, 1968.

oil companies would have apoplexy; the car owners would either go broke switching to turbines or leave the sport.

USAC moved quickly to stop the building panic. While it could have simply banned turbine cars and been done with it, the USAC board of directors chose a more diplomatic course to avert being saddled with a public image as a reactionary group stubbornly holding back progress.

The board huddled with two panels of experts—one headed, oddly enough, by Ford Motor Company engineers, the other made up of turbine engineers—then disregarded the turbine experts' report and sliced the allowable horsepower potential of racing turbines by twenty-five percent. The piston-engine establishment was relieved, which proved to be only temporary.

Granatelli brought more turbine cars to Indianapolis in 1968, and almost won again.

The furor began anew. USAC was swifter and surer this time: The board slashed the turbine engine potential another twenty-five percent, banned the four-wheel-drive principle used on Granatelli's cars, and ruled out anything but "automotive" turbines —of which there were none at that time.

That got the job done. The turbines were defanged. All was right with commerce and industry in the world of USAC.

A similar story came to pass in 1970 when the brilliant Texan, driver-engineer Jim Hall, unveiled his unusual new Chaparral sports car to be raced in SCCA's Can-Am series. The curious car featured a reverse ground-effects system with two large fans sucking air from beneath the car to create a partial vacuum, giving the car extraordinary traction in the turns.

Hall's car brought the same kind of terror to the Can-Am circuit Granatelli's turbines had injected into the Indy-car scene. Unlike the turbines, though, Hall's Chaparral bore a standard engine, a Chevrolet, just like most of the other Can-Am cars. His troubles originated with the other car builders, especially the European factory teams that had sunk large portions of their capital into the SCCA series and who didn't like the idea of literally eating the dust of Hall's radical machine.

SCCA, worried the loss of the Chaparral might cut into the attendance at the increasingly humdrum Can-Am events, resisted the protests from the team managers. But the issue was carried

Dennis Hulme (5), Peter Revson (7), and Jackie Stewart (1) at a 1971 Can-Am race at Mid-Ohio Raceway.

Bruce McLaren (4) and Denis Hulme (5) at the Michigan International Speedway for the 1969 Can-Am.

to the Federation Internationale de l'Automobile, which governs international racing, and the "vacuum sweeper" Chaparral was ruled out of Can-Am competition.

NASCAR, too, had its headaches in 1970. Chrysler Motor Company was racing with a lineup of new Plymouths and Dodges that featured high, thin wings rising above the rear fenders. The wings —a concept Jim Hall pioneered on his earlier Chaparrals of the mid-60s—gave the Chrysler cars greater stability at the blazing speeds generated on the high-banked Southern superspeedways and put the wingless Fords and Mercurys on the NASCAR circuit at a distinct disadvantage.

The elevated wings, a common sight on SCCA's Can-Am and Formula A machines until the FIA swooped down and removed them in 1969, were sternly dealt with in NASCAR racing. The balance of power was maintained by forbidding the entry of any new winged cars for 1971 and making the ones that were already on the circuit compete with considerably smaller engines.

Through all the controversies, the sanctioning bodies defended their actions by saying they were keeping racing competitive and holding down the costs to racing's participants. The latter undoubtedly was true. Most of the established car owners could not afford to buy and/or build turbine cars or vacuum-sweeper cars, although several were thinking seriously about it before the innovations were legislated out of existence. The first argument, however, raised a number of basic questions about the nature of the sport of auto racing. For when the sanctioning bodies talked of making their races competitive, they generally meant trying to keep the various cars as similar as possible. The less the cars differed, they reasoned, the closer the competition would be.

The logic was hard to dispute, and the truism of similarity breeding competition was applied religiously by the sanctioners. Of course, the enforcement of that axiom also meant the automotive companies at the core of racing's bankroll were sheltered from any violent upheavals brought on by would-be innovations, even those perpetrated by one of their own number.

But at the same time, it raised the bothersome issue of whether different drivers piloting near-identical cars was really what racing was all about. There were reasons to suspect that racing, in its purest sense, also involved the presence of cars that were decidedly different, cars that were clearly bold departures from the norm.

Those suspicions rested primarily with a racing group that actually had invested more time and money in the sport than all of the automotive companies combined. Racing fans, whose ticket purchases fed millions of dollars into racing's coffers each year, had repeatedly demonstrated their affection for the unorthodox, the unusual, the spectacular in racing machinery, at the place where it counted, the ticket window. They had been enthralled by the flashy, innovative cars, whether the turbines, the vacuum-sweeper cars, the winged cars, or the Novis of an earlier era. They swarmed to race tracks, ticket money gripped in their eager fists, just to see and hear them.

The sanctioning bodies knew the fans wanted the new cars to stay, but they could not risk undermining their economic foundations. They chose simply to protect the corporate investments rather than the individual ones, and confidently told themselves the fans would still come to the races. They were right, of course, since racing fans will go anywhere, anytime, to see anything resembling a race.

After the storm died down, the fans continued to flock to race tracks in record numbers. But there was a marked increase in the amount of grumbling in the grandstands at those races, as at least some of the more volatile spectators began to voice genuine bitterness and hostility toward the sanctioning bodies.

The grumbling was the loudest at USAC's smaller races, particularly its sprint car events, where the club's apparent penchant for making unpopular decisions gave the disgruntled fans an easy opportunity to vent their anger unrestrainedly, and sometimes riotously.

One of the more graphic examples of the direction the fans' feelings were taking occurred in the summer of 1968, only a short time after the USAC board had delivered its fatal decree on the turbine issue. The site was the clean half-mile dirt track at the Vigo County Fairgrounds, just outside Terre Haute, Indiana. The promoters had nicknamed the place "The Action Track" and this particular afternoon they got more action than they bargained for.

The sprint car program had gone smoothly until the start of

the feature event, when a car piloted by California driver George Snider spun and stalled in the first turn. USAC's usual procedure in the event of a spin or crash on the first lap of a feature race had been to call for a restart of the event, with the false start not officially counted.

Under USAC rules, article 9.13 in the 1968 competition rulebook, a restart calls for the cars to line up two abreast in the original starting positions they held on the false start, with no penalty to the car or cars involved in the first-lap spin. Otherwise, the cars would be lined up in single file, resuming competition with the spun cars relegated to the rear of the line.

At Terre Haute, USAC officials signaled for the cars to line up two abreast, normal in a restart, and Snider rejoined the field in his original starting slot. The field was given the green flag in that alignment and Snider quickly worked his way into the lead position. The Californian was still in front about two-thirds of the way through the race when the incredible news filtered down to his crew—the race officials had ruled the race had not been restarted officially, but had been continued under the yellow flag after Snider's first-lap spin.

This meant that Snider was technically way behind the field instead of way ahead, having been penalized the lap it had taken to get his machine moving again after the spin. The ruling was not announced to the crowd, but it did not remain a secret long. When a yellow flag came out late in the race and Snider was obliged to pull up at the rear of the pack, the fans began to detect something wrong. As the checkered flag fell and Larry Dickson, not George Snider, was ushered into the winner's circle, the picture took shape. Outraged by the apparent injustice, hundreds of fans stormed down from the grandstands and stomped angrily toward the judges' stand located at the rear of the pit area.

With the nervous USAC officials peering helplessly through the windows at the top of the stand, the incensed crowd surrounded the structure, shook their fists at the officials above, booed and loudly chanted "We want Snider!"

The officials managed to escape without injury only by waiting

Standing on the roll cage to his car, driver
Larry Cannon looks on as the mechanic works.

until the shouting mob had lost its steam and dispersed before making their departure.

The Terre Haute incident was not an isolated case. The part-time and low-paid USAC workers officiating at the smaller tracks often were booed soundly by fans for what appeared to be inept and unfair decisions.

Though refusing to admit to any trouble, the club quietly took steps to overcome the bad publicity it was receiving as racing entered the 1970's. In the fall of 1969, USAC handed the job to Bill Smyth, a barrel-chested man with a soothing voice, formerly the administrative assistant to millionaire John Mecom Jr., and a past Internal Revenue Service accountant.

As the club's executive director and its first real administrator, he began almost immediately to mold USAC into an efficient and streamlined business operation. In the first twelve months under Smyth's guidance, USAC signed its first multi-race television contract, whipped together a free-wheeling public relations effort, and landed a big-money sponsor for its Indy-car series.

Still, the presence of Smyth effected no great change in the club's basic philosophies and motives. Even now, the efficacious executive director dutifully defends the club's attitudes, even dismissing the idea that its image had suffered greatly from its past brouhahas.

"I've been for USAC from the beginning," he relates, "I had been on the board of directors and I think I had a pretty good knowledge of what it was all about before I came in as executive director. USAC's approach is rather conservative; that's not necessarily a bad thing, though.

"Sometimes you get so involved with something you don't realize the little criticisms you get aren't the feelings of the whole world. I found that USAC's reputation wasn't as bad as a lot of people thought it was. I got to talk to a lot of people and I don't think USAC and/or auto racing suffered from the bad reputation some people thought it had. I really think USAC has enjoyed a good reputation, for the most part."

The club's much-debated turbine decision also gets no argument from Smyth, although he generally sidesteps the main issue in his public comments on the subject: "I don't know, this all came up while I was off the board of directors," he says, when asked for his views on the turbine question. "I'm not an engineer, so I don't have an opinion one way or the other."

Of the critics of the USAC turbine stand, Smyth says, "They are generally people who have no investment in racing. I can't say that across the board, of course, because Andy (Granatelli) certainly has put a lot of money into racing, but there's a helluva lot of money invested by a lot of people in this and you have to consider that."

While he speaks of USAC's image with much stubborn optimism, Smyth concedes the club was in desperate need of a public relations boost when he arrived on the scene. He had quickly plucked energetic young publicity man Linn Hendershot from the Atlanta Falcons organization to head up a USAC public relations push, featuring a multitude of publicity gimmicks, club publications, and sponsor-promotion projects. "I felt there was a great void there," Smyth says of the public relations situation. "I felt we had been beaten to the punch by some of the competing sanctioning bodies too often."

Bolstered by the public relations upswing, Smyth went to work to consummate a rich television contract which put some of the club's Indy-car races on a nationwide hookup. He next lured Marlboro cigarettes, whose ads had been bumped from television by the growing anti-smoking campaign, into USAC racing as the main sponsor of the championship circuit.

Smyth then broke down the Indy-car division into three separate series of races, with a dozen oval track events—including the 500-milers at Indianapolis, Pocono, and Ontario—elevated to the top of USAC's pyramid of glittering championships. The road-race and dirt-track events, previously thrown in with the oval races on the championship schedule, were set apart from the top-line series. This trimmed down the number of races entrants were forced to run in pursuit of a particular championship crown and added new tracks in the east and southwest to the club's ever increasing race offerings.

"What we're trying to do is race fewer times for more money," observes Smyth, "and we're working to make it safer for the drivers, to get them more money, and make racing more popular in areas where we haven't been before. If we can accomplish those things, we'll do all right."

With Smyth at the helm, USAC picked up steam heading into the Seventies as the proficient administrator put the club's affairs in order. There were, however, some casualties along the way.

Former Indy driver Henry Banks, the club's competition director who had been singled out by critics as the architect of USAC's reactionary stance, was promptly kicked upstairs as a liaison man between the club and participating manufacturers and sponsors. Frank Bain, the club's business manager, walked out, claiming Smyth's policies were heading the club into bankruptcy. Bill Taylor, the vigorous stock car supervisor who inherited some of Banks' old duties, tired of the political in-fighting and resigned. Even Hendershot eventually left, as did two of his assistants.

The evidences of internal discord did not disturb Smyth and company, though. With much aplomb, the USAC manipulators sluffed off with cool, reassuring smiles any suggestions that there was any real dissatisfaction within the new order.

If the USAC philosophy was enunciated with meretricious composure, its neighbor to the south, NASCAR, ejaculated its particular position with a heavy-handed clout.

NASCAR, nurtured in the swampy South, has little use for the cosmetic public-relations palaver dished out at USAC. Below the Mason-Dixon line, auto races run one way, NASCAR's way, or they don't run at all. And NASCAR's way, to be more exact, is whatever Bill France, Sr., says it is.

A lumbering giant of a man, France reigns unchallenged over NASCAR. Nowhere else in racing does so much power rest with one man.

France, whose six-foot-five, over-200-pound frame belies his 60-plus years, made all of the important decisions in his long years as NASCAR president, ruling with benevolence when things went smoothly and with an iron fist when they didn't. Even after he stepped down from the presidency in 1972, he kept much of his power intact behind the scenes.

Technically, the top decision-maker in the NASCAR hierarchy is its commissioner. Until his death early in 1971, South Carolina Congressman Mendel Rivers, himself quite an expert on the acquisition and exercise of power, held the title, but not even Bill France can convince anyone close to the action that the commissioner is the final authority.

"There always is someone people have to bring their com-

Bill France, Sr. (center) on the old
Daytona beach course in the early 1950s.

Stock car racing at Winchester (Indiana) Speedway in 1971.

plaints to and I happen to be the one who usually takes the brunt in that department," France reported, with suitable humility, before Rivers' death. "Our top man is the Honorable Mendel Rivers —he's our commissioner and he has the final say-so. I'm not the top man, he is."

Despite his denials, France is recognized by those who watch him in operation as the de facto ruler of NASCAR, the man who runs things on a day-to-day basis. The totality of his control has been such, in fact, that many have tagged him "the czar of American stock car racing," a designation which France flatly rejects. "It's an erroneous label," he asserts. "I was instrumental in getting the organization started, that's true, but no one person can run the organization now." And no one person does, really. France has had a vice-president to help him oversee the southern

stock car plantation. The vice-president's name, oddly enough, was Bill France, Jr.

Reluctant to admit his lofty position, Bill France, Sr., nonetheless does not hesitate to evaluate his realm with the firm, confident resolve of a true patriarch. "We think our type of racing is the most practical and, while we don't talk about safety, the safest as well," he begins.

"I believe that NASCAR's future probably is as good, if not better than any other racing organization's future, for several reasons," he forecasts. "The main reason is that we believe we have concentrated on one kind of event and have done better with that one type of event than anyone else."

The latter statement would be almost impossible to dispute. NASCAR has perfected late-model stock car racing to such a degree it thrives all across the Southland, to the exclusion of almost all other forms of racing. And even today NASCAR continues to refine the art of staging stock car races. In 1970, France sent one of his stars, Tiny Lund, overseas to spread the gospel and drum up a few new attractions for future NASCAR events by entering stock car races in Germany and Japan. "The emphasis behind this is to add interest to our type of sport," France relates. "It added interest to the German event, for example, by having Tiny over there and possibly someday the Germans will want to come over here and run some events and this will add interest to our events.

"I can see someday that, at Daytona or at Ontario or Riverside, we would have an invasion of several drivers that represent the championships of various countries," he adds. And, not long after Lund's initial trips, top German and Japanese drivers did begin showing up for some of the bigger NASCAR go-rounds.

While his international relations were moving along nicely, France was having troubles on the domestic scene. The NASCAR drivers had gotten out of hand. Not completely convinced their interests were always at the heart of France's and the track promoters' policies, the top drivers formed the Professional Drivers Association. That move automatically put the drivers on a collision course with Bill France, who braced himself for the inevitable showdown with the upstart alliance.

That showdown came in September of 1969. The setting for the colossal confrontation was the gleaming new superspeedway Bill France himself had built at Talladega, Alabama, just east of Birmingham.

Talladega was France's brainchild—a steep-banked, over two-and-one-half-mile speedrome he had poured his thoughts, his money, his insides, into. When it stood completed, shining in the Alabama sun, he proudly showed it off to people like George Wallace and scheduled the inaugural race for September, 1969.

It was to be an historic race, but not for the reasons Bill France had hoped. The rumblings of discontent began as soon as the first car took to the super-fast Talladega track. The drivers, already upset over the fact that the purse for the race at Bill France's own track was one of the lowest for a NASCAR 500-miler, quickly complained that the high speeds reached on the

An overall look at the old Daytona race course.

new speedway were ripping their tires apart after only a few laps.

Some drivers also reported they were suffering physical side-effects resembling those incurred by jet pilots and astronauts from the sustained 190-mile-per-hour driving. The issue of whether the race could be run safely was voiced casually at first, then with growing conviction that it couldn't.

The furor grew steadily until, on the day before the Talladega race was to be run, the drivers boldly told Bill France they

couldn't race until new tires were developed to handle the greater speeds necessary at the new track. France, needless to say, did not welcome the news.

Most of the Saturday before the race day, France tramped around the pit area talking to small clusters of drivers, trying to get them back in line in time to save the race at his track.

France took a soft line initially, debating the matter with the drivers in a calm, reasonable tone, then hardened as his patience wore thin. When the PDA drivers refused to budge, France held back his anger and frustration with clenched teeth and resolutely told them, "There will be a race tomorrow, gentlemen."

And there indeed was a race the next day. It was not the race France and the paying spectators had anticipated, however.

By Sunday morning, the PDA members, including most of the top-name drivers, had packed up and left. So had several of the factory cars.

Bill France scurried around the garage area dragging out some of the entries from the previous day's Grand American pony-car race to fill out the field for Sunday's headliner. The race was run as promised. It was won by an obscure independent driver named Richard Brickhouse, but nearly everybody walked away from Talladega very disenchanted.

The PDA boycott made a shambles of the Talladega debut, something which would stick in Bill France's craw for a long time after. Over a year later, with two Talladega 500-milers run with only a smattering of gripes about the tire-ripping speeds, the unyielding NASCAR president still could not talk about the boycott without passionately disclaiming the idea that his sparkling edifice in Alabama could have ever been considered unsafe.

"That wasn't really the problem," he still contends. "I just don't think one of the motor companies wanted to compete. Had that motor company wanted to run, that race would have been run with no problems." Just which motor company perpetrated the boycott—Ford seemed the best candidate—and what its reasons were, France doesn't say. He simply knows the issue of tire wear was a smoke screen.

"We don't have any different problem with tires at Talladega

Auto racing—Daytona Beach style.

than they did at Ontario," he declares. "There, they just drove according to the limitations of the tires. There have been tire problems at Daytona, or Indianapolis, or in the Can-Am series, so the people driving the automobiles recognized the problem and drove accordingly.

"There aren't any more tire problems at Talladega than anywhere else," he continues. "The question is whether a man has the ability to control the car knowing the conditions of the situation he's got to control, and Talladega, then, is no more of a problem than any other track.

"I don't think it will happen again," France firmly forecasts. "Were this sort of a continuous walkout of contestants to occur a second time, I think the general public which has been buying tickets to the races would get so damned disgusted they would stop going to races. These people travel a lot of miles to get to these tracks. They want to see a race when they get there; that's why we ran a race at Talladega. There was no reason for anyone to walk away from Talladega."

Just how deep the scars of Talladega go becomes clear when France talks of the Professional Drivers Association: "Racing is unique in that a driver needs a team behind him; he doesn't make it on his own athletic prowess," he starts off, harshly. "When a driver enters a race, he can't enter without a car, and when he signs the entry blank he agrees to run the race. He knows what the conditions are before he arrives at the track.

"If the contestant wants to belong to the Knights of Columbus or the Shrine or any other fraternal organization, that's fine with us," he adds, bitter sarcasm creeping into his voice. "Just so long as he understands he's going to run according to NASCAR rules or he's not going to be accepted."

To guard against a repeat of the Talladega debacle, France inserted a new clause into the NASCAR entry blanks making it mandatory for cars, if not drivers, entered and qualified for a given race to start that race.

That action, coupled with the development of special tires for Talladega and the installation by NASCAR of a small plate in the carburetors of all Grand National cars to keep their speeds down and their engines together, smoothed over the controversy at least temporarily.

NASCAR rolled on, with the memory of the Talladega boycott only a nagging reminder of the drivers' uneasiness. In February of 1972, France handed the NASCAR presidency to his son, Bill Jr., when he stepped down to manage the campaign of presidential hopeful, George Wallace.

Compared with the soft-soap of USAC and the bossism of NASCAR, SCCA operated with impotent acumen—more progressive, low-key, somewhat naive in the ways of racing politics, and tormented by a persistent identity crisis.

For two decades, SCCA primarily dealt with amateur racing. With the exception of its sanctions of the U. S. Grand Prix each year at Watkins Glen, the sports car marathons at Daytona and Sebring, and its semi-professional U. S. Road Racing Championship, the club had little real experience in conducting full-blown professional programs. But in 1966, SCCA officials made a bold leap into professional racing, setting up two pro road-racing series for American and Canadian audiences.

Bill France, Jr.

When the allure of European road-racing finally was communicated to American fans via television, the club moved to capitalize on that twisting and turning style of competition that had been its particular love from the beginning. And when it launched its Canadian-American Challenge Cup series for the all-powerful Group 7 sports cars, the club found the North American race-going public ready for professional road-racing on a grand scale.

The Can-Am races, with their beautiful full-fendered sports machines and top drivers from both sides of the ocean, drew some 40,000 spectators per race that first year, 1966, and the series has never drawn much less in its five-year history.

The other series introduced in 1966, the Trans-American sedan championship for the new American automotive phenomenon, pony cars, was less successful at first, drawing only 4,500 onlookers per race in 1966. The club's third pro series, the Continental championship for Formula A machines, had the same initial reception in 1967.

By 1970, though, both those circuits were doing a healthy business, the Trans-Am drawing around 20,000 per race and the Continentals about 13,000.

Oddly enough, club officials were worried more about the Can-Am series than the Trans-Am or Continental. The Trans-Am and Continental both had fierce, close competition, even if their crowds were smaller, and were growing in popularity, while the Can-Am was getting dull competitively and its appeal was leveling off.

The immaculately prepared orange cars of Team McLaren had completely dominated the Can-Am since 1966. Driven by driver-builder Bruce McLaren and fellow New Zealander Denis Hulme, both seasoned grand prix competitors, the team racked off four straight Can-Am championships. They won all the races in 1969. In 1970, after McLaren was killed testing the new Can-Am car in England, Hulme teamed with American Dan Gurney and Briton Peter Gethin to win all but one for the McLaren stable.

The indomitable McLaren cars won so often and with such ease, often finishing one-two, the racing fans who continued to attend the Can-Am on the outside chance someone would beat the unbeatables, began to lose hope. SCCA officials were getting edgy, too; in racing, hope is a thing with ticket-money in its hand.

"Certainly we're looking at that—there has been domination by one team, but I think that domination is going to be increasingly difficult to maintain," SCCA's pro racing director Jim Kaser said of the situation near the end of the 1970 campaign. "There are some people who are getting serious about this thing and are going to do something about it, I think."

Kaser pointed to Jim Hall's "vacuum sweeper" Chaparral—which he labeled "a spectacular automobile"—the British entries from the March and BRM racing factories, and the titanium-based machine put together by the Autocoast operation in California. All had shown potential for challenging the McLarens, but all had for one reason or another been unable to pull it off.

Kaser's optimism was more wishful thinking than anything else. At the end of the 1970 season, FIA ruled out the Chaparral over SCCA's support of the controversial machine, and the other would-be winners seemed likely to remain that important split-second behind the always-advancing McLaren entries.

Then, as the 1971 season approached, SCCA's other two professional series were suddenly in trouble. With the national economy in a nosedive, four of the five factory teams pulled out of the Trans-Am circuit, leaving only the American Motors' Javelin team to play with the game but outclassed raft of independent entrants.

The Continental was headed for a trying season too. With USAC setting up a separate road-race circuit for its championship cars, SCCA's Formula A series was set in direct competition with the big-name Indy stars and cars for the first time. The prospects for the Continental's less-famous cars and drivers overcoming the heavier USAC appeal were disheartening, but SCCA officials refused to give up.

"It won't have any effect on our programs," Kaser commented on the USAC road-race plan, bristling slightly. "We concentrate on building up our programs rather than looking over our shoulders at other people's programs."

It proved to be a wise approach, as USAC's road-racing venture flopped, while the Continental series rolled on.

In addition to the fundamental ills threatening the three pro series, SCCA was beginning to show other symptoms of its growing pains. The club, which had suffered few major controversies in the early years of its professional adventures, was peppered by a barrage of squabbles and flareups. The most publicized incident occurred during the 1970 Can-Am at the Elkhart Lake Road America layout. There, Denis Hulme's apparent victory was wiped out when race judges ruled the McLaren driver had been given an illegal push start by corner workers—themselves part of the SCCA chain of command—after his machine spun off one of the turns. Hulme, who reported the corner workers had pushed him against his will, protested the ruling loudly, charging the SCCA officials were "a bunch of little Hitlers."

Earlier in the same season, some Trans-Am entrants had voiced objections to the club's rulings on the homologation of their 1970 machines—prescribing which production models and accessories would be permitted and which would not. One, the always-outspoken Indy veteran, Parnelli Jones, claimed the club was out to keep his particular mount, Ford's Mustang, from winning the series championship.

Cars lined up for the NASCAR 400 miler at the Michigan International Speedway.

There were other, smaller altercations, too. Officials disqualified what proved to be the wrong car at Sebring for causing a wreck. Fender-mashing incidents in both the Can-Am and Trans-Am ignited tempers and put SCCA officials in the middle of shouting matches between the drivers involved.

But SCCA leaders attributed much of the flak to sour grapes and sided with their officiating teams. "A certain amount of this is inevitable, especially when the decision goes against someone. We've got to live with a certain amount of that sort of thing," Jim Kaser commented. "I must say that, as a standard, the quality of officiating of SCCA events is really excellent. Sure, once in awhile an official is going to call one wrong, or one that on hindsight appears to be wrong, but we think the level is really good," Kaser continued, "I think I would say that no pro race has been won or lost because of an improper decision by an official."

Though plagued with many of the embarrassments common to the other top sanctioning bodies, SCCA still was the only one to

Sponsor and accessory decals on Indianapolis-type race car.

seriously consider whether the internal combustion engine was headed for the scrap heap, as the nation's growing antipollution forces claimed.

While USAC was toying with the idea of sanctioning, but not applying, the results of the Clean-Air Race competition to find a viable alternative to the internal combustion engine, SCCA was preparing to integrate the more pollution-free powerplants— the turbines, steam engines, electric cars, et al.—into its programs.

"I'd like to see something stimulated in the area of competition between cars that either meet or exceed the new emissions control standards, either in the form of a special rally with special stages or all-out racing events," Kaser revealed in mid-1970. "This is strictly in the thinking stages, but I wouldn't put it in the never-never land. I think it could be done in the very near future."

Despite its soft-sell approach, SCCA found it had to come to grips with the cruel realities of politics. The club did not walk away from politics but waded in fearlessly.

The tenor of SCCA's political attitude changed shortly after Jim Kaser handed in his resignation at the close of the 1970 season. Early in 1971, the club abruptly sent away two long-time staffers, club racing director Jim Patterson and public relations man Dic Van der Feen. Almost immediately followed the announcement that the club's headquarters would be uprooted from its quaint Connecticut setting and replanted somewhere in the Midwest, closer to the racing action. Closer, too, the club leaders could have added, to Detroit and Akron, the home bases of the nation's two largest automotive-related industries.

On down the ladder of sanctioning bodies, the lesser versions of USAC, NASCAR, and SCCA were plodding along in similar fashions.

IMCA was still around, running a handful of late-model stock car and sprint car races at small tracks in the Midwest, South, and Southwest as a prime farm club of the top-of-the-line circuits.

The Automobile Racing Club of America, meanwhile, had moved alongside IMCA in the ranks of second-string sanctioners. ARCA, specializing in the late-models, put on its programs at tracks in the eastern half of the country, often running as preliminaries to the bigger NASCAR main events.

Two new sanctioning bodies also were struggling to bring their particular types of racing to a level of national acceptance. The International Motor Sports Association was trying to make a go of Formula Ford racing and other sports car competition in the South but found the stock car-oriented Dixie fans reluctant, and the National Championship Racing Association was organizing a series of supermodified programs at dirt tracks in Kansas, Oklahoma, and Texas early in 1971.

On down the line, a multitude of regional racing bodies handled the late-models, sportsmans, modifieds, supermodifieds, midgets, sprint cars, or what-have-you, for their respective geographical areas, ranging from the United Racing Club in the northeast corner of the country to the California Racing Association on the West Coast.

Most of the clubs and associations had the same handicaps and hangups the Big Three sanctioners did. But, operating away from the glare of a national spotlight, the smaller organizations functioned under less pressure and their eccentricities were less institutionalized.

Isolated somewhat from the track-racing groups was the drag racing world. There in the land of smoking tires, Christmas-tree starting lights, and braking parachutes, the National Hot Rod Association and the American Hot Rod Association held sway over the hordes of drag-race enthusiasts who tinkered with their curious-looking cars all winter in dimly-lit garages just to blast down a quarter-mile asphalt strip at full acceleration.

NHRA, based in Los Angeles, and AHRA, headquartered in Kansas City, staged series of "Nationals" or championship drag meets across the country for professional and amateur drag racers. The two associations, whose followings were growing as rapidly as anyone's, seemed to have an easy time of it with their built-in solution for handling any radical innovations dreamed up by their competitors. Anytime a new idea popped up, they simply created a new competition class and kept right on going.

That paradise of straight-line racing was not immune to political division, though. In the spring of 1971, a third sanctioner, the International Hot Rod Association, came into existence to further fragment the market and the stability of the drag-racing genre.

From one end of the racing spectrum to the other, the stench of political dissection hung in the air like the smell of formaldehyde in a biology lab. Racing was sliced up into a score of fragments, and the fragments were not inclined to recognize they had all been carved from the same body.

They, instead, belittled each other in private, and publicly stood together to denounce their common critics who said their policies were antiquated and their priorities mixed-up.

Those critics surmised that as racing grew into a major sport its politics and its vested interests produced a tilted scale of priorities. First preference went to the automotive companies and sponsors, followed by the track owners, car owners, the sanctioners' own workers, mechanics and drivers, and, finally, the fans.

The critics charged that most racing decisions were made in light of their effects on the investments of the big-business interests rather than the good of the sport, which was not always the same thing. But no one denied that the system worked. It did, by the very nature of the top and bottom of the priorities ladder.

The automotive companies were the most fickle, putting in and pulling out their investments at the drop of a point on the stock exchange, and the fans were the least fickle, willing to withstand almost any indignity to see colorful cars chase each other around a track. And, whatever their faults, the sanctioning bodies managed to give the fans good races most of the time. So the fans kept coming, and the automotive companies inevitably had to come back where the fans were.

That perpetual cycle kept the wheels turning, but without shifting the sanctioners' focus from the money and its investors to the money of its audiences. The cash the fans handed across the ticket counter went into race purses and the pockets of the track owners. The money from the manufacturers was what passed through the hands of the sanctioning bodies. It was the money they actually saw, the money they touched and felt the texture and weight of, the money they built their programs on.

What the critics denied was the ability of the system to carry auto racing into the Seventies as a truly major-league sport, equalling pro football and baseball in its appeal, its approach, and its success. So long as racing remained a patchwork collection of politically autonomous special interest groups, they argued, it could never muster enough momentum to reach the majors.

Many of the critics, including some who had been top men with the various sanctioning bodies or automotive firms before pulling out, proposed the creation of a single sanctioning body with a racing commissioner to amalgamate the widespread and diversified aspects of the sport.

The proposal for a centralized racing government failed to gain much early support. The sanctioning bodies who would have to accept, if not lead, the changeover were not too impressed

Bobby Unser is clocked by crewman during
a practice run at Indianapolis in 1971.

with the idea. "There's no way for it to happen, in my opinion, because there's no way for one organization to handle it all," snorted Bill France. "Each organization has its own set of stars and if you combined them all you'd only have one set. You couldn't run a bunch of events with one set of stars. You need more than that."

"I doubt if it will happen," Bill Smyth chimed in. "Nothing is impossible, of course, but I think it would have to come a helluva lot further down the road than it is now."

"Racing is not like the other sports. It has some things in common, true, but it has some things that are fundamentally different," Jim Kaser added. "Auto racing, by its very nature, with the roles of the car owner, the man who operates the race track, the manufacturer, is not going to end up structured like the other major sports in this country. In general terms, I would agree that a national authority will evolve which will have, at least in certain areas, jurisdiction over the individual organizations in racing," Kaser did admit, however.

As the promising new decade began, therefore, there had been no real movement to unify auto racing. The crazy-quilt of sanctioning bodies continued on as it had before. Each ran its own races in its own way. The fans moaned occasionally when the officials called one wrong and the contestants screamed from time to time for what they felt was the same reason. Still, everyone generally accepted things as they were. After all, the U.S. sanctioning bodies stood four-square for The Flag, Mom, Apple Pie, and Crewcuts, so they couldn't be all that bad. Yet there were a few subtle signs of lingering dissatisfaction.

Along the north side of Indy's Gasoline Alley, the tall and dark-haired driver stood, hands on hips, and listened to one of the aged race officials explain the procedure he would have to follow to get his car checked out before he could put it onto the track. The driver, a product of the sports car circuits, listened patiently as the paunchy man dictated the complex rules to him.

Then, when the old official finished and turned to walk away, the driver graphically demonstrated his feelings about the prison warden attitude of the speedway overseer. His jaw hardened. His mouth twisted up in an exaggerated snarl. His arm shot out defiantly toward the departing official's back.

He raised his hand in that ageless and universal sign of defiance and disdain, "Up yours, buddy. Just up yours."

3. A Time for Reaping

THE awkward-looking white car skidded out toward the concrete retaining wall. Its tail rammed hard into the wall and the car tumbled crazily down the track, passing beneath a wooden pedestrian walkway. A black car swung to its left to avoid the somersaulting machine. As it cut back to the right, its rear wheels lost their traction and the black car slid into a dark blue machine which overturned in the middle of the track. A sleek gun-metal blue racer screamed out of the turn, its driver hunched forward in the deep cockpit. The swirling tableau of crashing cars suddenly unfolded in front of him.

The dark blue car was sliding, upside-down, along the track. The other blue car, rapidly-approaching, darted to the right, aiming for a narrow opening between the wreckage and the retaining wall. The overturned blue car edged up toward the wall, pinching off the other racer's escape route. The metallic blue car no longer had enough room to get by; its front wheel struck the skidding hulk.

The nose of the roaring car lifted into the air and the car pitched over the wall. It landed outside the wall on its nose, then on its tail, as it cartwheeled away from the track. As the machine bounced end-over-end through the air, it snapped off the top of a telephone pole. Finally, at the end of its flight, it slammed down with gruesome finality on its topside in a shower of dust, metal fragments, and flames. A man's arm protruded limply from beneath the smashed race car.

The driver, Bill Vukovich, was dead before the car ever came to rest. His skull had been crushed when it struck the telephone pole.

The three drivers in the battered cars left back on the track were all injured, though all would live to race again.

The whole sequence, from the time the first car careened into the wall, to the conclusion of Vukovich's lethal plunge to earth, had taken only a few seconds. The same number of seconds before, Bill Vukovich had been racing away to his third straight victory in the Indianapolis 500. The most supremely aggressive driver to ever race at Indianapolis, Vukovich was again completely in control of the race as he rumbled through the second turn and accelerated headlong into his destiny.

That swift and irreversible intervention of fate which snuffed out Vukovich's life is something all men who race cars live with. Around any curve at any track on any day, they know death may be waiting to cut them down.

From the moment he sees his first fatal crash, a race driver recognizes the risk he is taking. He may not see it at first, when he is filled with his own enthusiasm for the speed and competition of racing, but once he has seen someone die in a race car he knows the same thing can happen to him.

It is something every racing driver must grapple with early in his career. And, to the man, each ends up accepting it, coldly and calmly. If he didn't, he could never climb back into a race car.

Lee Kunzman, a talented young sprint car driver, put it as well as anyone could: "I think that any driver that goes into racing has to admit it's dangerous. It's a hazard of the sport, it's there and you have to look it straight in the eye. You have to recognize it's there or you're foolish, but I think most drivers sacrifice the dangers that are there for the pleasure of driving."

They accept the danger because, if they are to continue racing, they must. The compulsion to race, to compete, to excel, is so great they are willing to risk their lives doing it. And once they accept the hazards, they seldom worry about them. They view them with the pragmatic resignation of the fatalists they truly are. They are convinced their fates are predetermined and incontrovertible, that when "a man's time is up" there is no court of last resort. If it's their time to die, they can't prevent it; if it isn't they will survive to race again another day.

Consumed by this unyielding predestination, there is no necessity for concern about their personal safety. It is almost as if they believe they can drive as fast and as recklessly as they wish without fear, since only when their time is up will it cost them their lives.

Their fatalism not only relieves them of having second thoughts about the dangers inherent in racing, but it breeds in them a strange optimism that emerges whenever they might be tempted to have those second thoughts.

When the inevitable crashes come, the drivers who survive them always manage to find something to be thankful for, even when they have just barely survived.

If he narrowly misses being involved in a bad crash, a driver considers himself fortunate to have come through it. If he is in a wreck but escapes without injury, he is thankful for remaining whole and healthy. If he emerges with only minor injuries, he is quick to note "it could have been a lot worse." And if his body is smashed and broken in a racing accident, he still talks of how lucky he is "just to be alive."

God and Luck—in racing, they're the same thing—ride with racing drivers. One only has to look at the twisted and multilated remains of their crashed cars to see why they believe that.

The monstrous smashups they somehow live through, when they do, perpetuate the idea that they are protected until their particular time comes.

In a 1966 Indy-car race at Phoenix, Bobby Unser's machine shot under the guardrail after losing a wheel. There seemed to be no possible way he could have avoided being decapitated by the steel rail, but he did. The car was a shambles; Unser had only a sore finger.

During a Can-Am race at Las Vegas in 1968, Jim Hall's Chaparral rammed another car and soared into the desert, disintegrating as it bounded along the ground. The twisted carcass came to rest tail-first, with Hall still seated in what had been the cockpit. His legs were smashed, but he was alive.

Jerry Unser, eldest of the now-famous Unser brothers, sailed over the Indianapolis wall in 1958 in much the same fashion Vukovich had three years before. But Unser walked away with only a dislocated shoulder for his trouble.

A year later, however, Jerry Unser's car crashed less spectacularly into the Indy wall. The machine caught fire and Unser, pinned inside the cockpit, was fatally burned.

The saints of racing work in mysterious and unpredictable ways. There is no rational explanation for their method of selecting which lives will be given back and which will be taken away. The skill and experience of the drivers seem to have little bearing on how the keen-edged pendulum swings. It strikes down the mightiest, and the lowliest.

All three of the other drivers in Vukovich's crash were young men just learning the ropes at Indy. Any one of them could have been killed in that pileup, but none of them was. Bill Vukovich was the best driver on the track that day, but all of his talents and instincts meant nothing when he rushed into that death-dealing whirlpool on Indy's backstretch.

Jerry Unser was only an aspiring young racer when he twice collided with destiny and won only the first brief victory.

There is some tendency to believe that the longer a driver survives, the less likely he is to meet his end on a race track. The

deaths of such hardened veterans as Vukovich, Jimmy Bryan, Fireball Roberts, Jimmy Clark, Eddie Sachs—the list is almost endless—has diluted the concept considerably, but there is still some small validity to the belief.

It is strictly a matter of odds. By the time he reaches the top rungs of the racing ladder, a driver has already had his share of close brushes with doom. He has taken his lumps in those bad cars on those bad tracks he drove on the way up and, with better cars and better tracks, his experience shifts the odds slightly in his favor. He is by no means a sure thing even then, however. And, should a driver get by without the usual close calls, there are whispers that he is pushing his luck to its limits.

Bob Sweikert, who won the race Vukovich died in, nipped the Indy wall the following year in almost the same spot where Vukovich's car had leaped over the concrete barrier. Sweikert later claimed it was the first time he had ever crashed in a race car. It wasn't even really a crash; he continued on and finished the 500-mile event. A few weeks later on an Indiana sprint car track, Sweikert had his second, and last, crash. His car hurtled off the track and killed him. The odds have a harsh way of evening things up.

Sweikert was a rarity. Few men rise to the upper plateaus of racing without taking the hard knocks that form the basic education in the risks of their profession. Many carry the physical reminders of the bumpy road they traveled—the shoulder that aches periodically, the leg that stiffens when the weather changes, the recurring headaches, the jagged scars.

Those who were taught the sternest lessons offer the grimmest evidence of the gauntlet that is run. They are racing's walking wounded, the men with the game legs, fire-ravaged arms and hands, smashed and twisted faces.

They are at all the tracks along the way. They stick out like sore thumbs. Every circuit, large or small, has its legion of disfigured casualties, its bandy-legged Jim Halls, its fire-scarred Jim Hurtubises and Lou Sells, its limbless Jimmy Maguires.

Though NASCAR and SCCA have their share, it is USAC, with

USAC midget driver Danny Brown lost his leg when it was pinned between the bumpers of two passenger cars.

its slashing open-cockpit cars, which invariably produces the most mutations. The sheer power of its Indy-cars, sprinters, and midgets, their physical delicacy, and the higher frequency of competition seem to hold the greatest potential for marring its men.

Even Lou Sell, an SCCA driver, suffered his terrible burns in a USAC arena. His car tumbled over a ledge during a 1968 Indy-car race at Riverside, California. Jimmy Maguire lost his right arm in a 1964 USAC sprint car event. Hurtubise's arms and face were roasted in an Indy-car crash at Milwaukee the same year. Mel Kenyon's left hand and half of his nose were burned off in a 1965 Indy-car crackup at Langhorne, Pennsylvania. Norm Brown's face was devastated by flames in the 1968 Milwaukee pileup which killed Ronnie Duman. Johnny Rutherford's arms were twisted and scarred, first in a sprint car crash and then in an Indy-car blaze. Lee Kunzman's face and hands were seared in a fiery 1970 sprint car wreck.

As ghastly as even this partial list is, these were the more fortunate ones. All of them, even Maguire, came back to race again. With all their painful and crippling injuries, and the prognostications of their doctors that they would never race again, they put their aching bodies back into the cockpits of racing cars and roared on.

Throw in young Danny Brown, a USAC midget driver who lost his leg between the bumpers of two passenger cars away from the race track, and you have a squadron of living testimonies of the hold racing has on its people. With recuperative powers even competent physicians and surgeons cannot explain, they always come back for more of the same, if humanly possible.

It isn't possible in all cases. At the same USAC races where Kenyon or Rutherford or one of the others overrides his medical history, there may be one or two men who paid too great a price to be physically able to pick up where they left off.

They are men like Johnny White and Bob Hurt, both of whom now steer wheelchairs instead of race cars. Both were paralyzed by spinal injuries—White in a sprint car crash after being "Rookie of the Year" at Indianapolis in 1964 and Hurt in a 1968 encounter with the Indy wall while trying to qualify for the 500.

Still, Johnny White and Bob Hurt go as far as they can. White owns and works on a sprint car that runs the USAC sprint schedule. Hurt pledges to drive again. His doctors tell him it is impossible, but he thinks they are mistaken.

The presence of White and Hurt, along with the still-walking wounded, does not have the chilling effect that might be expected. Their appearance at race tracks does strike a pathetic note with the fans, yes. There is always a slightly heavier tone to the applause for Kenyon, Hurtubise, and the rest of those who carry on. But their physical deformities don't unnerve the racing fraternity. Some may marvel at the doggedness of those who come back from monstrous crashes, but they are not likely to be intimidated by the graphic evidence of what can happen to one of their number. It is simply part of the business, something that is accepted as such without agonizing over the possibility it could happen to them. "It's like anyone who participates in anything else. It's just one of those things," says Ted Hartley, who survived over 40 years as a top midget driver. "Like a football player, he's liable to get hurt but he doesn't quit because of it. You just don't worry about it."

It's just one of those things, the breaks of the game. And even when the demons do trip you up, you simply shrug it off. "As far as what it felt like when I first got upside down in a race car, the first time it happened to me, I got knocked out, so I don't know," Hartley reports nonchalantly.

The coolness with which racing drivers deal with their crashes is almost frightening in itself. Either they are truly steel-nerved or they quickly conceal their momentary fears when they start recalling their death-defying episodes.

Bob Veith smashed into the guardrail at Daytona in 1959. His Indy-car flipped over on its top and slid some 900 feet along the track, but the idea of being hurt apparently never entered his mind. "In that kind of darkness down there I just kept hoping I didn't hit anything, but I did manage to get the fuel line and the ignition shut off before it stopped sliding," Veith recalls, casually. "Your mind's still going pretty fast, you don't quit thinking. Your biggest concern is fire, but you don't really think you'll get hurt when you hit."

It is a phenomenal faith in his own immortality, in the benevolence of God and luck, in the conviction that his "time" hasn't come yet, that keeps a race driver on an even keel. That supreme faith does not prevent him from seeing the dangers he faces. It only frees him to pursue his chosen vocation with a clear conscience. "You have to really want to do this, because it is something that's a little bit dangerous," Rodger Ward, one of the drivers involved in the Vukovich crash and later a winner at Indy, once said. "It's a profession you have to want to do pretty badly, because there's lots of other ways to make a living."

"You're really sticking your neck out sometimes, I guess," adds Darl Harrison, now a veteran of nine seasons in the deadly sprint cars. "If you like the sport well enough, you're going to run the dangerous tracks and everything. I don't know why a guy does it, it's pretty ridiculous sometimes, but he does."

Ridiculous, dangerous, fatal—racing is all those things for the men who drive race cars, but they do it anyway. They climb into those rumbling cars and calmly urge them onto the tarck, knowing they could go home in a pine box. But they are doing something magical, something that makes them feel whole. If they have to die, this is how they want to go. The glory, the power, the fight for supremacy, is worth the risk.

They are too busy to worry about what is around the next corner. They are thinking about how to drive this turn, how to get around the car in front of them, how to catch the cars up ahead. They do not have the time to be worrying about anything else.

4. Watch Your Language

AUTO RACING, if we may call it that for just a moment, has a language all its own.

From the days when auto racing ads promised prospective fans "Chills, Thrills, and Spills," the sport has evolved a lexicon of words and phrases with as much color, glamour, and gaudiness as one of today's shiny racing machines—now known as "bullets," "dreadnoughts," "fire-breathers" or "juggernaughts," depending on your frame of reference.

Racing's inhabitants, or more precisely those who write its stories, have forged a curious collection of slang, colloquialisms, and figures of speech designed to match or surpass the growing "hipness" of the sport.

Just as race cars are no longer called race cars, nothing else is what it seems in the parlance of racing's participants and pen-pushers.

A race car, for example, no longer just goes fast. It now goes "like stink" and, when it does, it gains the title of "screamer" or "honker" or "Mister Quick."

When two such screamers then find themselves side-by-side on a race track, they do not, as in past eras, "battle" or "challenge" one another. Today, dipping into the vocabularies of the kitchen and the Middle Ages, these very same competing cars are said to "dice" or "joust."

Now should those same two cars—make that screamers—get a little overanxious and smack into each other physically, they would be thought to have had a "crash" or "wreck," right?

Wrong. They have had a "shunt"—a term borrowed from railroading—and have added a few "wrinkles," "creases," or "ripples" to their body metal. In the old days, they called them dents.

Next consider the age-old practice of spinning a race car. On seeing such an incident in bygone days, one would usually comment that the driver "spun" or, more elaborately, he "spun out."

Now, though, that same erring driver would be given the courtesy of having it said he "did a no-no" or he "looped it" or he "swapped ends." In other words, he spun (out).

Continuing on, if that same driver did a no-no on a road course and his spin carried him into the grassy portion of the layout, he "took an excursion into the grasslands" or "took the scenic route" or "visited the high grass."

So much for "driver error." Now let us move into the land of mechanical malfunction.

The most common failure that can befall a racing engine is detonation, a nice way of saying the powerplant has come apart at the seams and spilled its innards on the race track. Starting with the simplest way of saying it, one would declare that the engine "blew." The next step is to say the driver "cooked" the engine.

Moving up the ladder, one could exclaim that he "lunched" the engine or, shifting the blame slightly, the engine "lost its lunch." Then, since that last phrase is really a euphemism, you can say— those who dislike coarse language read no further—the driver "puked" the engine. Isn't etymology wonderful?

Turning to those brave men who pilot those four-wheeled fire-breathers, once known simply as racing drivers, a whole scrabble-board-full of names has been contrived by the pitside press corps. Depending on the individual, a driver may now be referred to as a "hotshoe"—although that one's about ready for the scrap heap —a "stormer," an "asphalt aviator," or a "brake burner."

For more specific references, anytime you are talking about a British driver, any other person who enters into the story has to be either a "bloke" or a "blighter."

And if you want to mention a young racer endowed with just the right combination of talent, wit, ego, money, and charm, you most certainly must speak of him as "that irrepressible individual, Sam Posey."

The various verbal inventions of the self-ordained motorsport lexicographers do not stop there, of course, though some might wish otherwise.

At any given moment, you may hear or see another of their creations somewhere, things like "wishbone" (a suspension part), "four-banger" (an Offy engine), "pod" (crash helmet), "soup" (rain on the course), "Jacob's ladder" (another suspension part), "carnival" (what all of racing is, supposedly), ad infinitum.

Collect all of those curious terms together and you probably would have enough for some sort of racing dictionary, which really might not do you much good in the pits, since no one there uses those quaint words and phrases, and the noise level would keep you from hearing most of them anyway. But it could be invaluable when you pick up just about any of the racing magazines currently on the newsstands and try to read the stories about the races you didn't go to. It might even help you figure out who won them.

5. *Rendering Unto God*

"THEY are all God-fearing men. All the ones I know are, anyway," Roger McCluskey answered, that May afternoon at Indianapolis when he was asked about his religious attitudes and those of his racing colleagues.

"God-fearing men"—that was the phrase McCluskey used, and it is as apt as any to describe the approach most racing drivers take to God.

Men who drive racing cars are religious men, as McCluskey's observation indicated. But they are not theologians. Their steadfast belief in God is not founded on the intellectual doctrines of academicians and philosophers.

Their proofs for the existence of a benevolent God are not rooted in the evidences of cosmology or teleology—most of them don't even know what those things are.

The existence of God, for a racing driver, finds its proof in less abstract things. It is found in the crash that is escaped, the wound that is healed and overcome, the race that is won.

As "God-fearing" men, race drivers do not think of their God in metaphysical terms, as Unmoved Mover or Prime Cause. He is not a vague abstraction. He is a personal reality, a divine body-guard who rides along in the cockpit with racing drivers and watches over them.

He is the protector who keeps the men of a deadly profession alive, and he can prevail upon even the most self-assured of them to humble themselves before him to give thanks for past blessings and to pray for future ones.

In racing, God is the object of a straightforward, if somewhat silent, reverence. It takes voice only when a racer, an uncompli-cated man who is often inarticulate on non-racing subjects,

makes a simple acknowldgement of his role in a particular success or survival.

Few racing men find the words to explain the religious aspects
of their racing experience. One who can, and often does, is Mel
Kenyon.

The Spirit of the Lord had hit the Apostle Paul on the road to
Damascus; it hit Mel Kenyon at Langhorne.

On a summer afternoon of 1965, Kenyon, already a national
midget champion, was running one of his first Indy-car races on
the always-treacherous Langhorne oval. His roadster was caught
up in a jarring crash. The car erupted in flames and Kenyon was
badly burned.

The doctors first doubted he would live and, when he indicated
he would, they declared that he would never drive a race car
again. The fingers of one hand had been burned off; his face had
been disfigured by the fire.

But in the months he spent in a hospital bed afterward, Mel
Kenyon found the one thing that could overcome the physicians'
prognoses and put him back in the cockpit of a race car. "My stay
in the hospital was really when I became an active Christian,"
Kenyon recalls. "I was brought up in the church and all that, but I
never became an active Christian until then. I feel my crash was
. . . a reminder, I guess you'd say."

The faith he mustered from that reminder brought Mel from
the threshold of death to the rebirth of his racing career in less
than a year. Racing again early in 1966, he quickly recorded successes in midgets and Indy-cars even greater than those achieved
prior to his Langhorne transformation. "I sometimes wonder if
it would have been possible without my faith, but I don't think
so," Mel now admits.

His submersion in his new-found religious experience was so
total that now Mel Kenyon, whose own spiritual rebirth grew
from the ashes of a near-fatal accident, can ruefully criticize
those fellow drivers who "are religious only when they have to
be, when they're about to die or something. It's all the time, from
the time you get up to the time you go to bed. It's not on and off,
not with me anyway," he says intently.

Shortly after he and his family moved from Iowa to Lebanon,

Indiana, in 1967, Kenyon joined a Lutheran church in nearby Indianapolis, where he takes his family every Sunday a rigorous racing schedule will permit. "If we're on the road going to a race on Sunday, it's a little difficult, of course," Mel relates, "And, working 16 hours a day on our cars, we don't have much time to be very active in the church itself. Of course, I don't believe you *have* to go to church," he adds, thoughtfully. "Because He's all right around you all the time."

Where Kenyon feels the presence of God most intensely is in the limitless isolation of the cockpit. He has felt God's hand at work there many times, most recently when he qualified for the 1971 Indianapolis 500 on the final Sunday of time trials: "When the time got right, the track was just right and I was all alone out there, everything just felt right.

"I generally can look back and tell you what I did at a certain time on a certain lap, and yet those four laps didn't seem like four laps at all. I don't really know what I was doing, almost like somebody else was doing it for me. It had to be something like that. It's kind of difficult to put in words."

The words which came most immediately were those Kenyon spoke over the Indy public address system as soon as he rolled to a stop in the pit lane at the end of his qualifying run: "I want to thank my crew, my car owner, and everybody else who helped us get here. And I want to thank our Lord and Saviour, Jesus Christ, without whose help I wouldn't be here at all."

If Kenyon's religious philosophy is the outpouring of racing's most basic and simplistic articles of faith, it is also the foundation for the religious stances of racing's worldliest figures.

The fundamentalist concepts that flourish in the bruising bottomlands of American racing carry over into its loftier realms. Protection from harm, literal divine guidance, and heavenly sanction of success lie at the heart of the faith of such "God-fearing" men regardless of their relative degrees of sophistication. They are the underlying tenets even for men like Mario Andretti, one of America's most polished and erudite racing drivers. "I'd like to consider myself a religious person," Andretti reports, easily, "I feel I have been helped a lot from upstairs—when I've won a race or when I've had a close call.

"The odds are against you, frankly, when it comes to staying in one piece, so you need some of that kind of help," he continues. "When you're in a bad wreck, you don't really have time to think about it. You're too busy then, but it sort of hits you later, especially when you examine it, see it on film. Only then do you realize just how lucky you've been."

Bad crashes Mario Andretti has had, but he has always managed to avoid the really serious injuries inherent in such incidents. His worst crash in recent years came at Indianapolis in 1969, when his Lotus swerved into the wall at 160 miles an hour and virtually disintegrated around him. Andretti escaped with only small facial burns under his eyes and later in the month won the Indianapolis race in another car.

He sees no ethical contradictions in a religious posture based so heavily on the persistent threats of bodily harm which characterize auto racing. "It's just like you find people turning to God in times of conflict and stress, like war," Andretti notes. "This is my war. I'm going to war every weekend. And I'm not ashamed to admit I say a little prayer before a race," he adds, with obvious conviction.

When he is not fighting his war in the trenches of Monte Carlo or Indianapolis or Langhorne, Andretti and his family are in regular attendance at Holy Family Catholic Church in his hometown of Nazareth, Pennsylvania. "We try to keep up the religious life as much as we can," explains Andretti.

Andretti's peace with God, fashioned from the atrocities of his own personal war, is articulated with only slightly more eloquence and perception than Kenyon's. But they are the same peace. The are both built on the hard realities of auto racing, the unmistakable extremes of agony and ecstacy native to racing life and racing death. They rest on the simple faith, the undiluted trust unintellectual men must rely on to succeed, and to survive.

They do not begin in reflections on cosmology and teleology. And they do not conclude with profound social doctrines for enveloping a man and his fellow men in a constructive religious framework.

Religion, for a racing driver, begins and ends within the narrow and deadly confines of the only world he knows and understands. It does not extend into such far-reaching spheres as sociology, moral philosophy, human ecology, or humanistic metaphysics.

Those are matters for theologians and ministers, not for "God-fearing" men. Not for racing drivers.

6. Rendering Unto Caesar

THE FOUR young people stand at the endge of the sprawling freeway. The three young men, their sun-bleached hair falling well past their collars, wear the anomalous uniforms of today's commune dwellers—an old Army fatigue jacket and threadbare brown corduroys, a brown body-shirt open to just above the navel and faded green bellbottoms, a flowered shirt and floppy-cuffed bluejeans. One sports a full beard of gnarled brown hair, another a bushy, drooping mustache.

The young girl wears a buckskin jacket and long, flaring bluejeans. Her face, bony and pink, squeezes out from between two cascades of straight brown hair held in place by a beaded headband.

Each of the four bears a metal teardrop-shaped peace medal dangling from a chain. Each wears brown sandals on dusty feet.

The belongings of the four young nomads lay at their feet in an assortment of knapsacks, bedrolls, and crudely-tied bundles.

In the distance, a pickup truck moves smoothly through the sweeping freeway curve. It rumbles out of the curve, loses speed momentarily, then picks up its steady pace again.

As it approaches the four roadside travelers, the truck slants toward the outside lane. Its horn breaks into a steady blare and the truck takes aim at the four motionless figures.

With the truck bearing down on them, the four young people scramble for the safety of the freeway guardrail. Their collection of bundles is left at the side of the highway.

The pickup truck swings onto the safety strip. Its right wheels are lined up with the cluster of knapsacks and bedrolls and deftly steamroller over each meager clump of belongings.

As the bundles dance, the truck edges smoothly onto the highway again and falls back into the rhythm of the freeway traffic. The four young people kneel beside their crushed and tattered possessions and watch the truck disappear in the distance, their faces torn between anger and bewilderment.

They have just had their first taste of the closest thing to "political action" a racing man is capable of.

The driver of the pickup truck is one of the country's top racing drivers. He smiles to himself as he motors on down the freeway, satisfied his "protest demonstration" had hit its mark.

It was not the first time the driver, who handled the wheel of a race car well enough to win some of racing's biggest prizes, had applied his skills to the paraphernalia of young wanderers who happened onto the same freeway with him.

This personal form of protest has become near-legend among his fellow racers. And when they tell of his freeway forays, they do it in voices filled as much with admiration as anything else.

For he is no freak, no wild-eyed political fanatic in an otherwise-calm occupational brotherhood. He is only a reflection of the basic political posture of his sport, and his practice of "pickup-truck diplomacy" speaks for the great majority of his racing colleagues.

Racing's general approach to politics is a simplistic one, one which parallels that of other men who spend their working hours in or under automotive vehicles—truck drivers, cab drivers, garage mechanics, and so on. The greater sophistication of racing machines—over trucks, taxicabs, and Corvairs—and of the skills necessary to handle them does not carry over into the political philosophies of the drivers, mechanics, car owners, and officials. They remain as medieval, as hard-hat as the other groups. They are patently anti-hippies, pro-police, anti-welfare, pro-Vietnam, anti-civil rights, pro-states rights, anti-free love, pro-apple pie.

They are most likely to think Lt. Calley should be given a medal for My Lai, Eisenhower was the only great president in their lifetimes, Haynesworth and Carswell should have made it on to the Supreme Court, and *Okie from Muskogee* was the most meaningful and significant piece of music written in the 20th Century.

If they were polled on the public figures they most respect, the most-frequently named would be George Wallace and Ronald Reagan. President Nixon, Spiro Agnew, J. Edgar Hoover, and Billy Graham would get their share of the votes, too.

Highly individualistic themselves, racing people tend to honor those politicians, like Wallace and Reagan, who have made the preservation of so-called "traditional American values" a personal crusade in the face of swelling cries for a new social order. They admire the uncomprising obstinacy such public figures exhibit in defending those values. That they, too, cherish those same values becomes almost secondary to the heroic stubbornness of a Wallace or a Reagan in upholding them against their common enemies.

"I really think Reagan's trying to do a good job, if they'd just let him," a veteran driver from California says of his state's governor. "I think he's got some good ideas for solving this ridiculous welfare mess," he adds, sipping his fifth Bloody Mary before lunch.

The sedimentary nature of racing politics varies only slightly from one stratum to the next. The lines of demarcation are indistinct, the shadings barely distinguishable.

The fewest deviations are found among the oval-track crowd, the most among the sports car set. But even on the road-racing circuit, it's a long way from Woodstock.

Long hair—generally disdained by the stock car, Indy-car, sprint car, etc., populace as unmasculine—is fairly commonplace among the road racers, but even some of the shaggiest of those hold to the conservative political viewpoints of their better-barbared compatriots.

Even one of the most cosmopolitan American drivers openly defends the U. S. presence in Vietnam, advocating a fight-to-win policy there long after even the most hawkish politicians have relinquished that stance, and then goes on to admit he is nauseated by the new young commune-builders, because they are "dirty" and they "screw in the streets."

That same driver also confesses that he has little sympathy with the welfare system or the black man's cries for equality.

Not that he looks down on the good black men, he notes, but he feels any black man who wants equality can get it if he is willing to work for it.

This outlook on the black plight is, again, characteristic of most of racing. Operating in an almost completely white community, the men in racing have little understanding or feeling for the black struggle for equality, dignity, and identity.

"You know they really get upset when you call one of them 'boy'," a burly veteran from the Southwest, confided in his companion one afternoon at Indy, "Down home, I called one of them 'boy' and, listen, he was ready to fight me right then."

"I was thinking, 'Now's your chance, boy, give'em a good show'," a young driver was telling a newspaper reporter who asked him about his feelings just before his first Indy race.

"Uh, you better scratch that 'boy' there. We're not supposed to say that anymore," he hurriedly added with exaggerated embarrassment.

Curiously enough, the sudden self-consciousness over the use of the word "boy" has been somewhat symptomatic of a subtle softening in racing's attitude toward the black man. Insulated from black people for so long—partly by the nature of the sport, partly by design—racing has had to come to grips, however hesitatingly, with the growing black presence in its ranks.

More and more blacks, finally able to afford and enjoy auto racing, have come as spectators. Some blacks have begun to appear on the racing crews of such luminaries as Andy Granatelli and Dan Gurney. One black driver, former moonshine runner Wendell Scott, has become a fixture on the NASCAR Grand National circuit.

For the most part, the blacks who have filtered into racing have been accepted, and will be in the future, because they have earned their places there through skill and hard work, more hard work probably than would be required of a white man. That acceptance actually does very little to change the fundamental view of more-universal black problems, just as the appearance of a few long-hairs in their midst has had no real effect on racing people's dislike for the scruffy, free-loving kids who riot on campus and shed their clothes at rock festivals.

In the privacy of the pits or the garages, conversations among racing men are still often laced with most of the language's uglier ethnic slurs, the old assortment of jokes, and snidely-cast aspersions about the manhood of those who don't visit the barbershop twice a month.

Racing remains at odds with the supposed new order, but its opposition is an impotent one. For the worship of "rugged individualism" which makes the politics of racing people so reactionary also cancels out any concrete effects those politics might have.

Coupled with their preoccupation with racing, the individualism of racing men keeps them away from the instruments which could put force behind their political ideas. They shy away from organizations, political or otherwise. They tend not to be interested in seeking public office, or campaigning for those who do. They do not have the time or inclination to work actively with local political party units.

Racing and the actual practice of politics are mutually exclusive, both requiring the total energies and attention of those who would pursue the particular promises of each.

Racing men race and leave politics to the politicians. They have their own opinions on the subject, to be sure, and they voice them when the occasion arises, but their political involvement rarely goes beyond that.

The closest they can come to political action is when they occasionally run their pickup trucks over the personal effects of a handful of "hippie-types" along a stretch of freeway, smile to themselves, and briefly wonder why the kids are trying to tear down this great country of theirs.

II THE PEOPLE

7. *They Call Him Everything but Mister 500*

ANDY GRANATELLI is a hustler. He's the original carnival mid-way huckster, the Brooklyn Bridge salesman, the Alaskan icebox peddler, the guy at the pool hall who innocently explains, "Well, I haven't had a cue in my hand for years, but I guess I could play a few racks."

He sells things. He sells magical elixirs he says will make your car run better; he sells radical new ideas that are supposed to revolutionize auto racing but never seem to do it; he sells the images of his backers, his drivers, his brothers, his racing ventures, his sport, to the paying public; but, above all else, he sells Andy Granatelli.

He's been beating the drum for himself, and a whole raft of enterprises, schemes, and ideas, most of his life. He began as a plucky Sicilian kid on the back streets of Chicago, convincing stranded motorists on cold, blustery mornings that he and his brothers, Joe and Vince, could get their cars started for the meager price of a dime.

From that humble beginning—if anything about Andy Granatelli is humble—he moved to hawking speed equipment to Chicago hot-rodders. That enterprise eventually provided him with the springboard he needed to do some real big-time selling.

He sold hot-rodding across the Midwest; he sold roadster racing at Soldier Field to Chicago sports fans; he sold his automotive ideas to the front offices of the Detroit carmakers. He sold himself as "Antonio the Great, Italian Speed Ace" to unsuspecting inhabitants of hick towns along the barnstorming circuit.

He sold his way into the upper reaches of the automotive world, and ultimately became the world's greatest super-salesman by taking a little-known oil additive called STP and building it into a multimillion dollar empire with himself, naturally, perched atop it.

With that kind of talent for promotion and salesmanship, auto racing was a natural for Andy Granatelli. And since he moved in on it, racing hasn't been the same.

He and the Brothers Granatelli came to Indianapolis after World War II to try their mechanical skills in the great Memorial Day 500. Their debut, as with their later efforts, had that certain Granatelli touch to it.

Andy and company created an instant stir at the Indianapolis speedway by pulling into Gasoline Alley for the first time in their Miller-Ford with an Illinois license plate hung on the back of it. They had, to the amazement of the Indianapolis regulars, driven their race car down from Chicago, completely decked out with headlights and license plate!

That was only the beginning of the Granatelli adventure in auto racing. For about a dozen years afterward, the three Granatelli brothers brought an assortment of weird race cars to Indianapolis, most of them powered by souped-up stockblock engines put together in their Chicago speed shop.

The Granatellis and their cars became one of the annual oddities for which the Indianapolis race has always been famous. The Indy oldtimers had many a good laugh over the flamboyant antics of Andy, Joe, and Vince, or "those crazy guys from Chicago," as they came to be known.

They were poor then, and not much of a threat to win the race, so it was easy for the Indy establishment to take a kindly attitude toward them. But it was an attitude which would not last.

Andy, who had been retired as an aspiring race driver when he crashed one of those first Indy-cars and broke nearly every bone in his body, was beginning to make his mark as a businessman. When he took over STP and ballyhooed it into the nation's fastest-selling oil treatment, he was able to begin thinking about making a serious attempt to win Indianapolis. Not that he hadn't been serious about it before, but now he didn't have to rely exclusively on enthusiasm.

The Granatellis were no longer poor and they were about to become a threat at Indianapolis. They also were about to become the most controversial figures in the history of American auto racing.

They started out by buying the famous Novis—those noble, growling fire-breathers originally created by Ed and Bud Winfield in the forties. They were the loudest, most powerful, most exciting cars that ever raced at Indianapolis. They also had the worst luck of any other cars at Indy, which naturally made them the most popular cars as well. That fact undoubtedly did not go unnoticed by Andy Granatelli as he stuck his big red and white STP decals on the sides of the brutish machines.

The Novis, under Granatelli's supervision, stayed true to form. They were loud and exciting, but they didn't win. They did, however, push the booming sales of STP even higher.

The Novis also boosted Andy Granatelli's stock with those legions of perennial Indy fans who take to anything with a little extra flair. And flair always was Andy's strong suit.

He dressed his pit crews in spectacular pajama-like uniforms plastered from top to bottom with those haunting red ovals with STP printed on them in big white letters. He bounced his 275-pound frame up and down the pit lane and brought roars of sympathetic laughter from the crowd when, on occasions and on cue, he broke into a waddling run in plain view of his doting audience.

But it was not enough. There was a difference between being an interesting curiosity and being a winner. So when the Novis failed to win, Andy tried something else.

What he tried, true to the old Granatelli gift for the unusual, would shake the Indianapolis fraternity to its very foundation. It would also bring to an end, firmly and finally, the fatherly benevolence with which the people in racing had looked upon his enterprises.

In May 1967, Andy came to Indianapolis with a bulbous bright-orange race car which had as its power source a turbine engine much like those used to power airplanes. From the moment the car rolled onto the track with its eerie whistling rustle, it was roundly condemned by racing's old guard. "That's not a race car, it's a goddam airplane," was the first and most frequent complaint lodged against the silent invader.

Race car or airplane, the lopsided machine—made all the more competitive by its side-by-side construction which put the turbine

President of the STP Corporation and colorful Indianapolis race car owner, Andy Granatelli.

powerplant alongside the cockpit, its four-wheel-drive system, and the magnificent driving talents of rugged Indy winner Parnelli Jones—totally dominated the month of May 1967, at the Indianapolis speedway. All eyes were on the STP turbocar from the time practice began the first of the month to the agonizing final laps of racing at month's end.

With Jones driving brilliantly, the turbine car—Andy Granatelli's turbine car—swept into the lead at the outset of the race and with awesome precision left its piston-engined challengers miles behind. But, with just four laps, ten miles, to go, a six-dollar bearing in the gear case gave out and the car rolled to a stop, Jones throwing up his hands in dismay as a glum Granatelli trotted up to the disabled racer.

The turbine car, though it did not win, threw a genuine scare into the racing community. The cries to ban the unorthodox

Indianapolis 1968—Joe Leonard in Granatelli turbine engine car, leaving the pits to set new qualifying record.

machine were immediate and continuous, and, before 1967 was over, the issue was carried to USAC's board of directors.

Surprisingly, the USAC board did not flatly ban the turbocar. The board did impose further physical limitations on the turbine powerplant, however, cutting back its power potential by twenty-five percent.

Andy was indignant. The new restrictions had effectively banned the turbine, he screamed, charging the USAC board with "stan'ling in the way of progress."

Then he did the one unforgiveable thing that could set the racing rank-and-file against him and make him forever an outcast within the sport. He refused to accept the USAC ruling. He sued USAC and the ensuing court battle—a long, loud, and expensive one—drew the kind of sordid headlines the people in racing came to resent bitterly. "He never should have taken it to court," one later said, expressing the general feelings of others. "He hurt everybody in racing when he did that."

The suit gained Andy little—the court upheld USAC's right to make or change its own rules—and cost him the friendship of many of his colleagues.

It didn't end there, either. The level of ill feeling toward Granatelli grew even more when the 1968 Indianapolis race came along.

While his court suit was hanging fire, Andy talked with Colin Chapman, the guiding force of the English-based Lotus racing cars whose Indy entries Granatelli had backed before. He asked Chapman to design a new chassis to house his turbine engines, whether they had to comply with the challenged USAC edict or not.

Chapman, an Englishman with a quiet genius for designing light, delicate, winning racing cars, handled the assignment with dazzling brilliance. Incorporating aerodynamic styling to the utmost as he sculptured the new chassis, Chapman produced a stable of dramatic wedge-shaped race cars that, after Granatelli pasted on his famous decals, looked like glowing red STP doorstops on wheels.

The new Lotus cars, like the first turbocar, used the four-wheel-drive system, which the USAC board had already said it intended to outlaw the following year, and carried Granatelli's turbine engines behind the cockpit. Aesthetically, they were breathtaking; functionally, they were nothing short of perfection.

Though the turbine powerplants were less potent than before and the Granatelli-Chapman combine was rocked early by the loss of four of its assigned drivers—the great Jim Clark was killed in Europe in April, fellow Scot Jackie Stewart broke his wrist in Spain a couple of weeks later, British driver Mike Spence died when his turbine car crashed in practice, and Jones withdrew when the original turbocar couldn't cut it—the doorstop cars dominated the month of May in much the same way the first Granatelli turbine had the year before.

In an awesome display of quiet power, ex-motorcycle champ Joe Leonard and grand prix champion Graham Hill qualified for the first two spots in the lineup, and Art Pollard lined up the third Lotus-STP machine a few rows back. It was beginning to look, as it had in 1967, like Andy Granatelli had it sewed up.

That fact in itself put him even more at odds with his competition. The hostility of Gasoline Alley inhabitants toward Andy deepened when the new turbine cars ran so superbly. Andy had said the new USAC restrictions would put the turbines out of business, they pointed out, and their latest performance just proved that, at the very least, Andy had been "poor-mouthing" or, at the very most, had been telling a bald-faced lie.

Whatever he had been doing, he still lost. None of the three turbocars finished that 1968 race, with Leonard's machine expiring while in the lead with eight laps remaining. It was 1967 all over again, only in spades.

It was 1967 all over in more ways than one. Again, though the cars did not win, everyone with a stake in the piston-engine monopoly of racing went after Granatelli's turbines with renewed vengeance. Everyone was against them—even God, according to the driver who ended up winning the 1968 Indy race. "God didn't want the turbines to win," Bobby Unser proclaimed from Victory Lane.

Moving as if it indeed had divine sanction, the USAC board finally completed the job on the turbine cars it started to do the first time. The board cut back the engine potential another twenty-five percent, formally banned four-wheel drive, and struck down the use of industrial turbines like the ones Andy

Indianapolis 1969—Mario Andretti and Lotus designer
Colin Chapman after a practice run in the Lotus.

had used in favor of automotive turbines, the only known models
of which were about as useful for powering an Indy-car as a
Volkswagen engine.

Andy perfunctorily announced that the edict had legislated his
turbines out of racing—which no one, of course, believed—and
quietly scrapped the controversial cars at the close of the 1968
season.

The Great Turbine Controversy was over. But racing's war
with Andy Granatelli wasn't. Without even putting a car on the
track, Andy again rankled his contemporaries.

Between the 1968 and 1969 seasons, Andy published his autobiography. In the book, he traced his rise from the days of starting cars for a dime to the present days of selling eighty-six million dollars worth of STP a year, including his versions of the many racing controversies in which he had been embroiled.

Strangely enough, it was not Granatelli's defense of the turbine cars and his other disputed projects that upset the racing crowd. It was the title of the book that infuriated them. He titled it *They Call Me Mister 500* and many in racing took instant offense at the idea that so flattering a title as "Mister 500" could be arbitrarily conferred on the man who had repeatedly disrupted the sport of auto racing.

"I've heard him called a lot of things, but never that," snapped one Indy regular. "The only people I know of who could rightfully be called that are Tony Hulman and maybe Wilbur Shaw, when he was at the speedway," observed another. *"They Call Him Horatio Hornblower* would have been more like it," added one of the better-read racing observers.

Mister 500 or Horatio Hornblower, Andy rolled on, undaunted. He came to Indianapolis in 1969 with a powerful if somewhat conventional lineup of cars. He entered eleven cars, the most ever entered by one car owner. "If he has to enter thirty-three cars to win the thing, then he'll probably do it," was the inevitable reaction from along pit row as people began to talk about how Andy was trying to buy the race since his attempt to steal it with the turbines had failed.

Andy didn't need eleven cars, as it turned out. He didn't even need all of the three he got into the race. He only needed the one very special car he had added to his collection.

During the off-season, he had picked up the racing operation manned by nonpareil driver Mario Andretti and masterful mechanic Clint Brawner.

Driving first a sleek new Lotus, then Brawner's year old Hawk-Ford after the Lotus crashed, Andretti brought the Granatelli dream to fruition. Both Andretti and the Hawk performed flawlessly on race day and finally got Andy Granatelli into Victory Lane.

Andy, of course, could not let the occasion pass without an appropriate display of the old Granatelli chutzpah. When he ar-

At work in the garage area at Indianapolis, Andy Granatelli
is on hand to oversee all work done on his race cars.

rived at Victory Lane, he grabbed Andretti firmly by the jaw and
solidly planted a kiss on his cheek.

It was the most beautiful piece of showmanship ever witnessed. With a rare combination of honest emotion and an uncanny instinct for theatrics, Andy kissed his way onto the front
pages of America's newspapers. The scene would reappear hundreds of times in the following months as the centerpiece of a
long line of STP advertisements.

Andretti did his part, too. Speaking over the speedway public
address system from Victory Lane, the resourceful winner explained his victory by saying for all to hear, "I guess we just had
more STP in our Ford engine than the other guys."

Andy couldn't have said it better himself. Mario's perfectly-
timed words would pour from a million radio and television sets,

followed by Andy's jovial sales pitch for STP, "The Racer's Edge."

The whole thing was ironic, really. Andy had tried to win Indianapolis with everything but a motorized bathtub and, when he finally pulled it off, he did it with a car little different from everybody else's. He won it their way, by the book, and with only the slightest rumbles of controversy.

Almost apologetically, Andy began immediately to undo the basically self-made legend of his continual failures at Indy. He played his twenty-two straight losses at Indy into a juicy melodrama for the newsmen and his own ad writers, and suddenly he had to figure out what to do for an encore.

With typical Granatelli candor, he confidently announced that he intended to try for a second consecutive Indy win. "After all, I lost for twenty-two years so I figure I'm entitled to win for twenty-two to be even. Why not?" he said, with the kind of preposterous logic only he could get away with.

But almost as soon as he had said it, he suffered another setback. At the end of the 1969 season, Clint Brawner and his young partner, Jim McGee, abruptly quit Granatelli.

Andy's shenanigans brought him trouble again. Brawner, the durable veteran with thirty-eight seasons under his belt, made it clear he and McGee were irked when their mechanical accomplishments were overshadowed by Granatelli's horseplay. "I never did see a good picture of us in Victory Lane last year," observed a bitter Brawner as he and McGee started work on building a new Indy-car operation. "I know I could have gone home and just called it quits," Brawner continued, his face firm, his eyes set, "but I decided to go ahead with this new car to show I could beat that damned Granatelli."

With Brawner gone, the Granatellis were forced to close ranks as their circle of associates narrowed down to family members and old cronies. Andy tried, in his cheerleading way, to rally his forces as brother Vince, tough and wiry, was moved into Brawner's former slot as chief mechanic and brother Joe, as always, remained the ever-present, balding figure standing quietly in the background. "Joe's the brains, Vince's the hands, and Andy's

Andy Granatelli at work on his race car.

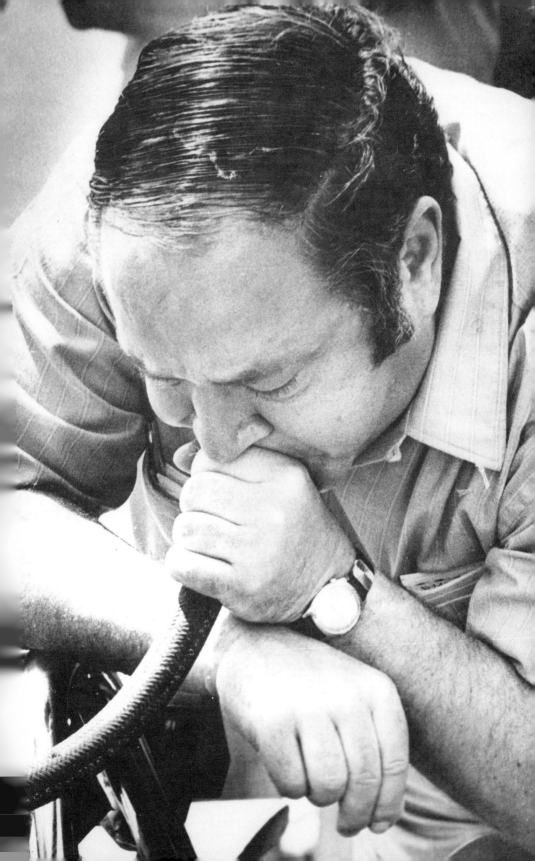

the mouth," one racing insider had said of the brotherly arrangement, and as the Granatellis prepared for the 1970 racing season it seemed to be an accurate evaluation.

But as the year wore on, there seemed to be a subtle change in the mouth portion of the threesome. It laughed less and less, and frowned more and more. Andy's controversies began to haunt him. His zany stunts sold a lot of STP, but made him an outsider with the racing stalwarts, many of whom had been his friends in earlier days. He was alone, except for his brothers and a handful of long-time friends.

Yet, Granatelli had made his indelible mark on auto racing. His cars and his wild antics would be remembered long afterward. His stormy turbine car phase was still being talked about some two years after the cars disappeared from the racing scene. Most of the talk was angry or bitter, but a few—those who were involved with the turbines, or those who saw them as harbingers of progress, as Andy apparently did—spoke wistfully of the swooshing red machines. "The turbine gives you a fantastic ride. I've driven the wedge with a Ford in it instead of the turbine and it still gives you a nice ride, but it pops and sputters a lot," commented Joe Leonard, who probably would have been a staunch opponent of Andy's turbines had he not been driving one. "Comparing a piston engine with a turbine is like comparing a Mustang with a Thunderbird, or a Chevy with a Cadillac."

The kind comments were too few and far between, however, to comfort Andy in 1970. He had to somehow reconcile himself to the consistent cheers that erupted from the stands anytime one of his cars ran into trouble in a race. And, worst of all, he had to learn to lose all over again.

In 1970, Andy's cars lost, at Indy and elsewhere, winning only once all season. The experience sobered him and, as if to prove he was more than a mouthy clown, he began to take his racing more seriously, spending more time hunched over his cars with his mechanics.

Still, on occasions he could show some of the old Granatelli gift for warmth and humor. "It's not that I like Mario because he's Italian," he quipped about Andretti in one of his more flippant moments with newsmen, "I like him because I'm Italian."

For the most part, though, he was more businesslike than

before, less rollicking, as he seemed determined to take his new failures with the solemn grace of a dethroned champion.

Things got no better in 1971, even though Andy lured McGee back into the fold, trying to put the magic back into his cars. He still took his lumps; his cars seldom finished races and won none.

He hit bottom at the end of the 1971 season. Andretti, yearning for victory again, left. McGee went with him. The face of Andy Granatelli grew longer, darker and more somber.

But 1972 was ahead, and one could easily suspect that Andy would not stay so subdued for much longer.

He was still a hustler, remember. One could almost see him standing there in a smoke filled pool hall, firmly chalking his cue after losing out to the local pool shark. "Well, I guess you beat me that time," he would be saying, "But I suppose I could play another game.

"Uhhhh . . . and by the way, why don't we jack up the stakes a little bit this time, just to make it interesting?" Andy Granatelli, hustler, would then say, carefully examining the tip of his pool cue and wearing the straightest damned face you ever saw.

8. Trial by Fire

LEE KUNZMAN stirred his coffee carefully as he sat at the small table in the cafeteria at the Indianapolis Motor Speedway. He glanced down at the white cup for a moment before withdrawing the spoon and sliding it onto the table.

Across the table from him, a newspaper reporter pulled a ballpoint pen from his breast pocket and scribbled something at the top of a long canary tablet. A photographer, extracting a roll of film from his camera and replacing it with a fresh one, straddled a chair cocked at an angle to the table. The fourth chair was unoccupied.

Kunzman looked the part of the aspiring young racing driver.

Lee Kunzman

His hair was thick and black; his good looks were classically Mid-western, virile but fresh-scrubbed; his arms and hands were meaty and masculine.

He sipped at his coffee as the reporter looked up from his tablet and asked, "Okay, Lee, you ready to start?"

Kunzman nodded casually. It wasn't his first press interview, but it still was something he had not done too many times before. Even though he had been impressive driving stock cars around his native Guttenberg, Iowa, and on the IMCA sprint car circuit and had won the first USAC race he entered—a midget program at Davenport, Iowa, in the fall of 1968—he still was, in May of 1969, recognized only by those newsmen who religiously followed the midget and sprint car trails.

"Well, I guess the first question is: What are you doing here at Indianapolis?" the reporter began.

"I'm definitely a spectator this year," Kunzman answered quickly, smoothly. "I want to learn as much about this place as possible, because when and if I run here I want to be competitive. I'd only been here once before—I came to see qualifications one day a couple of years ago but they were rained out—and everything is so vast that you can't hardly grasp the whole thing in a few days. I've really got the impression of the complexity of everything here. The organization of the thing is unreal, everybody has their own thing to do and they don't cross over into each other's areas. And the precautions they take before they ever let a man get on the race track—that's pretty impressive, too."

He sipped at the coffee again while the reporter asked about his feelings on being at a race track and not actually racing. "I definitely have that urge that I want to be running but, as I said, I would want to be able to be competitive," he related, "and I think a fellow could be more competitive if he understands the whole thing real well first."

The photographer, squinting through the viewfinder, aimed his camera at Kunzman and clicked the shutter methodically as the reporter turned the conversation to Kunzman's sizeable success in only a few months of USAC racing. That success included the win at Davenport, the subsequent victory in one of the featured midget races inside the Houston Astrodome, and consistently good finishes in a handful of USAC sprint car races.

The sprint car achievements included decent finishes on the awesome high-banked paved tracks at Dayton, Ohio, and Salem and Winchester, Indiana, a kind of monster they don't have in Iowa.

"I hadn't run very much pavement when I came to USAC," he confessed. "My first time on the high banks was at Dayton and I wasn't sure whether I liked it or not, but we did some things to the car and got it working at Salem. I'm getting to like the paved banks almost as much as the dirt now, but I grew up on dirt and I'm more accustomed to it," he added.

Next the interview moved to Kunzman's plans for the future, after his month of watching things at Indianapolis. "Well, I'm seriously looking for a championship ride so I can run the Speedway next May," he said, smiling, "and I would like to try a stock car again. I've always liked to drive them. I think a race driver should try to drive every kind of race car and I just want to try to drive as many as possible. Every type of car drives differently, of course, but racing is pretty much racing."

As he talked, a girl, probably in her early twenties, her face pleasantly tanned and her dark hair falling neatly past her brown shoulders, walked over to the table and edged onto the vacant chair. "Hi, Lee Kunzman, whadja doin'?" she said, pertly.

"Oh, just finishing up a newspaper interview," Kunzman replied, motioning toward the two men at the table with him.

"Oh, okay, I won't interrupt. See ya in a little bit?" she said, standing up again.

"Yeah, I should be done here in a few minutes," Kunzman assured the girl, who bounded off toward a table in a corner of the cafeteria.

"Okay, now where were we?" the bachelor driver asked, turning to the reporter.

"I think I was about to ask you how, and why, you got into this business in the first place," the man behind the canary tablet reported.

"Yes, right. Well, I used to go to stock car races when I was younger and I was very enthusiastic over them," Kunzman recalled. "Then, one day I went to an IMCA sprint race and it was the only sprint race I had seen. And when I saw that I thought this was what I just had to do. It's a hard thing to explain, but the other things I've done I never had a burning desire to do like I do with racing. You're satisfying a part of your personality you don't seem to be able to do with another occupation."

When Kunzman completed that statement, the reporter paused, staring at his scribble-filled tablet and tapping his pencil rapidly on the tabletop. "Well, I guess that's it, Lee. I've run out of questions."

"Okay, good enough," Kunzman said as the three men rose from their chairs.

He shook the hands of the two newspaper men, then moved toward the table where the tan-faced girl sat.

"Hey, he's alright," the photographer said quietly as he and the reporter sat back down at the table. "I didn't think race drivers were supposed to be that bright."

"Well, they're not always," the reporter confided, "I have a feeling he's kinda part of the new breed of guys we're getting in racing."

Lee Kunzman, at 24, is indicative of a new breed of racing drivers—bright, articulate, poised, determined. From that interview session in May 1969, he continued on his way, demonstrating that his personal polish took nothing away from his talent for manhandling a race car.

He won some half-dozen midget races in the last half of that season, and continued to finish well in the sprint cars. He got his Indy-car ride late in the season and handled it steadily, if somewhat unspectacularly.

He came, as promised, to Indianapolis the following May with a car to drive. It was not the best equipment around, but it was good enough to get him through the rookie's test required of all

Lee Kunzman with his crew waiting for the start of a sprint car race at Eldora Speedway.

newcomers to the Speedway. It was not good enough, though, to get him into the race.

Still, Lee Kunzman was generally viewed as a young driver with great potential. As he left for a sprint car race in Missouri a week after Indy, there was little doubt he would make his big breakthrough in the Indy-car ranks before the season was over.

But a place called Odessa, Missouri, changed all that. A new paved track had been built there, and the USAC sprint cars went there early in June to baptize the facility.

The Odessa oval was clean and fast, but the engineers had made a horrendous mistake. The concrete retaining wall at its rim was perpendicular to the ground, instead of perpendicular to the surface of the banked track. With that feature, cars that hit the wall tended to climb right up the concrete and sail over it.

Three cars did just that the night the USAC sprint cars ran there. The third car was Kunzman's. The car's accelerator jammed, and the machine charged the wall at full speed. It slammed hard into the wall, rose in the air, and soared over the structure, plowing through a wire fence and landing upside-down in flames. With the smashed car enveloped in fire and smoke, there seemed to be little hope Kunzman could escape alive. But like a modern-day Shadrach, he was spared from death in that fiery furnace. Badly burned and with his neck and right arm broken, he somehow managed to crawl clear of the burning wreckage. He was still in grave danger even then, though. One wrong move could leave him paralyzed. But Dr. Ward Dunseth, a southern Indiana physician and owner of a sprint car that Kunzman himself had driven for awhile, reached the injured driver in time to prevent that and to administer first aid for his burns.

Kunzman then laid in a hospital bed for weeks while doctors attempted to put his smashed, scorched body back in working order. Initially, they claimed he would never race again, but later conceded he probably would. The doctors worked on Kunzman's burns while his neck slowly healed. They reconstructed the once-handsome face as best they could, then labored at returning the strength to the injured neck. For weeks after Kunzman left the hospital, he periodically returned for neck therapy and additional facial repairs. By December, he was sufficiently healed to begin talking confidently of his return to racing. "I'm hoping it will be like January or February. That's what I'm guessing right now. I could race right now if it wasn't for my neck still being pretty weak."

He talked, too, of the Odessa race track that brought him as close to death as he cared to come. "It's a fine race facility," he observed, with no trace of bitterness. "It's a beautifully laid-out race track, but they kind of goofed when they built the wall perpendicular to the ground instead of perpendicular to the banking. That way, the wall acts like a ramp and pitches you right out of the ballpark. It was a mistake probably to run the track until they got it straightened out, but we race on a lot of tracks that probably are more dangerous."

He quickly dismissed any suggestion his injuries would interfere with his plans to resume racing. "I don't think they're going to affect me when I start racing again."

He also dismissed the idea his terrifying crash would cut into his enthusiasm for driving racing cars. "It gives you a lot of time to think it over and figure out if this is really what you want to do for a living. It's really a test of just how bad you want to be a race driver. Personally, I want to race as much now as I ever did, or more so. I just can't wait to get back in a race car."

He did have to wait a little longer than he thought. He did not race in January or February of 1971, but he finally did in late April of that year.

At Tri-County Speedway, a dirt oval north of Cincinnati, Lee Kunzman climbed back onto the horse that had thrown him. And, as he had in his first USAC midget race back in Davenport, he left no doubt about the quality of his fibre.

He won at Tri-County. He drove as efficiently, as confidently as he had before, without a trace of any swerving from the plans and desires he had outlined so reasonably across that table in the Indianapolis Motor Speedway cafeteria a year and a half before. There was, in fact, no evidence that he had come anywhere near death, that he had suffered long and violent pain, or that his climb toward racing success had been interrupted at all.

9. Jim's Town

FOR SOME five centuries, Duns enjoyed the peaceful anonymity of most small Scottish towns. It raised its sheep without fanfare, ran its shops to the tune of soft tinkling doorbells, built its houses with rough stone that grew chalky through the years. It went about its business gently, pleasantly, with no notice whatever from the outside world.

But for less than a decade of its 500-year history, the rural burgh a few miles east of Edinburgh with its 1,800 townspeople was washed in the blinding spotlight of international fame.

For close to eight years, Duns was mentioned almost daily in newspapers and magazines around the world. Its name was shouted through a million loudspeakers, modulated over a thousand radio and television signals. The sequence was always the same. The name of the obscure little town invariably followed the name of the quiet young man who lived out at the farm on Edington Mains, a short distance from the town proper.

It was always written, in newspapers and race programs: "Jimmy Clark, Duns, Scotland." It was always pronounced, through scratchy loudspeakers and radio receivers: "The race winner, Jimmy Clark of Duns, Scotland."

Most of the people who read or heard the names knew more about the man than the town. They knew much of Jim Clark, for he had won races from Nurburgring to Indianapolis, had won more grands prix than even the legendary Argentine, Juan Fangio, and had almost single-handedly uplifted the public image of men who make their living racing cars.

Racing followers knew the soft-spoken dark-haired bachelor with the burning eyes and toothy smile. They had seen him turn the chaotic sounds and sights of a motor race into a symphony of one man's complete control over a piece of racing machinery.

They had, in fact, seen more of Jimmy Clark in the later years than the people in Duns. As a world champion, there were more races to go to and less time to spend in the big pleasant house at Edington Mains.

Only rarely was Jim Clark spotted walking the Berwickshire countryside, alone or with a friend, among the lazy herds of coal-faced, whimpering sheep. Few were the times when he was glimpsed flashing by on a leisurely drive over the narrow roads in and around Duns.

And when, in April of 1968, his broken body was brought back to the house at Edington Mains for the last time, his life could only be recalled by the townspeople in a misty series of such brief and distant recollections.

They had given him up to the world, and when they buried him they felt the world owed them an explanation, an accounting for the lost years of his short life. Others had known him, or at least a side of him, better than his own people, but they surrendered him when it came time to mourn, to sum up.

It fell to the town's leaders to put into intelligible words the feelings of Jim Clark's people, who had only known him as the boy from Edington Mains, not the champion race driver. It was the burgh provost, Thomas Lennie, who tried to set forth the official version of the intertwined stories of Jim Clark's life, his people, his town. "We in Duns felt the loss most grievously because he was one of us. His home was within a few miles of Duns, his farming interests were here, and he was an honorary burgess of this ancient Scottish burgh."

Sitting in his small office in the newly-acquired Burgh Chambers, the man, whose duties correspond to those of a mayor in an American town, closed his eyes thoughtfully and recounted the early beginnings of Jim Clark. "He was not actually born in Berwickshire. He was born in Fife, but when he was six years old his family moved to Duns and took over the farm at Edington Mains.

"He was always interested in mechanical things and his first attempts at motor driving were at the tender age of nine, when, without his family's knowledge, he drove a small Austin Seven," the provost rambled on. "His next attempts were on a big Alvis, much too big for him, but he managed to drive it in his own way. By degrees, he moved to larger cars and to racing on local tracks and eventually to grand prix racing."

It wasn't really necessary for Lennie to recount Jim Clark's accomplishments from that point on. It was common knowledge to all who had followed his career: He had won two world championships, one Indianapolis jackpot, and the stature of a racing great before his car slithered off a wet track in Germany and catapulted into a clump of trees.

What Lennie did recount was a Jim Clark triumph which had taken place not on a race track but in the crowded, cluttered streets of Duns. "My most impressive recollection of Jim Clark is connected with the occasion on September 21, 1965, when he was admitted as an honorary burgess of Duns. And I, as provost, had the privilege and the pleasure of performing the ceremony.

"This is an honorary title bestowed by a Scottish town on a person whom the town wishes to honor and it is indeed the highest honor a Scottish burgh can bestow on anyone. Duns is a very ancient burgh, its history going back five hundred years, and Jim Clark was the first and only burgess honored in all that time.

"I have most pleasant and thrilling memories of that unique occasion in our town—the ceremony itself, the drive with Jim through the streets lined with cheering people, his charming company at the banquet which followed and, in the midst of all the adulation showered upon him, his modest and unassuming bearing as though he felt quite undeserving of it all.

"During the tour of the town, he was besieged by autograph hunters and must have signed his name hundreds of times that evening. Yet when he had to leave the street to enter the hotel, his reluctance to disappoint those who were still clamouring was most obvious. His modesty in the midst of all this hero-worship was what impressed me most and put upon Jim the stamp of a really fine man."

Pausing for a moment at the end of his reminiscence, Lennie then stood and moved casually into another, larger room of the town hall building, a room lined with glass cases filled with silvery trophies, plaques, and the like. "There was never any doubt that the people of Duns would want to provide some kind of memorial to the young man who had brought fame not only to himself but to this part of Scotland. And when his parents and family offered a large number of his trophies to the town to be put on permanent display, it seemed appropriate that a fitting memorial would be premises in which the collection of trophies and prizes could be adequately and properly displayed.

"The town council and the people are deeply grateful to Jim Clark's parents and family for the generous gift they have made to the town as it marks the close association which the former world champion had with Duns," he added, his voice taking on an official air as he strolled along the display cases, some of them still unfinished. "The cups and trophies number over one hundred and include some of the most beautiful and valuable pieces of silverware one could image. In its own way, it is the most unique collection in the world."

The sunlight shooting in through the windows splashed across the shining trophies of various sizes, the plaques and the photographs in the memorial display, the tribute put together by the town that drew its brief days of glory from a man named Jim Clark.

Looking through a window at the far end of the room, one could make out the pudgy forms of nodding sheep, grazing indifferently on a green hillside at the edge of the town.

10. They Take Him Seriously Now

FOR A LONG time, people mainly talked about George Eaton's long hair, his money, his girlfriends, and his sometimes indiscreet behavior behind the wheel of a racing car.

Of late, however, there has been less talk about those things—though George's hair is still shoulder-length, his financial status still monumental, and his girls still the shapliest in the pit area—and more talk about his maturation as a first-class young driving talent and potential international superstar of the future.

The mop-haired Canadian, youngest son of the owner of the Eaton's of Canada department store chain—which compares with "Sears, on a Canadian scale," by George's own description

—spent his first few years in racing living up to the old stereo-type of the rich kid who plays around with racing for kicks. His pit was always flashy and frantic, flooded with comely females, and his driving efforts were valiant and enthusiastic but marked with signs of immaturity. Photographers split their time between snapping George with his trackside lovelies and getting shots of his car slithering off the race course and whirling around in the grass.

In 1969, that changed. Running the fast and fastidious Can-Am sports car circuit, George Eaton forced observers to take him seriously. Wheeling a three-year-old car he had purchased from the McLaren works, George became the pride of the Can-Am in-dependents, finishing well in seven of the eleven races held and placing fifth in the series standings behind the factory drivers for McLaren, Lola, and Porsche.

Though he was still a "rich kid" with long yellow locks, a Jimmy Boyd babyface, and an apparent preoccupation for the opposite sex, George had matured as a racing driver. In his formative season, 1969, he showed real poise behind the wheel, and avoided the embarrassing off-course excursions he had been known for in his earlier years.

His striking development as a first-rate driver did not go un-noticed, either. Before the 1969 season had been completed, he had been given the chance to break into the pre-eminent road racing circuit, the international grand prix series.

Officials of the British Racing Motors stable, an inveterate mar-quee on the grand prix tour, signed George on as their third team driver—behind veteran stars Pedro Rodriguez and Jackie Oliver —for the final two races of the 1969 season and the full 1970 calendar. The BRM management also paired George with Rodri-guez as the drivers for the two new sports cars being constructed for entry into the rich Can-Am competition.

In less than a season, George Eaton erased his image as the Peck's Bad Boy of North American racing and was plunged into the midst of the world's most glamorous racing scene, running on the same tracks with the most colorful, talented drivers in the world—men like Jack Brabham, Graham Hill, Jackie Stewart, and Jochen Rindt.

The situation was one which might have tempted an eager 24-

year-old driver to try to show the world he could outrace these established stars, many of whom were already legends in their own time. But George had already been through his foolhardy period and was determined to control his natural impulses and make his evolution into a Formula One contender a smooth one.

"In Formula One, I'll have to get used to it first," he said, shortly after he had made his debut in grand prix racing. "It's not the place where you just start right out winning, so I think consistency is what I'll be striving for, although not at the sacrifice of speed. You still have to be quick just to run with them."

His cautious approach to grand prix racing, however, did not stop George from thinking about expanding his driving interests in the best tradition of an international racer. "I would like to get in some extra racing when my schedule permits. It depends on how much testing time I get in. It's mostly a matter of logistics and time. I'm committed to 26 races with the two series and I'll have to see what other racing I can fit in."

With his relatively early rise to the grand prix plateau, George appeared to have a lot of years left to try many other types of racing. And he enthusiastically pledged he would try them all, including NASCAR's superspeedway stock cars and USAC's Indy-car oval races. "I've never really done any oval racing, but I think you have to give credit where it's due. And there are some awfully good races on ovals."

George even voiced an interest in tackling USAC's dirt-track brand of big-car competition, a racing form usually disdained by products of the road-racing wars. "Oh sure, I'd like to try those," he exclaimed with the exuberance of a small boy who had just seen his first ferris wheel. "I want to race everything. But, first off I want to run Formula One and see if I can make it."

So, at the opening of the 1970 season, off went George Eaton to find his place in the world of international racing. And, at last, people didn't talk as much about his long hair, his bank book, and his feminine followers as they did about his growing ability as a racing driver. His hair still managed to raise a few extra comments, particularly at the more plebian U. S. racing haunts. George quickly made it clear, though, that his lengthy locks did not make him one of the hippie-yippie-peacenik types who protest the evils of the world. "I don't have many protests to make."

11. Down the Up Staircase

ONLY Jigger Sirois could have found something to be grateful for in the whole mess. There he was, on the second most exciting day of May, the opening day of Indianapolis time trials, rattling onto the big oval as the very first man to try to qualify for the 1969 race. With some 200,000 pairs of eyes on him, the man, who looks more like a school teacher than a racing driver, aimed his white-and-green car straight toward the starting line, where the green flag was held in stiff readiness.

He was a rookie driver at Indianapolis and the tenseness of his situation showed. His car skittered through at least one turn of each lap as he tried harder than he should have to live up to the promise of the moment.

His first two laps were clocked in the 161-mile-per-hour range, the third up into the 162-mph bracket. It was not fast enough. Almost everyone had agreed it would take a 164-mph average or better to make the field for the Memorial Day race.

Chief mechanic Bob Higman and car owner Myron Caves looked at each other for only a moment before reaching for the yellow flag to wave off the qualifying run as Sirois wiggled through the fourth turn.

While Sirois slowly made his way back into the pits, Arnie Knepper drove onto the track and cut his first lap at a respectable 166-mph clip. But as Knepper moved around on his second lap and Sirois stepped wearily from his car, drops of rain started to speckle the gray Indianapolis oval. The rhythm of the raindrops picked up quickly and Knepper was flagged off the track before he could complete another lap. It rained the rest of that day; no other cars took to the track on the day when the coveted pole position is usually won.

The turn of events instantly made a celebrity of Jigger Sirois, a bespectacled 34-year-old known only to faithful followers of the dingy midget circuits. Newsmen, many of whom had never heard of him, hustled Jigger into an impromptu press conference

Jigger Sirois

as soon as it was clear that he, and he alone, could have taken the pole position that rainy Saturday afternoon but hadn't.

From atop a long table in the speedway pressroom, the young driver with the peculiar name dazzled the press corps with warm, articulate spontaneity rarely found in the tough and unpolished world of racing people. He pranced around his makeshift platform, answering questions directly and honestly. He talked of the disappointment of the day, but still managed to smile philosophically about it and joked heartily with the reporters who, hungry for a good story on an otherwise dismal news day, hung on every word.

It rained the next day, too, and for the next week only Jigger could talk about the pole position, the one he almost won. He, Higman, and Caves all were quick to note, though, that the pole spot they could have won on that rain-shortened opening day of time trials would have been a temporary one since they almost certainly would have been bumped from the lineup with their weak 161-162 average speed.

By the end of the next weekend, when thirty three drivers and cars qualified for the Memorial Day field, they were clearly mistaken.

The official race-day field did not include Jigger Sirois—whose last-minute bid to finally crack the lineup was thwarted by a mechanical failure—but did include two entries that qualified with 160-mph averages, over one full mile-per-hour slower than the speed Jigger was set to post on opening day when Higman and Caves unfurled the yellow flag.

The chilling fact was that Jigger would have won the pole, and would have kept it. The solemn realization of what had been in the palm of his hand and had slipped away was enough to embitter most men. But, as the newsmen learned at that press conference, Jigger wasn't the bitter type. "I was disappointed I wasn't able to make the run, of course, but I'm still thankful to Caves and Bob Higman for getting the driver's test in. It's just like everything else. You just have to keep going. That's life, and maybe all this will work out all right in the long run.

"I'm still thankful I drew the number one qualifying spot," he went on, "because if I had been on down the line they still might have waved me off and I'd have been just another guy who didn't make the race. That way, I don't think anyone would have heard of me. Believe me, that can help when you're talking to people about rides. At least they know who I am, even if that wasn't the most impressive way to do it. I'd like to draw number one again next time, to be really honest with you."

Such enthusiasm in the face of a monumental heartbreak was unbelievable. But those who had encountered Jigger before that fateful day at Indianapolis had already found him refreshingly animated, candid, and genuinely human. With the face of a high school math teacher and the thick, strong shoulders of a truck driver, Jigger always found time to accommodate reporters, photographers, or fans who pestered him at the little speedways where he raced midget cars. Even when he didn't really have time, he patiently acknowledged the whims of everyone who cornered him and, when he simply had to get down to business, he excused himself with a smile and a polite apology.

Among the acrimony and roughness of much of racing his personal manner seemed almost out of place. But there was little real question about his belonging where he was. If his abilities with the midget cars weren't enough (but they often were) then his name and his heritage made it abundantly clear.

Leon Duray "Jigger" Sirois was the son of Frenchy Sirois, a racing mechanic back in the days when the mechanic rode along with the driver in case the car broke down out on the course. He was a Frenchman and a racer, and when his son was born in 1935 he selected a name that encompassed both facts.

He named his new son after Leon Duray, the pseudo-French driver of the 1920s who was actually an American named James Stewart. To make the picture complete, he added a nickname which saluted one of Frenchy's colleagues, famed riding mechanic Jigger Johnson.

With a name so steeped in racing history, it was inevitable that Jigger would entertain the thought of becoming a racing driver. "It wasn't that my family pushed me into it, they really didn't," Jigger now recalls. "But racing was a topic of everyday conversation around the house.

"Then one night I sat down with my dad and talked about what I wanted to do with my future. I said I wanted to be a race driver and my dad said, 'Boy, you don't know what you're letting yourself in for.'

"But I'm fortunate my family is behind me and they are willing to express their love and compassion for me. We have real good communication going for us."

The only obstacle created by his family turned out to be his name. Both before and after he went off to seek his fortune as a racing driver, that unwieldy handle provoked trouble. Most vivid in Jigger's memory is the time, back in his bachelor days, when a new girlfriend took him to her home to introduce him to her mother. When they arrived at the girl's house, which Jigger remembers was "very luxurious," he was ushered into the living room to meet mama, who was decked out in all the trappings of opulence and elegance, including a monocle. The girl introduced him as "Leon Jigger Sirois," promptly causing her mother to lower her monocle and exclaim, "Leon Jigger? My, that Jigger is a funny name. I don't believe I like that." That ended that romance.

The racing arena didn't shield Jigger from small embarrassments, either. Track announcers seemed to enjoy toying with his unique name. Many gave his last name a French pronunciation with the final *s* silent, which it isn't, and one even got so carried away that he introduced him as "Jigger Cirrhosis."

The problems with his name had little bearing on his racing, however. He survived long, hard years in the midgets, becoming a consistent competitor on that tough circuit. Not that he was a big winner, but neither was he a big loser.

He made the move to the Indy-cars in 1968 and in the inaugural USAC race at Michigan International Speedway he thrust himself into the spotlight by running second in a second-rate car before it broke down. It was that performance that brought him the ride in the Caves-Higman car for the 1969 season and ultimately the Indianapolis catastrophe.

After that disheartening May, everything went wrong. He lost the ride in the Caves car and had to rustle up whatever Indy-car assignments he could. The ones he got were only mediocre, and so were his finishes.

The disaster at Indianapolis haunted him elsewhere, too. He was having trouble getting a regular midget ride and no luck at all in lining up a stock car to drive.

He came back to Indianapolis in a tired car and never got up enough speed to even attempt a qualifying run. A few months later, he went to the new Ontario track with a better machine and was well on his way into the lineup when he spun and bumped the wall. He sat out that 500-miler as well.

At the close of the 1970 season, Jigger returned to his home in Hammond, Indiana, with little to be hopeful about. He had to work on construction jobs through the off-season to make ends meet for himself and his wife, Jan.

He had taken quite a slide down the razorblade of racing luck. But in true Jigger Sirois fashion, he was bloodied but unbowed. "What you're trying to say is my luck has gone all to hell, right?" he would gently scold when someone tried to talk about his misfortune in euphemistic terms. But he was having none of that sort of thing. Without missing a step, he was mustering his indefatigable supply of optimism for another try, and his recent failures couldn't get in the way.

"I was disappointed at the outcome of the Ontario thing. I didn't go out to see the scenery, I went to race. But I'm not at all discouraged," he asserted, a few weeks after the California venture.

Nor did the enthusiasm and confidence subside when he evaluated the prospects for the next trip to Indianapolis, even though the outlook for finding a car to drive there was discouraging. He was, as always, eager and optimistic. "I'm going to be a little more relaxed at the Speedway this year. I think it will make me go faster."

If anybody else said that, it would have been dismissed without a second thought. Jigger Sirois said it, and that meant he believed it. And even if you had your doubts, you wanted to believe it, too.

12. Who Is Pete Hamilton?

RACE DRIVERS are a beleaguered lot. They have to put up with all sorts of nuisances.

There was young Pete Hamilton, the blond baby-faced stock car driver, already sleeping soundly in his motel room at 8:30 P.M. on a spring Sunday night in 1970 after driving a grueling 500 miles around Atlanta Speedway, finishing third, and dragging his exhausted body back to the motel to sleep off the wear and tear of racing.

But for NASCAR's fastest rising young star, a night of solid well-deserved sleep was suddenly interrupted by the excruciating jangle of the telephone. On the other end, a racing columnist from someplace called Marion, Indiana, began explaining he

Pete Hamilton (right) and M. Petty, mechanic, Daytona 500 winners.

wanted some material for a story on Pete Hamilton, surprise winner of the Daytona 500 who was probably a stranger to his readers in Marion. "Sure," yawned bleary-eyed Pete, "be glad to answer your questions."

So the columnist jumped right in with what will surely go down as one of the most brilliant questions ever formulated: "Pete, how would you answer the question, who is Pete Hamilton?"

"Well, uh . . . I don't know," came the bewildered response. "They'll have to watch a race and find out."

The columnist blurted out another blockbuster: "How did it feel to win at Daytona?"

"Of course it's real good winning the big one, Daytona. There's no race we run quite equal to that one. It certainly has changed my life," added Pete, referring more to the national fame his Daytona win brought him than the strange phone calls he'd been getting lately.

Now the interviewer reeled off a series of more specific questions.

Q—"At what point during the Daytona race did you realize you had a chance to win?"

A—"About halfway through the race I began to realize that the car and the driver together could go all the way and everything went smoothly from there on."

Q—"What did Richard Petty (Hamilton's benefactor, boss, and teammate) say to you when you won?"

A—"He was just real happy and he came over and said, 'good job, Pete.' He doesn't say much, he's a quiet guy, but when he says something, he means it."

Q—"Have you encountered any real problems as a Yankee (he called Dedham, Massachusetts, home before moving down to Charlotte, North Carolina) in the Southern NASCAR ranks?"

A—"It hasn't been a problem so far. They accept me pretty much for what I am. A race driver is a race driver, that's all that matters to them."

Q—"Do you plan to move into any other type of racing in the future?"

A—"I'm trying to concentrate everything right now on running the Plymouth. Someday I might like to try something else, I don't know. Of course, I think stock car racing is pretty much the place to be."

At that point, the columnist hit upon a question Hamilton could get his teeth into, asking him to comment on the work done by the Petty crew in grooming the baby-blue winged Plymouth Superbird he drove.

"A driver's only as good as the car he's running, and I don't think there's anyone in NASCAR or in the USAC stocks that can put a car together that would compare with the one the Pettys put together. It's a pleasure to drive for people like that."

Then, as quickly as he had seemed to be on the verge of an interesting conversation, the interviewer slipped back into his more routine inquiries.

"Do you expect to win more races?"

"I don't know why not," Pete answered patiently, "I'm sure we're going to win some more, at least we're going to try."

Suddenly the columnist realized his interview was not going very well, that even if it had taken him almost a month to catch up with the sensational young racer, he was still entitled to a little sleep after a long and rugged afternoon of wrestling a couple tons of steel around a fast track.

Besides, the idea of identifying Pete Hamilton was ludicrous. He had sufficiently impressed Richard Petty with a solid string of wins in NASCAR's pony-car division the year before to be hired on as his understudy, hadn't he? What more was there to say?

So, in an apologetic tone, the interviewer thanked his sleepy subject and let him return to his dreams of stock car triumphs in that dark motel room in Georgia.

Who is Pete Hamilton? He's NASCAR's superstar of the future and a young man who sometimes has trouble getting a good night's sleep.

13. The Jimmy Maguire Story

IN THE summer of 1961, a young sprint car driver amazed eastern race fans by driving with a broken leg. A few seasons later, that same dark-haired young driver again set the racing world on its ear by outracing the fabled A. J. Foyt in a Pennsylvania sprint car contest. But even that was merely the beginning of the bizarre story of Jimmy Maguire, a story marked by extremes of agony and ecstacy, disappointment and determination.

It all began in 1958 when Jimmy Maguire drove his first race in a modified stock car. For the next two years, he honed his driving talents at grimy little tracks on the eastern modified stock circuit. Then in 1960, he went as a spectator to a sprint car race at Lebanon Valley, New York, the first sprint race he had seen and one in which a young Italian-born driver named Mario Andretti was to make his formal debut. It was also the race that made Jimmy Maguire decide he just had to drive those flashing open-cockpit cars.

So in 1961 he drove midgets, sprint cars, supermodifieds—"whatever I could get in," Jimmy recalls—at tracks in the East, and midway through the season he landed a regular ride on the United Racing Club's sprint car circuit, a respectable minor-league outfit which ran most of the half-mile tracks in New England, New York, and Pennsylvania.

That piece of good fortune appeared to have gone for naught, however, when Jimmy proceeded to break his leg in a supermodified crash a few weeks later.

But, displaying the grit which was to become a trademark of the youthful, dark-complexioned driver, Jimmy simply refused to accept the setback. With his leg in a cast, he climbed right back into the sprint car and kept on racing.

"I didn't want to lose that sprint ride," he later explained with a broad smile.

Once his leg had healed, Jimmy moved into the thick of the battle for URC's sprint car championship. He placed third in the standings for 1962 and the following year took the URC crown, winning 10 feature events along the way.

With the URC title salted away, Jimmy wandered over to Williams Grove, Pennsylvania, that fall to have a go at the stars of the United States Auto Club sprint car division, a division which featured such seasoned stalwarts as A. J. Foyt, Parnelli Jones, Jim Hurtubise, and Don Branson. And those who were there at the Pennsylvania dirt oval would not long forget what transpired that day.

From beginning to end, the Williams Grove race was a head-to-head confrontation between the relatively-unknown challenger from the East, Jimmy Maguire, and the pride of USAC, A. J. Foyt, who had already knocked down the first of his three Indianapolis 500 triumphs a year earlier. The two battled lap after lap, and when the dust finally settled, upstart Jimmy Maguire had flashed under the checkered flag a slim car-length in front of the ensconced Foyt.

It was a joyous, proud triumph for Jimmy, but it was to be short-lived. A post-race protest revealed the engine in Jimmy's car, built to URC standards, was nine cubic inches over the USAC maximum. Jimmy was disqualified and Foyt declared the winner.

His name was erased from the record books almost as quickly as it had gone in, but Jimmy's remarkable feat at Williams Grove was the talk of the racing crowd. "It was a disappointment, but it was worth it at the time because of all the publicity I got from it," Jimmy recollects.

When the 1964 season rolled around, Jimmy became a regular competitor on the USAC sprint car trail and "the fella who beat A. J. but it didn't count" set out to prove that Williams Grove was no fluke.

He ran second to Foyt in a sprint feature at Reading, Pennsylvania, then took third in a Williams Grove rematch. He had second place nailed down at Eldora Speedway in Ohio until his engine gave out.

The next stop on the sprint car calendar was at the New Bremen, Ohio, dirt oval. That race on a summer afternoon in 1964 would dramatically alter Jimmy's life and his part in the history of auto racing.

The New Bremen track, baked in the summer sun, was incredibly dusty that day, and the billowing clouds of dust rendered the sprint car pilots half-blind as they plowed around the half-mile ring. "It was a rough day for everybody," Jimmy still remembers. "Guys were crashing right and left; it was unbelievable."

Chuck Hulse, a tough little driver who was on the rise on the big-car circuit, was already on his way into the hospital and out of racing for several months when the New Bremen feature event started.

The pack of growling race cars hit the starting line in an explosion of sound and thick brown dust. As the slithering cluster moved around the track, a sandy haze hung like a curtain over the track surface, the cars knifing through in faint, blurred bursts.

Somewhere in that brown fog, Jimmy Maguire was churning along as best he could when he suddenly caught a glimpse of something amiss as he exited one of the turns. The something suddenly became clearer. It was a car spinning directly in front of him.

Jimmy swerved hard, but a split-second late, to try to miss the whirling machine. His front wheel clipped the other car; his car tilted up, then began a dizzying series of barrel-rolls down the track. The first roll knocked Jimmy unconscious. The last roll left the sprint car upside-down on the track, Jimmy's right arm pinned beneath the rollbar. His arm severed near the shoulder and bleeding profusely, Jimmy was administered to by a trackside doctor who rushed to the overturned race car and promptly stopped the bleeding. "He probably saved my life," Jimmy says of the rescuer, whose name he no longer even remembers.

Lifted gingerly from the wreckage, Jimmy was rushed to a nearby hospital, where he lay unconscious for two weeks. When he finally awoke, his arm had been amputated and so, it would have seemed, had his driving career.

But the thought of giving up as a race driver never entered Jimmy's mind. "I just remember waking up and smiling and I didn't wake up to any great shock. People had to tell me what happened; I didn't even remember going to the track that day."

"As far as my arm was concerned, I just thought to myself— well, it's going to be a whole new challenge. I just couldn't have gotten discouraged because everybody was so enthusiastic for me. I was just anxious to get out of the hospital and get going again."

It was some six months before he did get out of the hospital. During that time, he was fitted with an artificial arm and given tedious rehabilitation therapy to teach him how to use it. The therapists probably didn't realize it, but they were showing him how to be a race driver again.

Once out of the hospital, Jimmy set out immediately to see if he could, in fact, drive a race car with one arm. He devised a ball-and-socket receptacle which he bolted onto the steering wheel and, inserting the metal tip of his artificial arm, used it to help steer the car. The setup called for some major adjustments on Jimmy's part, but he made them with calculating determination. "All I had to do was start using my left arm as my driving arm. It was just like learning to drive all over again and using primarily my left arm, instead of my right. It takes a little bit of the strain off my left hand," he commented on the steering wheel gadget. "It gives me very good control and a very good feeling of the race car.

"You never lose the feeling that your arm is still there and working," he continued. "The nerves don't know the arm isn't there so you're turning the corner with normal coordination and balance. The most important thing for me is to make sure the car is comfortable before trying to run. If it isn't, the strain will wear out my left arm."

Once he became accustomed to the new steering system, Jimmy waded back into racing competition almost as if he'd never been away. Less than a year after losing his arm, he was racing, and winning, again. He jumped into three-quarter midget racing in the East in 1965, winning the first race he entered and two more a short time later. Before the year was over, he had moved into the full midgets. He drove both the three-quarters and full midgets with moderate success the following year.

For 1967 and much of 1968, Jimmy's racing ventures slacked off somewhat as he and his wife settled in their new house in Somerville, New Jersey. He still managed to squeeze in a dozen or so races, knocking down six seconds and a third in the midgets during 1968.

The winter of 1968, however, saw Jimmy take a giant step toward returning to full-time competition as he packed his bags and journeyed to Australia for the midget season there, a popular proving ground for young U. S. midget hopefuls. If he had anything to prove, he did it convincingly on that trip. In six races in Australia, where midget programs draw as many as 40,000 enthusiastic spectators, he won three feature events and left the Aussie fans buzzing about the "one-armed wonder" from America.

On the strength of his Australian performance, Jimmy suddenly found himself being wooed by USAC midget officials, who had previously refused to take his comeback efforts very seriously. The club officials extended an invitation to him to compete in the gala USAC midget show inside the Houston Astrodome in March of 1969, a by-invitation-only affair.

Though he didn't do particularly well at the Astrodome, Jimmy had his foot in the door, having erased some of the skepticism that accompanied his early attempts to become successful as a one-armed racing driver. "I knew people would laugh when I first came back, but when I showed them I could drive a race car then I guess they changed their minds."

Not that USAC was really convinced that they wanted Jimmy racing with them, but they did recognize there was no justifiable way to keep him out, and they conceded a one-armed driver might be a good drawing card. "We didn't want him to run, but we didn't know how to tell him," one USAC officer admitted later, however, after they found a way to tell him. The way came about as the result of something that happened shortly after the Astrodome race in a vacant house near Readington, New Jersey. But the racing community was not to find out about it until several weeks and a few Jimmy Maguire accomplishments later.

After the Astrodome, Jimmy ushered himself back into USAC racing by entering a number of the club's midget shows, including the rich "Night Before the 500" program in May at Indianapolis' Raceway Park. There, with some 80 cars and drivers battling for top spots, Jimmy qualified 14th fastest, putting him into the main event easily, but then had his problems on the long and fast five-eighths mile paved oval and finished last. "I wasn't really comfortable in the race car," he moaned afterward. "Raceway Park is a real fast track and the centrifugal force was so great it put all the strain on my left arm. For four or five laps I would go like blazes, but I just couldn't last. I just couldn't hold the wheel any longer."

The Raceway Park feature was to be Jimmy's last USAC race, as it turned out, but he still was to have two quick moments of glory with that organization.

A week after Raceway Park, the USAC Indy-cars were qualifying at the Milwaukee, Wisconsin, fairgrounds track in preparation for the 150-mile championship race the next day. Jimmy Maguire was there, too, pacing nervously around the pit area while the shrieking rear-engine cars made their qualifying runs. As the last qualifier pulled into the pits and shut off his engine, Jimmy zipped up his driving suit, pulled a thin black glove onto his left hand, tucked his crash helmet under his arm, and strode toward the starting line. There, a small knot of older, paunchy men with USAC armbands on their sleeves stood around a low-slung white race car.

Jimmy argued with the USAC officials for weeks to let him try an Indy-car, and they finally relented. They agreed to let him take one of the cars around the Milwaukee mile-long oval for ten laps or so, just to see how he handled it. It was only to be a test run and he would have to have several more like it before they would even consider his plea to actually compete on the big-car circuit.

Jimmy pulled his crash helmet onto his head and climbed into the cockpit. He methodically fastened the seat belts, inserted the tip of his artificial arm into the steering wheel receptacle, and waited for the engine to be started. After gunning the rough-idling powerplant a few times, he nodded for the car's crew to push him away from the starting line.

As the squat little car rolled along the track, all eyes, including those of every USAC official on hand, followed it closely. "I was scared stiff," Jimmy later revealed. "I knew that one mistake and I'd be out of there."

He moved his speed up steadily as he whipped around the Milwaukee oval, getting in about a dozen fast laps before the USAC officials flagged him off the track. Almost as soon as he stepped from the cockpit at Milwaukee, the ever-confident Jimmy predicted he could make it into the Indy-car ranks. "I know I can do it," he beamed, "It's an odd situation, but I know nobody's had the determination to try to do it before. I think it's just a matter of being patient."

Not everyone at Milwaukee was as optimistic, however. While Jimmy claimed he had been complimented on his performance by a number of established drivers, other observers said he had looked "squirrelly"—an old racing term used to describe erratic or incompetent driving.

Jimmy, his usual self-assurance buoyed by the Milwaukee test, countered that his critics simply did not want to admit that a one-armed man could succeed as a racing driver. "They have two arms and they don't know how my philosophy works, and just because nobody's done it before there's no reason why somebody can't do it," he said of his detractors. "They just don't like the idea that I can do with one arm what they have to use two arms for. Nobody should object just because they never have done it or they wouldn't want to do it themselves. There's no good reason why I shouldn't have the opportunity to do this so long as I go out there and I don't look like a wild man."

From Milwaukee, Jimmy traveled to the track which had dealt him such a painful setback five years before, New Bremen. He went to the New Bremen oval, paved since he last raced there, for another test run, this time in the unusual Ford-powered sprint car built by master mechanic A. J. Watson.

That test, like the one at Milwaukee, inflated Jimmy's exuberance. "What a race car that Watson car is, with that Ford engine! It ran like a rocketship!" he exclaimed after spending an afternoon wheeling Watson's creation around the New Bremen track.

Jimmy eagerly went to USAC officials after the test run and asked for clearance to compete in the upcoming sprint car program at New Bremen. But again he was turned down.

"I wanted to see if I could apply what I knew in my head to the race track, and I found I could," he rationalized after the USAC rejection. "My inner self has been satisfied. I know I can run with them."

His inner self knew it, certainly, but it was becoming clearer and clearer that Jimmy might never be able to run with the USAC sprints or Indy-cars unless the resistance of the club's officials weakened.

"I think they never thought I'd get this far," he said, tersely, of the hesitant officials. "Most of them have just heard about me; they haven't seen me run. If I could run a few of the races, then they could see first-hand and maybe they'd take notice.

"All I want to do is drive race cars—I wouldn't be happy unless I was doing it," he added. "I don't go out there to amaze anybody; I go out there to satisfy myself. I happen to enjoy going out and competing and trying to beat the other guys."

Shortly after the New Bremen experiment, Jimmy disappeared from the racing scene. He was seen a few times working with the Firestone tire crews at the Indy-car races as he had in the past, but he suddenly wasn't driving anymore. When asked why he wasn't running the midgets any longer, he would answer that he had been forced to go home to New Jersey because he had no steady ride on the midget trail. "I would've stayed in the Midwest if I'd had a car to run," he would say, adding that he was still looking for a midget assignment. "Of course, right at the moment it looks like I'm fishing in a lake that doesn't have any fish in it."

A more concrete reason for his absence from the midget scene soon became evident. The incident at Readington was finally coming to light, and his racing career was on the verge of collapsing.

In April, New Jersey state police arrested Jimmy and three other New Jersey men after four young runaway girls told them of a wild drinking and sex-filled party at an unoccupied house near Readington. According to the police reports, the four men and the young girls—the youngest was 11, the oldest 13—had broken into the vacant house, whose residents were vacationing, and partied long into the night. Jimmy was formally charged with the vicious-sounding offense of the carnal abuse of a 12-year-old girl.

When that news got back to USAC, it was all they needed to solve their long-standing dilemma over Jimmy Maguire. Apparently unaware of the old American concept of a man being presumed innocent until proved guilty, club officials pressured Jimmy into turning in his racing license. A USAC publication then piously announced that Jimmy had retired—at the age of twenty nine for no stated reasons. One of its most perplexing problems had at last been taken care of, neatly and finally.

Jimmy's court case dragged on for nearly a year in Huntertown County Court. Finally, in February of 1970, he was able to plead guilty to the lesser charge of contributing to the delinquency of a minor, was fined $500 and placed on probation for one year.

During the time the court case was pending and the first months of his probationary period, Jimmy continued to appear at USAC's Indy-car races as a member of the Firestone service crew. He worked silently, saying little about any part of his driving career. Most of those who knew what had happened in New Jersey whispered that his silence meant he had accepted the fact his driving days were over.

And so it seemed in 1970. But over the winter months, just a few weeks before his probation was scheduled to end, reports began to filter back from the East about a young man who was causing a stir in the newly-popular snowmobile racing circles of New England. Then, in February of 1971, a photograph appeared on the front page of a national racing publication, showing a smiling dark-haired young man at the controls of a fancy snowmobile. The man was dark-complexioned; his facial features were smooth and youthful. The shiny metallic tip of a mechanical arm protruded from his right coat sleeve.

Those who had seen him drive with a broken leg in 1961, or had seen him in the early days of his comeback after New Bremen, just smiled knowingly to themselves. They knew what Jimmy Maguire had done in the face of other seemingly insurmountable obstacles, and they knew he wasn't done yet. Not by a long-shot.

14. *The Flying Dutchman*

A RACE CAR was his brush, a dirt track his canvas, and a rooster-tail of flying dirt his masterpiece, this rugged-looking farmer from Pennsylvania who turned dirt-track racing into a fine art. A screaming race car moving around and around the track, pushing the cushion of dirt at the edge of the groove out toward the fence lap by lap and inch by inch until it could broadside around the track, its tail against the fence, in one fluid motion—that was the artistry of Tommy Hinnershitz.

When Tommy Hinnershitz returned to his farm near Reading in 1960, his art was being buried by tons of asphalt and now, a decade later, seems destined to be relegated to the archeology textbooks. Time, sadly, changes all things. "It isn't the same now. Your cars are quite a bit different and your tires are very much different, and the driving technique for most of them is different because most of the drivers now get a lot more of their racing on pavement," observes Hinnershitz, now almost 60, balding, and out of racing. "The driving technique for pavement carries over quite a bit onto dirt today and it's not as exciting as it used to be," he continues. "I like to see them on the dirt, broad-sliding around. It's something that's pretty hard to explain other than that."

But the man whose racing skills brought him over one hundred victories in sprint and championship cars through three decades of driving still hopes the form of racing he loves can survive. "I guess maybe I'm wishing more than anything else, but it seems these things run in cycles," he explains. "If the tracks are right, I don't think there's any better show, and I hope the dirt will make a comeback, at least on the half-mile ovals."

Working against the resurgence of dirt-track racing, according to Tommy, is the fact that dirt tracks are becoming hard to keep in good racing shape and race drivers, not called on to run dirt races as often, can't develop their technique as finely as he and the drivers he raced against could. "After you've done something for a long time, naturally you get to know more about it. I always looked my track over very closely and figured out what it might do in ten laps, twenty laps, and so on. You had to try and find something about the track the other drivers might not suspect which would help you get around a little quicker. A lot of times, it was a big guessing game. Sometimes I guessed right and sometimes I guessed wrong," says the man who guessed right often enough to win a phenomenal seven Eastern sprint car championships from 1949 to 1959, his last full season behind the wheel.

In the three decades he raced, Tommy competed against some of the most illustrious names in racing, both past and present. From the immortal Ted Horn, for whom he drove in the early days, to A. J. Foyt, from the great one-legged driver, Bill Schindler, to the monumentally courageous Jim Hurtubise, he ran against them all and always managed to win his share of the races, particularly when it came to his specialty, the dirt tracks.

Through all those years, all those races, the soft-spoken racer had the opportunity to weigh the skills of many fine drivers and his observations on that subject are penetrating and to the point when he compares the drivers of his early period in racing with those of a more recent era.

"At the time, Ted Horn was the outstanding competitor of them all," he recollects, "but, all-around, my own personal opinion is that Foyt is the finest we've ever had." Tommy's evalu-ations become a little less exacting when he's asked to recall his greatest moments in the auto racing world. "That would be hard to say, 'cause I had a lot of them," answers the man who thrilled hundreds of racing crowds with his mastery of the dirt-track technique through nearly two generations.

Even with all the thrills, Tommy finally had to step down as the acknowledged master of the dirt tracks. In 1960, the year after he had secured his seventh sprint car title in the East, "The Flying Dutchman," a nickname growing out of his Pennsylvania Dutch background, announced his retirement. "I always prom-ised myself that once I didn't enjoy driving anymore I was going to quit. A lot of people never realize how much strength it takes to drive a car around on the dirt and after awhile I just didn't feel I was doing the best possible job I could at times. When the car starts driving me, I know it's time to quit."

Though he stayed with racing as a mechanic for several years after his retirement, Hinnershitz finally left the sport in 1966 and now operates a garage for a truck fleet in Reading. At the same time, he continues to operate the farm near Oley which had given him his second racing nickname, "The Flying Farmer."

Tommy still follows the sport he entered in 1930 and came away from thirty years later. And as he looks back on those long, often-hard years, the rough spots get smoothed over by the fra-ternal nature of the auto racing carnival: "I wouldn't trade my experiences, especially getting to know so many swell people in racing. I wouldn't trade that for a couple of million dollars, but it really was a pretty tough way to make a living."

Tough though it was, the career of Tommy Hinnershitz was that of an artist whose talent brought a grace and beauty to auto racing that, though it disappears in a sea of cement and asphalt, remains for those who were lucky enough to be there, those who can still remember. A man and a machine, painting a mural of speed and motion in shades of brown—a masterpiece not easily forgotten, nor likely to be found soon again.

15. The Philadelphia Boys

THEY had just won the tough twenty-four hours of Daytona, but Mark Donohue and Roger Penske didn't have time to dwell on it. Sebring was only two weeks away, the Trans-Am opener a month and a half, Indianapolis two months. They had work to do.

There, in their suburban Philadelphia garage a week after Daytona, the two men who formed America's most successful road-racing team were already back at work. Mark Donohue, the crewcut graduate engineer who had become the country's finest road racer, and Roger Penske, the retired sports car driver who saw to it that Donohue's cars were prepared flawlessly, took only a few moments to relive the glory of Daytona, where they had surprised the eager Porsche factory entries with their three-year-old Lola-Chevy.

"We didn't really have too much of an idea what would happen at Daytona," Donohue reported casually. "We hadn't run the Lola for about two years, so we just took it down there to run it in practice and tried to find out as much as we could then.

"We did as much as could with the car, but we went down there without really knowing what we would be able to do. As it turned out, the Porsches were a little faster off the turns but we were just as fast on top speed and had better brakes, so it evened out pretty much."

The match appeared less even late in the endurance contest, though, when the Lola had to have a new exhaust manifold installed and fell some 200 miles behind the Porsches. "It looked pretty grim right then," Donohue observed. "Some of the fellas wanted to call it quits but Roger thought we ought to try to do twenty-four hours even if we didn't win and see what fell off the car. Roger always seems to know when to make the right decision, and he was right again."

The Porsches soon fell on hard times themselves, and Donohue was back in front when the sun rose. "They had trouble and we had trouble, but they had more," Donohue noted.

The Daytona-winning Lola sat to one side of the spiffy garage. Pieces of the Camaro with which the two Philadelphians intended to take their second straight Trans-Am championship filled the far wall. To the near side rested the shell of the Lola Indy-car, painted the familiar deep-blue of all Penske cars.

It was Indianapolis that Donohue and Penske were beginning to think most about then. They were going to the big race for the first time, and those who knew of Mark's driving skills and Roger's reputation for building durable machinery were already speculating about the impact the pair would have on the Indy scene.

The USAC Indy-car crowd knew only selected parts of the Penske-Donohue story. They knew of Penske's reputation for running a tight organization, preparing fast and durable racing

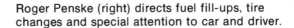

Roger Penske (right) directs fuel fill-ups, tire changes and special attention to car and driver.

Roger Penske and driver Mark Donahue.

machines and developing the pit stop into a masterpiece of speed and precision. The veteran hands remembered the lean, smooth-featured Penske from the days of USAC's old road-racing circuit, where he had been a first caliber driving star. Driving everything from Birdcage Maseratis to Fiats, Penske had become one of America's first road-racing greats, dominating USAC and SCCA sports car racing in the late '50s and early '60s.

Penske quit driving abruptly in 1964, took over a Chevrolet new car dealership in Philadelphia, and began puttering around with race cars for other people to drive. By 1969, he was viewed as the supreme team manager, turning the cars provided by such suppliers as Lola of England and Chevrolet of Detroit into immaculate pieces of racing machinery.

Along the way, he picked up a baby-faced, quiet-spoken young driver named Mark Donohue. About all the Indy fraternity knew of him was that he had entered his first USAC Indy-car race—at the Mosport road course in Ontario—the season before and finished third. A few may have known he had demolished the competition in the U. S. Road Racing Championship series the past two years, knocking down the last two titles of that scrapped SCCA enterprise. He also piloted the Penske-prepared Camaro to the 1968 Trans-American championship.

What they didn't know, if it mattered, was that, early in his career, Donohue had first run into Penske at an SCCA driving school. The experienced Penske was one of the two men who turned the amateur into a pro. The other man was the late Walt Hansgen, a pioneer in the history of American road racing and Donohue's advisor at that SCCA driving school. Together, the two expert drivers put Mark Donohue on the road to racing greatness.

By 1961, the same year Penske was *Sports Illustrated*'s "Driver of the Year," Donohue had won his first SCCA amateur championship. By 1965, he was Hansgen's driving partner in the sports car marathons at Sebring and Daytona. By 1966, he was a full-time race driver, taking Penske's Lola-Chevy into the thick of the Canadian-American Challenge Cup wars.

From that point on, people became used to seeing Donohue's name listed as a winner or near-winner of American road races.

They were beginning to recognize that he was a force to be reckoned with in the near future.

Even those who didn't know the full story were predicting the next "Rookie of the Year" at Indianapolis would be somebody named Mark Donohue.

"I don't really like to hear talk like that," Donohue snapped, "People put labels like that on you and then expect too much out of you. That's especially bad at Indianapolis, where you can blow an engine on the first lap and be out of it.

"We're just going to go out there and try our darndest to make the show," he continued, "I'd like to do a good job for Roger; I don't want to let him down as far as my performance goes. I don't know what I can deliver out there. I'm going with an open mind and do the best job I can."

As Penske, his black hair now tinged with gray at the temples, fiddled with something at a rear corner of the Indy Lola, Donohue went on with his appraisal of the upcoming venture at Indy, set to roll into action as soon as the gates opened the first day of May, 1969. "It appears even a month isn't really long enough to get ready for that one. It seems a shame to take a whole month for one race, but if you're not ready to go by May 1 you don't usually make the show."

Donohue next talked briefly of the painstaking work the Penske crew puts in on the cars he drives, whether for the big one at Indianapolis or a Trans-Am bash or the long Daytona marathon. "We have a certain approach to racing here," he explained, "we put as much time in on a Trans-American car for a three-hour race as we do for Indianapolis. As far as preparation, there's no difference at all."

Asked then about the recurring suggestions that he could find happiness in the luxurious grand prix circuit overseas, Donohue answered, "I'm not independently wealthy like some race drivers. I just couldn't pack up and go over there and announce I was ready to take over racing in Europe. There's plenty of good racing over here and I don't see why I should give that up and go over there where I can't make a living."

The "make a living" phrase struck a resonant chord. Donohue

The Sunoco-McLaren Special Indy car owned by Penske.

started out a few years before as an amateur road racer, competing on weekends for kicks. He became a professional racing driver shortly after that. As he stood there in a garage filled with some of the finest racing equipment in the world, Mark Donohue had no inclination to look back to those more carefree days. "No, I'm enjoying what I'm doing. It's hard work and it's time-consuming, but I don't know many people who enjoy what they're doing as much as I do."

16. Ralphie

RALPH LIGUORI is an anachronism, a throwback to racing's dark ages. He is outspoken, sometimes brash. He can be cantankerous, even angry. At a race track, he carries on like a brooding, surly barbarian. Car owners do not trust him with their race cars. Most of his fellow drivers cannot fathom him. Newcomers to racing view him as an uncivilized phantasm from a prehistoric age. His temperament has often made people wary of him. "I sure hope Ralph does well today," confided the wife of one of his crewmen before a big race. "If he doesn't, he'll be utter hell to live with on the way back home."

His career as a race driver has been punctuated by repeated frustrations and embarrassments. He has gone to Indianapolis thirteen straight years to try to put himself in the starting lineup, and has failed thirteen straight times. He has had some success in other big-car races and in sprint cars, but he seems to crash a lot, too—sometimes by his own indiscretions, sometimes by those of others.

He usually can be found at a race track sitting against the wheel of a race car, glumly scanning the activities in the pits or on the track in the aftermath of another misfortune, or in anticipation of an upcoming one. But despite all this, or rather because of it, Ralph Liguori is loved.

Crusty as he may be, he is loved by the racing fans, the eternal champions of underdogs and outcasts. To the pot-bellied, beer-slurping spectators at the primitive little race tracks where he often races, Ralph is something special, someone to pull for, someone to search out later in the pits to congratulate or, more often than not, console.

The affection for Liguori is a curious mixture of pity and worship. He is pathetic and at the same time admirable. With all his rough edges and endless misfortunes, he evokes a certain sympathetic response, a tenderness, from the racing fan, who then sums up his feelings by devising a nickname that captures the essence of this one-of-a-kind race driver. They call him "Ralphie the Racer" and, as such, he represents the true anti-hero of modern racing—the last vestige of the hard, plain-spoken individualists who peopled the sport through its early history.

In a day when race drivers are being honed into slick talking public relations types for mass media consumption, Ralph still drives with the primitive hunger of a barnstormer and makes no effort to gloss his trackside remarks with flowery phrases and snappy cliches. He races as he always has, with conviction and abandon, and he talks and acts the same way.

He looks the part. His coffee-brown skin and wrinkleless face belie his 45 years. With wavy black hair and steaming eyes, he has a definite Latin look about him. He walks with a relaxed, jaunty step, his shoulders slumped forward slightly, his hands jammed into the front pockets of his slacks. A loner, he normally can be seen sauntering along by himself, often seemingly engrossed in thought and stopping only occasionally to join in a conversation with other drivers and racing people. In street clothes, he wanders unnoticed by fans or newsmen and is genuinely startled when an unfamiliar fan or reporter suddenly intercepts him. When he does talk, he is candid, sometimes argumentative, with his facial expression alternating between a pinched frown and a half-moon smile. His arms flail continuously, pointing at his listeners, slapping together for emphasis.

His home is in Tampa, Florida, but he spends only a few months there each year. From late March to late September, he criss-crosses the country searching out the race tracks where sprint cars and championship cars hold forth. For some twenty-odd years now, he has religiously made that long, tough pilgrimage. For the past thirteen of those years, Liguori has taken one month each summer to wage his own personal war with that heartless speedway they call Indianapolis.

Liguori was only thirty-two years old when he first passed his driver's test at Indy. He was a young, eager, talented driver then, and by all rights should have had only a normal amount of trouble getting into that celebrated race. But Indy isn't a normal race track—it ages young men. It eats some alive, and others it gnaws silently, year after agonizing year.

The young Ralph Liguori failed to make the race that first year, 1959. He failed again in 1960, 1961, 1962, 1963, 1964, 1965, 1966, 1967, 1968, 1969, 1970, and 1971.

Each year, he traveled to that unique world on West 16th Street. Some years he had a car to drive, others he had only an ache in his guts and a crash helmet in his suitcase. But each year, come race day, his helmet was back in the suitcase and Ralph was sitting out another Indy race.

Ironically, his phenomenally rotten record at Indy has not stemmed so much from a lack of driving talent as from a lack of sound judgment. In his eagerness to be in the race, Ralph has perenially accepted rides in cars that can only charitably be called race cars. They are what racing people call "shitboxes," cars long since passed the time when they were competitive. Most rookies at Indy are offered these cars, but the smart ones turn them down. It is not an easy thing to do because most young men who come to Indy would give almost anything to have a chance to be in the starting lineup on Memorial Day.

Ralph succumbed to the temptation though, and in the process probably gave up his chance. He took the rides in those tired pieces of junk, entered every May just to be a part of the Indy carnival. Such cars tend to do one of two things when they are pushed for that little extra speed needed to make them competitive. They come apart at the seams or they break loose from the driver's control and crash. They did both to Ralph. He put more holes in engine blocks and black scars on speedway retaining walls than he cares to remember.

Even the one outstanding car he got his hands on refused to cooperate. The car was the fabulous Novi, the terrifyingly power-

Ralph Liguori

ful and star-crossed brute that electrified Indy crowds but seldom finished races. One May, Andy Granatelli put Ralph in one of his fiery-red Novis. It seemed like a natural combination from a sentimental angle—the man who should have made the race many times but hadn't in the car that should have won the race many times but hadn't.

From a practical standpoint, though, it was an ill-conceived move. Enraptured by the throaty roar of that beautiful V-8 engine, Ralph tried to fulfill the promise of the emotional match of man and machine in just a few laps around the unforgiving Indy oval. Flashing down the long backstretch, he became one of the few men ever to overtax the muscular powerplant created with such tender, loving care by Ed and Bud Winfield. The engine, with more power than any drive-train or chassis could take, exploded in a cloud of fire and smoke, spewing oil and metal in one ear-shattering regurgitation. Spinning in its own vomit, the Novi whirled around and around on the narrow track, Ralph frantically struggling to keep the runaway monster from smashing into the unyielding retaining wall. He lost that battle, too, and when he stepped from the smoldering carcass, his meteoric love affair with the Novi clearly was over.

He then returned to the less glamorous cars and merely repeated his earlier failures. Over a decade after he first tackled Indy, Ralph finally conceded no amount of desire could overcome the failings of second-class racing machinery. "I came here, at first, thinking I was a superman, but I'm not," he said in Gasoline Alley early in May 1969. "I'm just like anybody else. You can't do it on foot. I never thought I'd turn down a ride, but you've got to say no sometime."

So Ralph stopped climbing into the shitboxes, but it was too late. His past history now dogged him and no one made an offer he could say yes to. The owners of the better cars shied away from his record of a dozen Indy failures. "Liguori runs real good, but he's a hard-luck kind of guy," said one of those owners. "Bad luck I've got. He and I don't need to get together."

That's the final irony of Ralph's painful ordeal at Indianapolis. He had to pay the full price for bowing at the altar of the shitboxes. In the minds of the better car owners, he had become poison, even though he possessed one of the essential attributes of an Indy aspirant—experience. Despite the many black moments with the shabby cars, he had logged hundreds of laps on the difficult 2½-mile oval. "God knows how many laps I've run at this place. I've driven as many as some guys who've been in the race, that's for sure."

But the blown engines and crashes overshadowed all that, and he seldom even gets to sit in a car at Indy anymore. He stalks the garage area every day of the month, but the good offers don't come and he seldom has occasion to put his driving suit on.

Yet he clings tenaciously to his belief that he belongs in the race and talks unabashedly not only of starting the race but winning it as well.

His incomparable misfortunes didn't end with Indy. His record on the smaller tracks was a strange crazy-quilt of scattered success and considerable calamity. He has, on certain fortuitous days, shown flashes of true driving brilliance. Almost without exception, those days came when he was racing on dirt tracks, where he displayed a stunning virtuosity for that particular brute-strength and ragged-edge brand of racing.

One of those days came in 1957, when he won a sprint car race on the big Langhorne, Pennsylvania, oval. Ten years later, his consummate skill for dirt racing manifested itself twice as he triumphed in sprint car events at Tulsa, Oklahoma, and Granite City, Illinois. Still another three years passed before he scored again, at Williams Grove in Pennsylvania a few weeks after pulling down a second place in the Hoosier Hundred big-car race.

In all his years of racing, he has hit on the right combination only often enough to post a handful of wins and near-wins. For every good race there were a half-dozen when his luck was catastrophically miserable.

At the small half-mile tracks where the sprint cars race and the larger, but equally primeval, full-mile dirt tracks on the USAC big-car circuit, things keep happening to him—improbable, illogical, unexplainable things. People run into him and he runs into people. Tires go flat for no apparent reason. Wheels fly off. Fuel lines break. Radiators overheat. Brakes quit working. All of which leave Ralph empty-handed when they pass out the checks. If on a given day the Fates are totally unforgiving, they can hand Ralph more lumps than any one man deserves.

So it was on a spring day in 1969 when the USAC sprint cars came to Eldora Speedway, a crude half-mile dirt bowl in western Ohio. On that day at the steep-banked dish of dirt cut out of an Ohio cornfield, Ralph rolled double snake-eyes.

"It's a track you have to figure out and I like it because I can usually figure it out pretty well," Ralph has said of the Eldora track, but things were to happen to him that day no amount of figuring could foresee.

A notoriously poor qualifier, Ralph found himself in fifteenth place in the twenty-car field for the feature event. It was a long way to the front but not an impossible distance for a driver eager, and brave, enough to work at it. As the lineup hit the starting stripe, the cars broke into an uneven string and poured into the first turn, running high near the rim of the dusty bank. Down the short backstretch flashed the buzzing clothesline of colorful machines, then one by one they cocked sideways and sliced across the top of the next turn.

Suddenly, one car, a bright red blur, darted down to the middle of the bank, its tires grinding viciously in the loose dirt. The car moved past one, then two of its high-riding competitors, and glided smoothly into a gap in the line of roaring cars. Down into the first turn again, and the red car repeated the move, picking up two more places. The leaders were still several yards ahead, but all eyes now were on the slashing red car and its bold driver.

Ralph Liguori was working his spell on the Eldora audience, mesmerizing the now-standing crowd with his rhythmic performance of desire and daring.

Across the midsection of the turn, then out to the edge at the head of the backstretch, a quick straight burst, another grudging slice around the turn and down past the starting line with his engine screaming back at the crowd.

Before the race was half over, Ralph had passed the fourteen cars in front of him. He was in the lead and seemingly in a position to move out to a comfortable lead. But this was not to be a comfortable day for him, remember.

Riding through the first turn, the tail of his car slipped around farther than it should have and made a slow, lazy arc down to the bottom of the bank. "I just ran out of brains," Ralph candidly explained later.

Almost before he stopped spinning, he was waving his arms frantically for the push-truck to get him started again. It did, and he was off again to try to snatch back the victory that seemed certain only moments before. Cutting low on the track again, he began chewing his way through the field. Up to eighth quickly, he was watched with renewed awe by the already-spent Eldora spectators.

Then the awe turned first to fear, then apprehension, and finally to sadness. As Ralph came ripping onto the mainstretch, the race's lead car slowed, then stalled right in the middle of the first turn. The cars immediately behind scattered to avoid the disabled car, but Ralph, driving with vengeance, flew blindly into the turn. Only at the last second did he see the stalled car, and he cranked the steering wheel hard to the right to avoid the motionless machine. He missed it by inches, but his line was then carrying him inexorably into the rust-red steel guardrail. His car slammed heavily into it, its outside wheels climbing skyward. The car rose in the air and cartwheeled crazily down the banking —Ralph tossing around in the cockpit like a lifeless rag-doll.

When the car came to rest, its front wheels sheared off, Ralph was slumped forward in the cockpit.

The officials halted the race. The safety crews rushed to Ralph, unbuckled him from his safety harnass, and gingerly carried him to a waiting ambulance. With the race track in stunned silence, the ambulance's wailing siren cut through the air like a scream as it moved off the track, through the parking lot, and onto the highway leading to the hospital.

The race was restarted and an Illinois driver, Larry Cannon, declared the winner before word of Ralph's condition filtered back to the Eldora arena. First it was said he had a broken nose. Then a report came that he had a broken back. Later that night, an Associated Press story related that Ralph had announced his immediate retirement as a race driver from his hospital bed.

The next day, Ralph squelched that report with one blunt, unequivocal statement. "Hell no, I'm not retired," he grunted, already out of the hospital. "Everybody always makes these things out to be worse than they are for some reason. There really wasn't that much wrong. All I got was a scraped nose, and they made it out to be a broken nose, and a sore back, and they made that a broken back."

With those reports laid to rest, he turned back to the aspect of the peculiar day at Eldora that meant more than a few scrapes and bruises. "I knew I could win it and I was running to win."

He was running to win. It was as simple as that. He didn't win, but no one who was there that day could question his right to say he would have if destiny had not intervened.

Even the man who won the race admitted amazement at Ralph's ability to make a low groove work, something others tried that day with considerably less success. "I don't know how Liguori was working it," said Larry Cannon, "He must have been letting it all hang out."

That's exactly what he was doing. After all, that's why they called him "Ralphie the Racer" in the first place.

17. *No Stars in His Eyes*

FOR SOME strange reason, my father always calls him "Mario Amvetti." It has never been clear whether he pronounces it that way because he thinks that's really his name, or because he's making a joke, or because his bridgework is giving him trouble. But without fail he'll talk about "Amvetti" doing this or that at a race, and I've never had the heart to say anything to him about it.

His name, of course, is Mario Andretti. He is a short guy, a good half-foot short of six feet, wiry, wide-eyed, darkly handsome, and perhaps the most superbly gifted racing driver of the age. He has driven every kind of racing machinery there is to drive. He drives Indianapolis cars, grand prix cars, stock cars, sports cars, sprint cars, midgets. He has driven all the tracks there are to drive, from the crude dirt races at Reading, Pennsylvania, or Springfield, Illinois, to the luscious road-racing layouts at LeMans, France, or Kyalami, South Africa. He has raced up the side of Pike's Peak and through such aptly-named glens as Langhorne's "Puke Hollow" and Elkhart Lake's "Thunder Valley."

He's won almost every race there is to win. He's won Indianapolis, and more Indy-car races than anyone except A. J. Foyt; he's won Daytona, both through 24 hours of bleary-eyed sports car racing and three hours of fender-scraping Grand National combat; he's won champagne-drenched grand prix jousts at such places as Kyalami and Ontario.

And with all his driving, his winning, his traveling, his public acclaim, he has emerged as racing's first truly professional athlete —its first polished and poised statesman. At the same time he retains his raw driving instincts, Mario Andretti has developed the keen business sense and the fundamental *savoir-faire* athletes in other American sports began to exhibit some years ago.

Capable of earning as much as a half million dollars per season, he lays out his racing plans with the calm calculations of a stock broker. For the past few years, he held his USAC Indy-car treaty with flamboyant Andy Granatelli and his European grand prix and sports car alliance with Enzo Ferrari in a delicate balance, parlaying the two pacts into a year-round schedule of the biggest and richest races on both sides of the Atlantic. "Racing to me is definitely a business. I don't feel particularly attached to any one area. I owe a certain loyalty to USAC because this is where I got started, but, by the same token, I feel I'm a businessman at the same time and every year I'm going to weigh the situation and see which way to go. I'm too old to have stars in my eyes and I'm pretty practical about this thing."

On his relationship with the sometimes not-too-practical Granatelli, he added, "I think even though Andy and I don't always agree on our philosophy of racing, we made it pretty clear we're

Mario Andretti in the pits at Indianapolis in 1969.

going to put the emphasis on being practical instead of controversial. As long as we agree on that, we'll do all right."

They were doing fine in 1969 when Mario won at Indy and took
his third national Indy-car championship. They did less well the
next two years. By late 1971, Andretti's practical side got the best
of him, and he severed his relationship with Granatelli to do
more racing for Ferrari in Europe and join up with Al Unser and
Joe Leonard on the Indy-car team put together by ex-driver
Parnelli Jones.

Mario Andretti (left) and Jackie Ickx (right) after winning the
six hour Continental race at Daytona Beach in February 1972.

Meanwhile, on the banquet circuit Mario suitably impressed
the steak-and-salad crowd with his easy manner at the speaker's
podium and his warm wit. Not that he is a polished speaker, but
he is a long way from the axle-grease gorilla who mumbles a few
words into the microphone and hastily takes his seat behind the
flower bowl.

"I knew Andy was a very emotional kind of guy," he tells a
banquet crowd of the famous kiss Granatelli gave him at the con-

clusion of the 1969 Indy race, "and when I agreed to drive for him, we talked about a clause I wanted in my contract—positively no kissing. So he was almost under breach of contract there. Of course, I was so happy myself those legal things didn't bother me."

He speaks as glibly about the mental lapse he suffered late in that 1969 Indy contest, a lapse that sent his car skidding to within a foot of the outer wall and that a number of television cameramen recorded on film. "During the race, I didn't think anyone caught it, but they did. It's a long race; there's no scenery or mountains to look at or anything. It's not that you're loafing around or anything. It was just that I had to get off the pace a little and sometimes you're not mindful of everything that happens. From there on out, I guarantee you I was right on the ball."

Usually seated beside his bouncy wife, Deeann, at the head table before he is called to the podium, Mario always looks relaxed and composed, nattily dressed in a snug silk suit, the perfect picture of the businessman-athlete stereotype.

Yet there is still much of the basic racing passion left in the man. His brilliant driving, still the most spirited of all American drivers, and his exhausting pursuit of racing glory almost every week of the year prove he has not sold himself, body and soul, to practicality. If he had, he would probably have stopped racing and become a salesman.

"I enjoy it," he says of his busy racing calendar on one of his rare stays at his Nazareth, Pennsylvania, home. "I couldn't bear the idea of not racing, not even for a month. I can't just sit around that long. I get itchy after awhile."

It is a rare but logical combination—racer, businessman, public figure. Mario has become the model for all professional racing drivers, even in a subculture that retains much of its native coarseness and crudity.

Linda Vaughn, the blonde "Miss Hurst Golden Shifter" whose bosom measures almost as much as Mario does from top to bottom, stood along the chain-link fence behind the Indy pits, her mug on one side of the fence and her assets on the other. She watched as Mario prepared to take his car out on the track and exclaimed to her pretty, but less endowed companion, "There he is . . . there's Super-Wop." Super-Wop, that's what she had called him all right, and she kept on calling him that, smugly, as she stood there.

Mario obviously has not smoothed over all of racing's rough edges. He still hasn't led racing, by his example, to the trough of sophistication and refinement. He still has to get his business-man-athlete image through to a sunny-faced, impudent girl the guys back in the garage area privately call "Super-Tits" and a well-meaning father who insists on calling him "Mario Amvetti."

18. One Who Came Back

FREDDIE LORENZEN always was something of a non-conformist. So it was not too unnatural for him to be one of the few racing men to defy the old unwritten law that says once you leave the sport, don't try to come back. More than a handful of good men have been killed or at least broken proving the truth of that racing law, but Freddie Lorenzen, the flashy maverick, beat it.

Flamboyant, seemingly fearless, smoothly handsome, and massively talented, Lorenzen was NASCAR's greatest superstar in the early sixties, winning more long, fast races on the great superspeedways of the South than any driver before him. He had been the first man to complete a superspeedway "Grand Slam" by winning at each of the original five high-banked Southern speedbowls—Daytona, Darlington, Charlotte, Atlanta, and Rockingham. Twelve times he had throttled his sleek Ford past the checkered flag in NASCAR's most fabled high-speed races—the Daytona 500, Darlington's Rebel 300, the World 600 and National 400 at Charlotte, the Atlanta 500. (In 1966, the Rebel 300 was changed to the Rebel 400 and the National 400 became the National 500.) When, in 1966, he came home first in the American 500 at Rockingham, Fred put the finishing touch on the history-making "slam" he had started at Darlington five years before. Twelve superspeedway victories, the Slam, 14 wins on NASCAR's shorter tracks, 12 more on the USAC stock car circuit, two season championships in USAC—all were in the trophy case of the intense young bachelor from Elmhurst, Illinois, when his racing career hit full-stride in the mid-60s.

But the tensions and anxieties of racing ultimately began to fray the sensitive nerves of Fred Lorenzen. The powerful pressures of speed and success finally overwhelmed him, and in 1967 he called it quits at the age of 32. To wind down his jangled nerves, Fred went on an extended holiday, the usual playboy pursuits combined with some serious dabbling in the stock market. The big board of the stock exchange and the broads, beaches, and bright lights of America managed to hold his attention for some three years. But then Wall Street began to suck up his money; the leisurely life did the same to his spirit.

Finally, in 1970, the inevitable decision came. Freddie Lorenzen decided the frustrations of stock car racing were really less punishing—and more profitable—than the frustrations of stocks and bonds. In tandem with Richard Howard, energetic owner of Charlotte Speedway, Freddie came back.

At Howard's raceway and in Howard's race car, Lorenzen started his first race in three years. It was as if he had never even been away—he led the race, with no appreciable signs of the long layoff.

Whipping his winged Dodge around the Charlotte speedrome, the dimple-chinned repatriate found the lead on five different occasions in the long race before a blown engine sent him into a race-ending spin. It was an amazing performance in a sport where comebacks usually are fraught with apprehension and dark forebodings. Even Fred Lorenzen was a little flabbergasted by the whole thing.

"To tell the truth, yes I was surprised," he exclaimed after the Charlotte event, "hell, we were in pretty good shape to win the thing until the engine blew. It took a couple of days to get used to it again," Fred admitted, reflecting on his few days of practice before competing at Charlotte, "I thought it would take me longer, but it didn't."

Clearly, the three-year vacation had not left him fat, flabby, and fatigued, even though he admittedly didn't do much in the way of real work. "I didn't do much of anything—I did spend a

Fred Lorenzen

Buddy Baker (left) and Fred Lorenzen discuss strategy before the start of NASCAR's Firecracker 400 Grand National Stock Car race.

lot of time with the stock market—except water ski and . . . play, I guess you'd say. Of course, I kept myself in pretty good physical shape those three years. I did a lot of water skiing and exercise and so forth. I think I'm really in better shape now than I was before."

While his waistline stayed within the established limits for the duration of his hiatus, his overall appearance didn't. On his return, Fearless Freddie rocked the NASCAR establishment back on its collective heels with his rust-colored hair draped well down his neck and sporting the flashiest multicolored bellbottom pants and body shirts the fairly provincial stock car contingent had seen.

The hair, naturally, drew the most static from the straight-laced hierarchy in the NASCAR command. "There were comments, but they didn't order me to cut it," Freddie related defensively, "I've got it trimmed up now—in fact, I think it's too short. I caught a cold with it like this." It also posed no serious danger to the traditional he-man image of a racing driver, as far as Fred was concerned. "As long as you still look like a guy, then it's alright," he asserted, with a trace of righteous indignation.

Hair flowing in the wind, Fred turned from the Charlotte beginning to face his tough trek up the treacherous comeback trail. The first step firmly made, he readied his second step and focused his eyes on the long path ahead. "I'm hoping we can do well enough the rest of this season to land a good factory ride for next year," he said in mid-1970, "I've been talking with some of the factory people trying to line up something, but it's really too early to tell what will happen next season. I think the big thing right now is to make a good showing in this car," he added matter-of-factly.

Like Charlotte, the succeeding showings were good enough to keep Fred moving forward along the comeback route. Though he did not win any races, he led several and finished well up front frequently—more than enough to land him a good ride for the 1971 season. It came from another Illinois resident with his own reputation for flamboyance and flair, Andy Granatelli. The STP mogul provided the financial backing for a new Plymouth and placed the machine in Freddie's eager hands. Not exactly a factory ride, but easily the next best thing.

The STP Plymouth kept Fred running near the front of the NASCAR speed derbies, but it would not put him in the one spot he had been used to in his earlier racing days, the winner's circle. But, before the '71 season was over, he found his way into the cockpit of the famed Wood Brothers' Mercury, a car that could finally put him back on top, which had collected a passell of big wins with people like Cale Yarborough and Donnie Allison at the wheel. Even though he promptly piled up the Mercury on the Darlington wall in September, Fred was on his way. He was on the verge of being a winner again, he was carrying the Ford Motor Company banner again, and he was convinced he could pick up where he left off in 1967 and keep his racing career going for several more seasons. "I'll keep running until I see I don't have it anymore," he observed as he looked ahead, "It could be three or four years, I don't know."

So on he goes, repeating his personal saga at stock car tracks across the country, this man with the floppy hair, the colorful clothes, the still-youthful good looks—this Fred Lorenzen, the one who came back.

19. Togetherness

IT WAS A fairly ordinary hospital room. It had the sterile white appearance and antiseptic smell of all hospital rooms. Sunlight entered only in thin yellow shafts through narrow beige venetian blinds. Nurses marched into the room at regular intervals, bring-meal trays, straightening bed sheets and pillows, taking temperatures.

In one bed was a round-faced man in his early forties, his wavy brown hair streaked with silver. Gauze bandages covered two patches of skin on his face and one on his neck. Despite the bandages, his mouth still managed to curl up in a gentle smile as he spoke with his soft Texas accent.

In the other bed was a slender man, about ten years younger, his arm bandaged and his foot in a cast. His hairline receded far back on his forehead to closely-cropped brown hair and his crisp voice bore little trace of a regional accent.

The first man, the Texan, was Lloyd Ruby, a race driver. The second was New Jerseyite Wally Dallenbach, also a race driver.

Two men, two race drivers, lying in hospital beds in a Delaware hospital. They arrived here on consecutive days after crashing at the same race track and weren't really surprised to see each other. They had seen a lot of each other during the 1969 season. In fact, they were beginning to feel a lot like Siamese twins.

Ruby, the quiet, ageless veteran of the racing wars, and Dallenbach, a more recent addition to the upper rung of racing stardom, strung together parallel tales of initial successes followed by deepening misfortunes, all leading to the colorless confines of a Delaware hospital room.

It all began when they arrived at Indianapolis in May. Ruby, with second and third place finishes in the two pre-Indy championship races, was leading the USAC national point standings. And Dallenbach, with a second and a fifth in those races, was right behind him in the second spot on the points tally.

Qualifying for the Indy marathon, both turned in disappointing runs and landed side-by-side in the seventh starting row. The seventh row is a long way back at Indianapolis, but two men, Ruby and Dallenbach, were about to prove it was still in the ballpark.

From the fall of the green flag, the two sliced through the eighteen cars ahead of them like knives through apple butter. Ruby, then Dallenbach, would flash past one, two, maybe three cars on a straightaway. Then Dallenbach would pass Ruby, or vice versa, and together they would move past still another competitor.

Before the race was fifty laps old, the twin chargers passed everybody and each took his turn in the lead. By Dallenbach's count, they passed each other about thirty times while they were at it. "We just were having our own race out there," Wally later commented.

But neither Lloyd Ruby nor Wally Dallenbach won the race. Mario Andretti did. Before the race was half over, the two men who proved to be the most competitive with Andretti experienced their first mutual stroke of ill fortune.

On the eightieth lap, Dallenbach's sleek white car with the bright orange and chartreuse trim rolled to a stop in the infield grass, its clutch shattered. A few laps later, Ruby was stepping slowly from his bulbous yellow and red machine as it sat helplessly in his pits, gasoline pouring from its side after a hose fitting was ripped away during a routine pit stop.

Thus, the two drivers who had done the most driving on the Indy track that particular Memorial Day suddenly were mere spectators; the anticipated victory had eluded them both. "I believe we were really in good shape to win it," Ruby said. "If we hadn't fouled up there, it would have been a fairly easy run. I think if we'd kept running Andretti wouldn't have finished."

Dallenbach, too, would look back with longing and disappointment on that day: "I felt I had as good a chance of winning it as anyone."

From that point on, the two would get used to seeing each other on the sidelines before the completion of a championship race.

Ruby was the most immediately afflicted. In the thirteen championship events following Indy, he only finished two, and plunged from the top of the points ladder to fourteenth place.

Dallenbach, after finishing four of the first five post-Indy contests, saw the checkered flag fall only twice in the next eight races and traded his number-two slot in the points listing for seventh place rung.

The summer of their mutual bad luck was destined to culminate when they traveled to Dover, Delaware, in August to race in the first big-car race on a new high-banked track built over the past winter.

The big and fast Dover track proved to be too much of a strain on the sophisticated, fragile suspension systems of the rear-engined Indy cars, an effect not encountered by the brutish stock cars that raced there earlier in the year. And it was Ruby and Dallenbach who proved that unpleasant fact.

Again Ruby first felt the sting of the whip. Whistling around the steep banks of the spotless new Dover oval the day before the race, his car broke loose in the third turn, slammed into the retaining wall, and erupted in flames. Before he could extricate himself from the burning machine, he was scorched on the face and neck and minutes later was booked in at the local hospital.

It only took one day for Ruby to get company. Dallenbach joined him after slamming the second-turn wall during the running of the Dover race, hospitalized with a broken foot and burns on his arm.

The strange turn of events gave the injured racing drivers someone to talk to in the hospital, but each secretly began to wish he could break clear of the other's streak of bad luck. They were friendly and sympathetic toward one another, certainly, but both wanted to end their unusual brand of togetherness. "The last time I saw Lloyd was in the hospital and I said something to him about drawing a line about doing things together," Dallenbach would joke a few weeks after both he and Ruby had checked out of the Dover hospital.

Their racing wounds healed, the two drivers set out separately to reverse their own failing fortunes. Each hoped to put things sufficiently in order in the two remaining races of the year to get a running start for 1970.

For Ruby, all roads lead to Indianapolis, and the two races, at Phoenix and Riverside, were viewed as a testing ground for what he fervently hoped would be his long-sought victory at Indy. For Dallenbach, the pair of year-end events would serve the same basic purpose although his personal goal was two-pronged. "I've either got to win Indianapolis or the championship, and I'm not going to settle for anything less," the New Jersey driver said shortly before leaving for Phoenix.

The Phoenix race in early November then became the focal point of the pair's plans to shake the bad luck which had been plaguing them for over half the season and to demonstrate their readiness to head full-throttle into the next racing year.

Happily, they pulled it off, but not without a bizarre trace of the phenomenal proximity which had haunted them since early May. At the finish of the Phoenix race, Ruby had clearly rubbed out his run of bad luck in convincing fashion. He won, and did so without any hint of the year's earlier misfortunes.

Tagging along right behind him, taking second in the Phoenix event, was the smiling Easterner, the man on the other side of the Delaware hospital room, Wally Dallenbach.

For Ruby and Dallenbach, 1969 was a year of inexplicable and indelible togetherness.

20. *King of the Midgets*

THE SPEEDWAY announcer announced the first five drivers. Each received a polite round of applause from the crowd as he strode toward one of the humpbacked midget cars lined up in two neat rows on the track.

"Starting in sixth position, driving car number one," the announcer then blurted through the loudspeaker, "A three-time national midget champion and Indianapolis-500 veteran, from Lebanon, Indiana—here he is, fans . . . Mel Kenyon!" The tempo and volume of the applause was noticeably greater this time, with scattered whoops of excitement audible among the din from the tiers of gray bleachers along the front straightaway of the small oblong race track.

A black-haired man trotted onto the track as the crowd continued its applause. His left arm, a brown sock-like covering over his hand, went up into the air and waved stiffly in the direction of the bleachers. He stopped beside a blue car trimmed with white and, as the clamor subsided and the announcer introduced another driver, he reached into the cockpit, extracted his crash helmet and goggles, and methodically arranged the maze of straps and belts in the tiny driver's compartment.

Some minutes later, the two columns of cars marched out of the turn, their engines cracking like overgrown popcorn-poppers. Picking up speed in one great burst, the cars began to break ranks as they ripped past the dancing green flag at the starting line. The third car in the outside column, a blue car, suddenly shot into the narrow opening between the two cars in front of it. There was barely enough room for the third car; its wheels seemed only inches away from the other cars. As they moved into the first turn, the blue car edged out of the tight space and moved out in front.

Slicing out of the second turn, the blue car squeezed between a yellow car and the outer wall. As the pair ripped down the short straight stretch, the blue car slowly pulled past, diving into the next turn just in front of the yellow machine. The next time it came around the second turn, the blue car was right behind a gleaming black one. This time, the blue car darted down to the inside, moving beside the black car as they thundered toward the third turn. The two cars swung into the turn side-by-side, the blue one on the inside and the black one on the outside. When they reached the middle of the sweeping turn, the rear wheels of the black car skipped sideways ever so slightly on the black asphalt. The car hung suspended for a fraction of a second as the driver lifted the accelerator. The blue car leaped ahead, and the black one fell in behind as the two machines again moved onto the front straightaway.

Ten minutes later, the blue car rolled up to the starting line, where the speedway announcer, a beauty queen, and a shiny trophy stood. Mel Kenyon won another midget race.

After the announcer shook Mel's hand, the beauty queen kissed his grimy face, and both of them handed him the trophy. Mel Kenyon then moved through the milling crowd toward a dark pickup truck with a camper on its back. A swaying, topless trailer was hitched to the truck's bumper, and the blue number one midget was parked beside it.

For the next hour, he stood next to the truck sipping beer and talking with the streams of people who always crowd around him after a race, whether he wins or not. With him, sitting against the fender of the trailer, was his brother Don who handles the mechanical chores on all of Mel's race cars.

Now, after the race, in the pale-yellow glow of the track lights, Mel's once-handsome face takes on a ghostly aspect. It carries the grim evidence of the fiery Indy-car crash at Langhorne in 1965 which almost ended his life. The left side of his face is still badly scarred from the burns; his left nostril is a tattered flap of skin. There is yet another remnant of Langhorne disaster. Where his left hand should be is the fingerless glove with a ring of thin metal on the palm side. The ring slips over a peg on the steering wheel, allowing him to steer his race car without the fingers, amputated after the 1965 crash.

As he stands there, scarred and surrounded by well-wishers, Kenyon is the picture of a typical midget racer, a tough breed of man peculiar to the American way of racing. And in that rough-

and-tumble world of darting little cars and long, continuous hauls from race to race, he probably is the best there is.

First from his home in Davenport, Iowa, later from his new residence in Lebanon, Indiana, just north of Indianapolis, he has raced the midget circuit for over a dozen years. He has usually driven with the same flair and doggedness he had this particular night, and won over 60 midget races and three national midget championships in the process.

Mel Kenyon eats, sleeps, and breaths midget racing. You have to when you're running 50 to 60 races a summer, most of them at dirty little backwoods tracks where the take-home pay is a couple hundred bucks or less. You have to love it to survive. Mel thrives on it, and long after a race is over he talks with friends and strangers about midget racing. "I think it's about the only real fun in racing, mechanic-wise and driver-wise. With a championship car, you'll work for three weeks and run it once and then you work three more weeks. You put as much time in on a midget, but you might run three or four times a week. And, for the driver, they run much closer together on the race track, which makes for real good competition. Sometimes it does get to be quite a drag, I guess. Well, not a drag, really. Sometimes you'd just like to get a little more sleep."

He talks of the scrubby tracks, some paved and some dirt, where he races, making no clear distinction on his preference for one racing surface over the other. "Actually, I prefer them both. I like a good dirt race where you can run two or three grooves and give everybody good, close competition. And a good pavement race, I enjoy that also." He talks, if asked, about the metal ring that gives him the use of his disfigured left hand. "It has worked out real well. It's always a hinderance, a handicap, to a degree, but sometimes it works to my advantage."

He talks, too, of other kinds of racing, when there is no more midget racing to talk about. He will talk about his races at Indy, where he has driven more conservatively than usual and finished in the top five, three of his first four years there. "I try to stay up front, but I don't generally go for the lead. I think you have to *finish* that race."

He even talks about sprint car racing, where the cars, the money, and the danger are on a slightly larger scale than the midgets. "I drove a few sprints and found I could do real well, but I also found I didn't want to go that route because they seem to jump on too many guys' heads."

When the talking is done, and the crowds filter out through the track gates, Mel goes to the track office to pick up his paycheck. This night it is a relatively large one, $385. Some nights, it wouldn't buy enough gas to get home.

With the check in his pocket, he climbs aboard the pickup truck and heads off into the night, his thoughts already turning to the race tomorrow at some track hundreds of miles away. Mel Kenyon, midget driver, will be there, doing what he does best, and loving every minute of it.

21. Losing Is for the Other Guy

The Goodyear press man had a pensive look on his face when he walked into the reception room, his hand cupped behind his neck. After smoothing his straight black hair with a quick pass of the same hand, he smiled confidently as he looked around the spotless room with black and white checkered linoleum on the floor. Reporters, their opened notebooks in their laps, sat along three walls of the room on metal folding chairs. An empty mahogany chair with a thick beige cushion sat against the fourth wall. "Okay fellows, A. J. will be here in a minute," the Goodyear man said, "and don't worry, everything's alright. I just saw him and he's in a good mood."

The more successful he became, the more people talked about A. J. Foyt's temperament. If you caught him at the wrong time, he would snap at you, tell you to shove off, or simply ignore you, they said. The word soon went out, first to the press people, then to the race fans: if things aren't going well for A. J., steer clear of him. That directive was a sound one, for the hard-driving man from Houston did not enjoy losing. If he was losing on a given day, he was in no mood to exchange small talk with an inquisitive reporter or bystander. For A. J. Foyt, there is only one place that counts, first place. Anything else is strictly small potatoes, regardless of how much money it pays.

A. J. walked through the doorway into the room filled with reporters, tipping his black cowboy hat forward as he walked over to the beige-cushioned chair. He was dressed comfortably in a powder-blue turtleneck with matching slacks and suede loafers. He slumped down into the chair, threw one leg over the mahogany arm, and smiled at no one in particular.

He had just won the pole position for the 1969 Indianapolis 500. He was, as the Goodyear man promised, in a good mood. But as he began to talk with the reporters about his qualifying run, he seemed to be holding back just a little, lacing his answers with the guarded confidence of a man who still had work to do. "I felt we could have broken the record easy, the speeds we had been running," he said convincingly of his 170.568-mph pole-winning run a few hours earlier. "I really felt we could do 172.2, with maybe a lap at 173."

From the time he began racing, in Houston, Texas, A. J. accepted one of racing's oldest laws that says: Race to win, first of all, and if you can't do that, keep driving as if you could.

A. J., the thick-shouldered, jut-jawed man who always looked like he was on the verge of blushing, indeed raced to win. And win he did—more races than any other American driver—the Indianapolis 500 three times, the USAC national championship five times, the twenty-four hours of LeMans the one time he ran it, scattered stock-car, sprint-car, sports-car, and midget races scores of times. When he did not win, he hung in there as best he could. Often, when his car developed some minor malfunction, he pitched in with the crew to work five, ten, fifteen minutes—however long it took—to repair it, then jumped into the cockpit and roared back onto the track as if he were still battling for the lead. Or, if his car simply couldn't be fixed, he went to work with the crew on somebody else's car, a teammate or a friend, or just someone who needed h :lp.

Twice at Milwaukee, when his regular Indy-car broke down

While working on his car, Foyt gets fumes in his
eyes prior to the start of the 1969 Indy 500.

during practice, he unloaded his old dirt-track car, qualified it,
and ran it in the race. One of those times, he almost won the race
in the clumsy-looking dirt car to the wild delight of the fans and
the race promoters.

*"We had kind of sandbagged all week," A. J. was saying to
the reporters. "We never did put a full lap together so the other
guys wouldn't know what we were doing."*

*The main "other guy" was little Mario Andretti, who finally
qualified second-best to A. J. after disintegrating his best car
against the wall. "Mario won't give up; he's worse than I am
about that," A. J. said, smiling coyly.*

A. J. Foyt signing autographs for fans in Indy's Gasoline Alley.

The 20 or so drivers were lined up along the metal guardrail, some leaning against it, others sitting in the thin patch of grass in front of it. A. J. stood at one end of the group, his arms crossed tightly across his chest. He and the others listened patiently as an official with a yellow cap on his head and a clipboard under his arm dryly outlined the rules for the upcoming race. When he asked for questions or comments from the group, A. J. uncrossed his arms and spoke. "Yeah, I just wanted to say something to some of the newer fellows, like . . . ," he began, his eyes running down the line of drivers until they found a skinny young man sitting on one of the guardrail posts. "Are you the fellow who drives the green car?" Young Al Loquasto nodded. "Uh huh, well I noticed at Trenton that when I came up behind you, you seemed to take a different line into the corner every time. I don't know if you were aware of that or not, but it made it pretty hairy for the guys who were racing for position to get around you. I'm not trying to criticize, but if you could keep the same line each time or move the same way whenever somebody comes up to lap you, it would work out a lot better," A. J. told Loquasto, his tone firm but not unfriendly. "You're certainly entitled to run to finish out there, but if you could take the same line each time it would save some problems for the guys who are racing for position." Loquasto nodded quietly as A. J. talked, then looked down thoughtfully at his fingers as the drivers' meeting started to break up.

Someone was asking A. J. if winning the pole position had made him start looking at the upcoming 500 as the one most likely to give him his fourth Indy victory—an unprecedented feat. "It's just another race, really," he answered matter-of-factly. "Sure, I'd be honored to be the first four-time winner and I think we stand a good chance of doing it, but you never know."

A. J. seldom pulled his punches. He always answered reporters' questions directly, sometimes with startling bluntness. When he went about the task of getting ready to race, he did it with grim determination. And anything that got in the way ignited his temper.

When mechanics let him down, or he at least thought they had, there were blazing verbal battles. He ran through a lineup of racing's best mechanics before putting his cars in the hands of the one man he could trust explicitly, his father.

Reporters could get under his skin, too, especially when they misquoted him in their articles. Once, when a magazine article quoted him as calling the NASCAR drivers "hillbillies" and the European grand prix drivers "fags," A. J. threatened to take the author to court or to "Fist City," and made a lengthy apology for the article to the NASCAR drivers before the next race.

But A. J. still had his share of fun. When things were right and the pressure of winning races was off, he was as rollicking and good-natured as anyone. Anytime there was a circle of drivers standing around at a race track, A. J. usually was right in the middle, cracking up his colleagues with a joke or funny story.

A. J. was smiling broadly as he talked of teammate Roger McCluskey, who had gone out on his qualification run with a chance to knock A. J. out of the pole slot. "I was kind of needling him before he went out and told him that when he beat my speed I was going to wave the yellow flag on him."

The one and only time the ever-present Foyt poise had been shaken was the day A. J. agreed to participate in a publicity stunt at the DuQuoin, Illinois, fairgrounds track. His partner in the stunt was to be a furry, 385-pound, seemingly friendly lion. A. J., whose 185 pounds are spread over his five feet, eleven inch frame rather evenly except for a slight bulge at the waist, was to be knocked down playfully by the lion, which he was. But then the lion added an unexpected twist to the game by refusing to let A. J. up. When A. J. struggled to get up, the lion began nibbling at his uniform and by that time A. J. had had more than enough of that particular publicity stunt. Once the animal's trainer had rescued him, A. J. stumbled to his feet, visibly flustered, then managed a widening smile as he strolled back toward the pits alongside the lion, now securely on the end of the trainer's leash. Later the same day, A. J. ran a race and lost. At that point, he would have gladly wrestled the lion and probably could have whipped it.

"Okay fellows, is that it?" A. J. was asking as a lull hit the press conference. When no one offered another question, he pushed himself up from the chair, straightened his cowboy hat, and shook the Goodyear man's hand.

A. J. strode out through the door and headed toward the garage area gate. Through the press conference, he had been in a good mood, cordial, patient, and glib. He was obviously pleased with winning the race for Indy's pole position, though not as pleased as he could be.

The race that really counted was still a week away. Only if he won would A. J. be truly happy.

22. Capels and Capels

THE FIRST TIME you see him, this bushy-haired young man with the rugged good looks, he may be crouched beside a race car engine in a bright blue shirt and white mechanic's trousers, his hand cranking away with a wrench somewhere deep inside a maze of metal and wires. The second time you see him, even if it's the same day at the same track, he may be standing somewhere along the pit row, wearing a white driving uniform, snapping on a crash helmet, and climbing into the cockpit of another racing machine. Instinctively, you rub your eyes to make sure they're working properly. They are.

You next might want to think you had run into a case of identical twins, except you noticed both men had the same "Johnny" stitched over their breast pockets. The only remaining possibility is, of course split personality, and that's a little nearer the truth, although not in the strict textbook sense of split personality. The double life of Johnny Capels is not a product of a psychological quirk; it is a product of the psychology of a man whose mission in life is winning auto races.

Johnny Capels (right) talks with Joe Leonard
before the start of the 1972 Indianapolis 500.

Simply put, Johnny Capels has two separate and distinct jobs.
He is, first of all, a race car driver. He is also a race car mechanic.
Since he made his way from New Mexico to the Midwest late in
the 1968 season, his mechanical talents have brought him into the
winner's circle more often than his driving abilities.

Johnny, who whetted his racing appetite by matching his driving skills against a pair of brothers named Bobby and Al Unser
on many a dirt track in New Mexico, planted his seedling career
—along with his wife and two children—in Indianapolis, Indiana.
Armed only with a near-antique sprint car, an Al Unser castoff, he
set out to make his fortune as a racing driver. But being something of a realist, he took along his wrenches and other tools—
just in case.

Those wrenches and tools received a hearty workout. Not that

Johnny's driving effort was a failure—on the contrary, he performed remarkably well considering the age of the sprint car and even put it under the checkered flag first in a sprint feature at Hamburg, New York, in the fall of 1968.

But it takes more than one sprint car win to feed a wife and two growing children. So Johnny's wrenches were reluctantly taken out of their case and put to work on the Indy-car raced by Johnny's ex-competitor, benefactor, and friend, Al Unser. Working with venerable Indy-car mechanic George Bignotti and also with chassis experts from the Lola factory in England, Johnny quickly honed his mechanical skills to a level that carried him to the Indianapolis 500 considerably sooner than he would have made it as a driver.

Signed on with the crew of the car owned by Jim Robbins and to be driven by Indy sophomore Jim Malloy, Johnny sat at a table in the crowded speedway cafeteria in May of 1969, stirring a steaming cup of coffee, and put his mechanic's job into perspective. "My main reason for being here in Indiana during the racing season is to be a race driver. I don't want to be a mechanic. I'm a race driver and I want to be out there racing. I don't mind working on the cars, but my objective is to drive them. It really bothers me quite a bit being here. Every time I push Malloy off, I want to be up there getting pushed off myself.

"Of course, this is a great opportunity for me because I'm much more prepared for my first chance to drive here than I would be otherwise. I'm a driver who's interested in the machine itself, not just in whether or not it's a ride, and once I know what to do with one of these cars, what you have to work with, I feel when I get my chance to drive here I can be successful."

The prospect of returning to the mammoth Indianapolis speedway some May naturally turned Johnny's thoughts to the age-old problem that confronts those who try to move into the 500 fraternity: the hard and irreversible fact that at Indy the veteran drivers get the good cars and the newcomers get what's left. "I'd say possibly I'd have to take something less than the best, although there's a line I would draw. Of course, not-quite-the-best car can still be a good car. But I'm not at all interested in running a car that isn't competitive just to say I made the race. That's something I learned in the sprints: when you run back in the pack, it starts to work on you after awhile. Pretty soon you start thinking maybe it's not the car, maybe it's you. Besides, you have to drive so hard just to make the program in a poor car. It's no fun to know you're starting that far behind. I don't race for a hobby; I intend to be a champion driver. You've got to do it for one reason, to be Number One, or you shouldn't be doing it."

Moving to his encounters with the rugged, unyielding competition in the sprint car caravan, Johnny admitted to some problems keeping up with the more-experienced veterans of that circuit. "In USAC racing, it came hard for me because everybody here is a champion. But Hamburg showed that I might be able to equal the other boys. It was the greatest elation of my life. It was such an achievement after the mediocre start I made for the season."

That success late in 1968 set Johnny's mind to thinking of moving his driving ambitions from the half-mile ovals of the sprint car circuit to the full-mile circles of Indy-car competition for 1969, with May 1970 the target date for tackling the big one at Indy. "Possibly my start will come on the miles this year, which would pretty well school me for here next year," he said confidently there in the Indy speedway cafeteria that day in May 1969.

The hoped-for start on the mile tracks did not come that year, though, nor did it come the following year for Johnny. He returned to his wrench work for the Bignotti-Unser operation and, as he worked, the time for his own driving efforts became less and less. For Johnny, the collective success of the racing team he was with smothered the opportunity for him to seek his own individual success as a driver.

The gun-metal blue car with the yellow lightning bolts streaking back from its nose quickly became the most frequent visitor to Victory Lane along the USAC championship trail. With steady Al Unser handling the driving—later joined by Joe Leonard in a duplicate machine—co-owners Parnelli Jones and Vel Miletich providing the necessary cash, and Bignotti, Capels, and company tuning the machinery to perfection, the team collected exactly

Capels (left) with car owner, and former driver, Parnelli Jones.

half of the first-place trophies available during the latter portion
of the 1969 season and all of the 1970 campaign.

All the glittering glory of the Unser-Bignotti-Leonard-Jones-
Miletich-Capels organization did little, however, to temper
Johnny's longings for his own way into Victory Lane. Talking at
his home between the 1970 and 1971 seasons, he clearly harbored
the same personal desires he had back in 1969. "I haven't begun
to back off on that idea yet. I've never had anything else on my
mind."

There wasn't a moment's hesitation on Johnny's part to say he
would leave the success and security of the Bignotti stable to ply
his primary trade on the nation's race tracks. "That's what I
want to do, but I haven't come to that bridge yet," he reported
with only the slightest hint of impatience.

"It's tied me down," he reflected on his stay with the Bignotti
operation. "But at the same time, it's opened up some possibilities for me as a driver." These possibilities were, in fact, developing at the very time he talked of them. With George Bignotti
laying the groundwork behind the scenes, a brand-new championship dirt car was being created by capable car builder Grant King
for Johnny to pilot on the one-mile dirt tracks to be frequented
by the USAC troops in the summer of 1971.

The new dirt car represented the crucial turn in Johnny's career as a racing driver, but it was admittedly a mixed blessing.
With Johnny designated as both the crew chief for the new Bignotti creation assigned to Leonard in 1971 and a member of the
crew for Unser's dirt-track machine, it was going to be a hectic,
harrowing year. The dirt races in particular would test Johnny's
fortitude as he attempted to prepare Unser's car and drive his
own. "I want to try it at least," said an unruffled Johnny only
weeks before the ordeal would start. "I'll do whatever I have to.
I'll work overtime getting my own car ready, and Al's too, but I
think I can manage it. I still want to drive. If I can get inside the
door this way, I sure would be glad to put up my wrenches."

He never did get an opportunity to drive, though, that season.
While the King car was built and readied for delivery, Johnny
never turned a lap in it. In fact, he spent no time at all in the
cockpit of a race car the next year. All of the 1971 season was

spent over, around, and under the Jones-Bignotti car that Leonard drove to the USAC national championship.

The nature of Johnny's two racing jobs had run into their inevitable conflict, and he was finally forced to choose one over the other. And, on the eve of the 1972 season, there was a new tone to Johnny's comments as he talked of the demise of his driving plans and the growth of his mechanical success. "It was a total conflict; I couldn't work for Parnelli Jones and go off racing myself. So I had to make a commitment, to myself and the team.

"I doubt if I'll be driving this year," he confessed, "I'll be chief mechanic for Joe Leonard's new car, trying my best to win the championship again. I haven't formally retired from driving, but I seem to be going a lot farther the other way. It looks right now like my tools are the best thing I've got going for me.

"I just may be in too deep to get out now. I'm not really fighting it though, because it appears I might be able to make a name for myself this way, better than I ever could have as a driver. And, of course, I've got my two kids to consider, although I always did consider them when I was driving.

"I might drive again, if the situation arose, but I don't know if that will happen. I'd like to run my own operation someday—that's what I'm aiming for. If this is where I'm more successful, then I'd eventually want to have my own cars and my own shop."

And so, Johnny Capels' double life apparently has come to an end. For the time being, at least, he is taking on just one racing job, one racing uniform. Still, his eyes remain focused on the one thing he always aimed for, as driver or mechanic—winning auto races.

23. *The Revolution Maker*

JIM HALL is a quiet man. When he does talk, it is with a throaty Texas drawl and few wasted words. He is tall and lean, with a pale, gaunt face and bandy legs. He looks like neither a revolutionary nor a genius; however, in the world of American sports car racing, he has been both.

His ideas for building race cars are usually considered far-out when he first introduces them, but they almost always work. Some are so effective they completely change the direction of race car designing; others are so uncanny they send his competitors away in a quandary. And, whenever his latest idea is perfected—or is outlawed by the higher-ups—he simply withdraws to his shop in Midland, Texas, and thinks up a new one.

No one really suspected what was going to happen back in the late 50s, when Hall, the ink hardly dry on his engineering degree from the California Institute of Technology, took up road racing in earnest, driving sports cars and formula machines in SCCA events. His driving was competent, but it certainly didn't prepare the road racing crowd for the earth-shaking things he soon was going to do—the innovations which would drastically alter the face of auto racing.

The revolution began quietly enough in 1961, when Jim began to work on the first sports racing car of his own design. He unveiled it to the road racing world during the 1962 season. Like those that would follow, it was painted a clean white and bore the name Chaparral, in honor of the speedy southwestern bird also known as the roadrunner. Unlike future Chaparrals, this one was relatively conventional and did not throw racing into any great turmoil.

The first Chaparral, with its lightweight body and subtle suspension innovations, won some SCCA races but died at the 1963 Sebring 12-hour endurance event. Chaparral II came along in 1964 and with it, Jim Hall made it clear he was out to shake up the road racing establishment. This sleek white car featured a fiberglass chassis and an automatic transmission, something not before considered feasible for road racing, since drivers were continually shifting gears to navigate the twisting turns of the circuits they raced on.

Its feasibility was proven though, as Hall took top honors in the U.S. Road Race of Champions series in 1964 and barely missed the same title again the following season. The same proved true for the endurance races, as Hall and teammate Hap Sharp captured Sebring in 1965, beating the best that Ferrari,

Ford, and Porsche had to offer. They also defeated that formidable competition in the 1,000-kilometer marathon at Nurburgring, Germany, in 1966. The automatic transmission marked Jim Hall as a bright new innovator on the racing scene, but more, much more, was coming.

In 1966, Hall unveiled another new Chaparral, and it was a real blockbuster. This latest brainchild of Hall's was easily spotted—from the rear deck of his new car, atop two sturdy stilts, rose a wide airfoil, a thin wing much like those on a small airplane. The road racing crowd was aghast, and the more skeptical ones predicted the winged cars would fly off the track and land in the next county.

But when Hall and former world grand prix champion Phil Hill drove the new Chaparrals onto the track, the only things they flew past were speed limits, track records, and other cars. And, in the fourth race of the rich new Can-Am sports car series, Hill and his Chaparral made a perfect landing into the middle of the winner's circle at Laguna Seca, California.

The principle behind the Chaparral wing was simple enough. On an airplane, the wings are tilted slightly back so that, as they move through the air, the passing air strikes the bottom surface of the wings, exerting a lifting force on them. Hall simply reversed the procedure; the wing on his car was tilted slightly up, and the air struck the top surface, creating a downforce on the wing. The force held the rear of the Chaparral car to the ground, giving it greater traction and stability in the turns.

Hall had also added another clever twist—the wing was moveable and the driver could control it from the cockpit. By pushing a button, the driver could make the wing tilt up for the turns, then make it lay flat to reduce wind drag on fast straightaway sections of the race track. The "flipper" wing drove the fans, and the competition, along the Can-Am and endurance race trails wild, but persistent mechanical difficulties eventually forced Hall to drop the moveable wing and replace it with a stationary one.

If there were those who still doubted the worth of Hall's wings after their 1966 successes—and there were a few—Jim changed their viewpoint in 1967. With an updated version of the winged Chaparral, he gave champion Bruce McLaren his stiffest challenge on the road to the '67 Can-Am crown. Hall chased the New

Zealander home in the final two Can-Ams of the year, and posted an impressive victory in the BOAC 500 long-distance race in England.

By 1968, almost everyone had conceded that the wing concept was a sound one. And, when Hall's newest Chaparral rolled onto the Can-Am grid that season, it no longer was the only winged bird in the flock. Other teams were beginning to try wings on their entries, including the new Ferrari Can-Am car from that venerable Italian race car works. Jim Hall had won the battle of ideas.

The 1968 season was not a good one for Jim, however. His success on the Can-Am circuit was somewhat spotty and, in the last event on the calendar, his Chaparral finally did the one thing many had predicted right from the start. It flew—not into the next county, but into the desert alongside Stardust Raceway near Las Vegas. Launched into the air by a collision with another car, the Chaparral made a crash landing on its tail, with Hall suffering two badly broken legs, a dislocated jaw, and burns.

While the crash jeopardized his driving career, it surely didn't interfere with his car-designing ingenuity. For 1969, the year when almost all the Can-Am teams tacked Chaparral-style wings on the rears of their cars, Jim Hall turned in another direction. The car he produced that year was a radical departure from the previous Chaparrals. It was built low to the ground, with a smooth, sleek profile and plexiglass windows on each side of the sunken driver's compartment. Instead of an elevated wing, it had a thin, flat fin attached to its tail which made the car look like a graceful white fish.

Its performance did not match its grace, however, even with John Surtees, the former grand prix and Can-Am champion from England, at the controls. In the 1969 Can-Am series, the car failed to live up to the Chaparral tradition, even after Hall resorted to a giant elevated wing late in the season.

The dismal showing of the 1969 car brought the skeptics around again, suggesting that perhaps a combination of the Las Vegas crash and time had taken its toll on the Jim Hall genius. Still, between the 1969 and 1970 seasons, there were constant rumors that Hall was toying with an entirely new concept for his next Chaparral.

Jim Hall's 1969 Chaparral—his most unsuccessful
Chaparral—driven by John Surtees.

The rumors were quite correct, and when it came time for
Can-Am racing in 1970, Hall gave the racing world its first look
at the rumored new concept. It was a "reverse ground-effects
system," something which had been studied for possible use on
passenger cars many years before but had never been put to
practical use. Hall, backed up by the know-how of Chevrolet's
engineering department in Detroit, found a very practical use
for the system in his newest Chaparral and created the greatest
shock wave of his career in the process.

The basis of a reverse ground-effects system is the creation of
a partial vacuum beneath a vehicle, thereby lowering the atmospheric pressure under the car. The normal atmospheric pressure
above the car then tends to push down on it, holding the car to
the ground like a suction cup with wheels. Hall accomplished
this by installing two rotary fans at the rear of his new Chaparral
which sucked the air from beneath the car and exhausted it out
the back. A skirt of tough plastic was draped around the bottom
edge of the car to make the vacuum as complete as possible. The
setup virtually turned the car into a high-speed vacuum cleaner,
tightly hugging the track as it swept along.

Predictably, the "vacuum sweeper" Chaparral was the sensation of the 1970 racing season. Driven first by reigning grand prix
champion Jackie Stewart, later by Englishman Vic Elford, the
Hall creation smashed track records and posted top qualifying
times all along the Can-Am circuit. Though it did not win any of
the races, it clearly had the potential to do so once the bugs in the
ground-effects system could be ironed out.

It also clearly had the potential to cure one of the Can-Am's biggest problems. With the immaculate orange cars of Team Mc-Laren completely dominating the series season after season, spectator interest had been on the wane. When Hall brought out his spectacular new car, the fans started flocking back, which naturally made SCCA's officials and track owners a great deal happier.

But the other Can-Am car owners were far from happy—in fact, they were close to furious. If the reverse ground-effects Chaparral was allowed to continue in competition, they claimed, everyone would have to buy or build cars with this new system in order to keep up. That would raise the cost of Can-Am racing several thousand dollars, forcing some teams to pull out of the series, the argument went.

Led by Teddy Mayer, manager of Team McLaren, the car owners took their case to the SCCA board of directors, pleading for a ban on the ground-effects system. The SCCA board, which admittedly had bent the rules to let the new Chaparral race in the first place, debated the question for several weeks before announcing it would allow the car to race again in 1971. Jim Hall had won the first round.

But the fight wasn't over. Mayer then took the issue to the Commission Sportive Internationale, which lays down the rules and regulations for international racing events like the Can-Am. The CSI reversed SCCA's decision, decreeing that the Chaparral violated the rule against "moveable aerodynamic devices" and therefore could not compete.

So, Jim Hall and his sensational Chaparral were suddenly out of racing. As usual, Jim had very little to say about the turn of events. He merely packed up his revolutionary racing machine and headed back to Texas. It didn't take long for Jim to make racing news again, however. Over the winter, he began inquiring about the possibility of building a reverse ground-effects car for the Indianapolis 500. But USAC official detoured that idea by banning the system from its races.

With the ground-effects setup shelved, Jim simply didn't race in 1971. For the first time in ten seasons, a year went by without an appearance by Jim and one of his ingenious Chaparral cars. And this time there were no reports, or even rumors, about what his plans were for the future.

"I wonder what he's up to now," people would ask, when Hall's name came up in conversation. Most of them had their suspicions about what he was doing. Hall was down at his shop in Midland, where he had turned out race cars capable of beating those from the elaborate factories of the established car builders in Europe and North America.

He was undoubtedly thinking up something spectacular and new to try on his next race car. He was almost certainly planning a new revolution.

24. A Certain Breed

A LONG, needle-nosed car whistles across the Bonneville Salt Flats at over 300 miles per hour. A shiny stock car whips around the high banks of the Daytona International Speedway at 176 m.p.h. A growling Funny Car streaks down a quarter-mile dragstrip in less than seven seconds.

None of these three incidents would normally have made headlines; all had been done several times before. But each was a record-breaker because the drivers of the three cars were women.

A three-driver team enters the grueling twelve-hour Sebring marathon and finishes eighth in its class. A veteran drag racer takes a pro stock eliminator title at a Nationals meet. A sports car driver expresses a desire to race in the Indianapolis 500. Again, all are events that would not have ordinarily made much news, except for the fact that all the drivers involved were women.

Women, often restricted to segregated sideshows called "powderpuff derbies" and subsidiary roles as corner workers, scorers, or simply pit decorations, have started to make waves in the world of auto racing, so long an all-male domain. They have literally put themselves in the driver's seat and, though their numbers and achievements are still relatively small, women are increasingly making their presence felt on the speed scene.

Lee Breedlove, wife of former land-speed record holder Craig Breedlove, made the first significant dent in racing's all-male image in November 1965. At the wheel of her husband's "Spirit of America" jet-powered car, with which Craig would later break the six hundred mile per hour barrier, Lee skimmed across the Bonneville flats at 335.070 miles per hour, setting a world land-speed record for women.

Mrs. Breedlove's feat seemed to break the ice for racing's female contingent. One could sense that the women who worked with the safety crews at road races, who were scorers and timers with racing teams, or who drove in various sports car races and rallies were now going to move away from the old "pit popsy" stereotype which lumped them all together with the buxom bathing beauties brought in by track owners and accessory companies to add a cosmetic touch at trackside. They were ready, it seemed, to give the men a run for their money.

And it didn't take long for the ladies to make it clear they intended to do it on the competitive race track, not just on solo runs against the clock. One of American drag racing's first female competitors, "Dragon Lady" Shirley Sheehan, knocked down a national pro stock eliminator title. Three young female drivers, Rosemary Smith, Janet Guthrie, and Judy Kondratieff, drove their Healey Sprite to nineteenth place overall and eighth in the tough prototype class at Sebring.

The male racers were beginning to realize that the gals were quite serious about challenging their long-standing supremacy in racing. If there were any doubts about it, they were dispelled in 1969 by a slim Miami divorcee named Smokey Drolet. With one press announcement, she shook the entire racing fraternity.

Smokey, a veteran of numerous sports car and small sedan races, announced she planned to drive in the Indianapolis 500, and would take Indy and USAC officials to court if they barred her from entering. That statement sparked an immediate uproar in the Indy establishment.

"We would have to change the whole structure of our racing," complained one USAC official. "Women aren't even allowed in the pits and never have been."

Actually, the alarm over Ms. Drolet's announcement went beyond the fact that she was a woman. Much of the astonishment was based on the implication that she might demand to drive in the 500 with only limited racing experience in less-powerful racing machines. "We wouldn't have a problem. She would," said one official. "She would have to get the driving experience she needs to drive in this race."

"I don't know of anyone who could demand to drive in this race," commented another. "I don't know of a man who could demand to drive in it."

Even Andy Granatelli, who had sponsored the Studebaker that lady drivers Paula Murphy and Barbara Nieland drove to several production car speed records at Bonneville, questioned the implications of the Florida woman's proclamation. "She's going to have to get some experience in the championship cars. Nobody runs the 500 first.

"Of course, I think women ought to have equal rights. I think they should drive race cars," Andy quickly added, however.

The apparent threat of a female invasion of the Indy scene did not materialize, though. Smokey Drolet did not even show up at Indianapolis with a crash helmet let alone a court order and has said very little since then. But the Indy management still had to face the female push for recognition. In 1971, a magazine reporter from New York did take the speedway to court over its refusal to issue press credentials to women, and the speedway management promptly discarded that policy, permitting female reporters and photographers to roam at will through the pits and garage area for the first time in the track's history.

One of the next major accomplishments for a female driver was to come at a NASCAR stronghold, Daytona. Paula Murphy, again with the backing of Andy Granatelli, wheeled a Grand National stock car around the banks of Daytona, ripping off a couple of laps at 176 miles per hour establishing a new closed-course record for women. While her speeds were well below the 190-plus laps of NASCAR's top male pilots, they would have easily put her into the field for the next Daytona 500.

With the efforts of Paula Murphy, Lee Breedlove, and the rest of the women racers, almost every level of American racing has had its glimpse of the fast-driving ladies. Yet one particular racing form, drag racing, remains the most frequent stage for direct confrontations between the sexes. Often turning the presence of

female competitors to its advantage with high-powered publicity blurbs, drag racing has produced such popular women stars
as Shirley Sheehan, Della Woods, Judy Lilly, and possibly the
most successful of all the women drivers, Shirley "Cha Cha"
Muldowney.

Shirley "Cha Cha" Muldowney at work on her racer.

Shirley Muldowney began drag racing to stay out of jail. Admittedly "a tomboy when I was a kid," she drew the unwanted attention of the law in Schenectady, New York, with high-speed escapades in her supercharged Corvette. "I was just bad news— I was always getting into trouble," she recalls. "I was instructed by the police to go drag racing, so I wouldn't end up getting myself hurt."

Obeying the police order, Shirley started collecting trophies instead of traffic tickets. At a dusty eighth-mile dragstrip at nearby Fonda, New York, she created a sensation by beating some of the old regulars in the weekly drag meets. With the backing of her husband Jack, a Schenectady service garage operator, she gradually moved up to faster machines and the more glamorous tracks of the national drag-racing circuit.

In 1967, she became the first woman ever to receive a competition license to drive the super-powerful dragsters, the fastest, most dangerous type of cars in drag racing. Overcoming some initial reluctance from the race officials to let her compete, she showed she could handle a twin-engined Chevrolet gas dragster, turning in sound performances at national meets across the country.

In 1971, she moved into Funny Cars, those exotic hybrid cars of drag racing that feature hot supercharged engines and ultra-lightweight fiberglass bodies. Second only to the fuel dragsters in speed, the Funny Cars surely generate the most excitement for drag racing fans.

And Shirley Muldowney gave the Funny Car crowd all the excitement it wanted. She beat the best of the Funny Car drivers at the IHRA Summernationals at Rockingham, North Carolina, becoming the first woman to win a national Funny Car crown. Then, at the Lebanon Valley, New York, dragstrip, she became the first woman to crack the seven second barrier, charging her Chrysler hemi-powered Funny Car down the quarter-mile in 6.82 seconds and hitting a sizzling 219 miles per hour at the finish line. Later, at the NHRA Nationals at Indianapolis, she tripped the electric eye at 6.76 seconds in qualifying for the final eliminator rounds of that important meet.

The trim brunette had come a long way from the hot-rodding tomboy who had distressed Schenectady policemen years before.

At the age of thirty one, "Cha Cha" had proved women racers could keep up with, and occasionally beat, the men. Of course, the racing men had not always taken kindly to that idea.

"It caused problems with the men drivers in the beginning," she remembers of her early days at Fonda. "They used to really take it to heart when I'd walk off with the trophies they had been winning every week. But when I started running the hot cars, the dragsters and Funny Cars, then I ran into problems with the sanctioning organization, NHRA.

"It was something they hadn't had to deal with before, a woman in those kinds of cars, and I really think they were just afraid I might get killed and give the sport a bad name."

The procedure for keeping "Cha Cha" out of the faster cars was simple at first—sanctioning officials just returned her entry blanks stamped "Too Late" even if she mailed them weeks ahead of the deadline. Finally, she filed a lawsuit against NHRA, and the officials finally relented. That changed everything for "Cha Cha."

"I have had no trouble at all in the past few years. In fact, the fellas, the other drivers, are my best friends now. They give me help, advice and so on. They couldn't be nicer."

As as matter of fact, one of the male drag racers was almost too nice to "Cha Cha." Connie Kalitta, a top Funny Car racer, sold the lady driver her first Funny Car and helped her set it up for racing. Then she turned around and beat Kalitta with that same car on her way to the Rockingham Nationals championship.

But, when "Cha Cha" talks about the reasons for her success, the bulk of the credit goes to Kalitta and her husband. "It has taken a lot of hard work and help from people like my husband and Connie and a lot of others."

Doesn't her husband get upset with her taking off for drag meets around the country all the time? Not at all, says the racing wife and mother. "He loves it. You see, he has no conception of what it's like to do it, so he thinks it's marvelous. He does some of the work on the car and raises our fourteen-year-old son while I'm off racing. He's just terrific about it all."

And Jack Muldowney may have to be even more terrific about his wife's racing career, if she gets to do some of the things she wants. Shirley has big plans, and two of them involve record runs

Funny Cars ready to race at Indianapolis Raceway Park.

by two other lady racers. Not overly impressed with Lee Breedlove's land-speed record drive or Paula Murphy's Daytona high-speed laps, she is thinking about bettering both. "It wasn't that big a deal to run three hundred in that car," she says of Mrs. Breedlove's record. "I'd like to try to go over five hundred miles an hour. That's something I want to do very badly.

"I talked to Art Arfons, who held the record before Craig Breedlove broke it, about driving his rocket-powered car at the flats. He seemed to be willing to let me try it, but he crashed the car late last season, killing three people, and has retired as a driver. So, I may not get to do it."

Paula's one hundred seventy-six mile per hour tour at Daytona is another record for Shirley to break. According to the outspoken "Cha Cha," "That was just for two laps, not four hundred with other cars on the track. I don't know if a woman can make it in NASCAR racing, but I'd like to think if anyone can it's Shirley Muldowney.

"Honestly though, I don't think you will ever see NASCAR issue a driver's license to a woman. It's too strenuous, too grueling, for a woman. I think the same thing probably is involved at Indianapolis. But I'd like to find out for myself. I can't honestly say whether or not I could handle it. I really don't know, but I would like to try it—with the proper instruction, of course."

"Cha Cha" also has plans for the day when she gives up driving fast cars. "I do have one thing I want to do, if and when I decide to not drive anymore and am financially able to do it. I would like to own a Funny Car and have a driver, a man, for it.

"I know it sounds strange for me to say I'd want a man to drive my car, but I honestly believe in my heart that there's just a certain breed of gal who can deal with driving a race car. I frankly don't think most women could handle the two hundred-mile-per-hour cars."

With that statement, "Cha Cha" clearly deviates from the viewpoint of some of today's Women's Lib advocates, who might justifiably point to her success as a model for followers of the cause. Shirley Muldowney, whose press agents generally refer to her as "the plucky French drag racer with a 36-22-34 figure," has her own views on Women's Lib.

"I really go for the equal opportunity bit, because I went through it with the sanctioning bodies when I tried to move into the faster cars. But as far as burning my bra and that stuff, obviously I'm not in favor of it."

25. Reflections

A FATHER, wearing a blue racing jacket and smoking a cigarette, sat about three-fourths of the way up in the tall gray grandstand, his foot propped against the unoccupied seat in front of him. Beside him sat his son, a mop-haired seven-year-old with a bag of popcorn.

On the track—a grubby, rutted little dirt saucer—pushtrucks began shoving humpbacked little midget cars away from the starting line.

Father: "Okay, Kirk, who you pickin' in this race?"

Son (looking toward the track): "I'll take number one, Dad. He's gonna win, I bet."

Father (looking down at his program): "Okay, I'll take number twenty-five. He's a real good driver."

Son: "Yeah, but he can't beat number one!"

Father: "Why not?"

Son: "Well . . . his car just just looks faster, you know what I mean, Dad?"

Father: "That's true, Kirk, but that doesn't necessarily mean he'll win, you know."

When the checkered flag fell a few minutes later, car number one was first, some six lengths in front. Car number twenty-five finished fourth in the eight-car field.

Carl Hungness is a tall, gangling guy with dark hair and thick-rimmed glasses who, in his early twenties, probably still looks just like he did in his high school graduation picture.

Carl is a dreamer, a would-be race driver, a sometimes racing writer, an occasional public relations man, and, so far at least, a champion of lost causes.

He wandered from his native Colorado to sell his dream of a weekly racing paper to the mighty United States Auto Club. Amazingly, the organization went for it, and Carl was its editor.

But, dreams being dreams and organizations being organizations, it was only a year before the paper, and Carl with it, was sent packing.

He didn't travel far, though. Across the street from the USAC offices, he opened his own little office as a personal management and public relations representative for race drivers.

All the while, Carl was trying to become a race driver himself. He raced his own midget until it flipped him over the wall at a grimy "outlaw" track in Illinois.

Then he bought a Formula Ford car, and that circuit promptly went under. "I'm trying to sell my Formula Ford so I can buy a rear-engine Chevy to run in USAC's road-course division next year," he related, standing in the pits at Terre Haute. "Of course, in the meantime I've got to make some grocery money," Carl added, smiling as he reached into his pocket and pulled out a white decal with "Frostie's Truck Stop" crudely lettered across it. "If I can find somebody who needs a sponsor for this race, I can make $50 with this."

Looking around the pit area, he suddenly spotted something. "Hey, excuse me, but there's Bill Renshaw. He doesn't have a sponsor. I'll see ya later." And off trotted Carl Hungness, super-salesman, to talk of racing and Frostie's Truck Stop and big, big dreams.

It turned out to be one of racing's great put-ons. A day and a half before the 1969 Indianapolis spectacular, a race driver, a very illustrious race driver, named Mario Andretti, angered by an about-face ruling by speedway officials on his extra radiator, publicly announced he wanted no part of Mr. Hulman's race unless the officials reversed their stand. The officials did not relent. Andretti did, and proceeded to win the race in a breeze.

The next May, back at Indianapolis, Andretti good-naturedly scolded newsmen, many of whom had given the story big headlines, for putting so much stock in his threatened withdrawal. "You guys should have known better than to take it too seriously," Mario joked in his choppy trace-of-Trieste accent. "There was no way I wasn't going to be out there when it came time to race."

The photographer crouched down, leaning, twisting to one side as he aimed his telephoto lens at the young black-haired man standing next to the sparkling new sprint car.

The man in the racing uniform caught the motion of the photographer, glanced briefly, sternly in his direction, then self-consciously jerked his head around. The photographer persistently waddled around in a semi-circle to focus on the young man's face again.

The subject of the cameraman's attention glared again, then looked away again. He looked back momentarily; the photographer clicked the shutter, then rose from his crouched position smiling.

The race driver busied himself with checking out his helmet and gloves, while the photographer casually glanced up and down the pit area. Another man, older than the driver, dressed in street clothes, and apparently the owner of the race car the driver stood beside, approached the photographer.

"What're you doing?" he asked curiously.

"Just taking some headshots. I'm thinking about doing a story on him later this season," the cameraman replied, motioning toward the now-helmeted man nearby.

"Oh, okay," the other man murmured, "I just hope you don't jinx him."

"Oh no, everybody I take a picture of does great." The photographer laughed but was suddenly reminded of the old drivers' superstition against having their pictures taken before a race.

The young driver spun early in the consolation race, restarted, and finished fifth, missing the feature event by one position.

Bruce McLaren walked through the pit gate and, with a subtle limp left over from his childhood, sauntered through the short, wide concrete corridor to Gasoline Alley.

A young man, probably a teenager, wearing a blue turtleneck, crisply-creased blue slacks, and a dark sport coat, spotted McLaren and bounced from his position leaning against the wall at one corner of the grandstand exterior. Visibly steeling himself with self-confidence, the young man strode out and intercepted McLaren midway between the pit gate and the garage area.

"Hi Bruce, I'm . . . . . . It's good to see you," he proclaimed. "I just wanted to tell you I think your cars are fantastic."

"Well, thank you. Thank you very much," McLaren responded in soft, flowing New Zealand tones.

"Yessir, they're really beautiful," the young man continued, his confidence already evaporating. "Well, been good talking to you, Bruce. I sure would like to see you drive here sometime."

"Well, thank you. Maybe I will," McLaren said pleasantly, smiling broadly as the young man backed away toward the grandstand.

McLaren turned and walked briskly through the garage area gate and disappeared around the north end of the squat white garage buildings with green trim.

Five days later he died.

Standing on a broad, jutting tree root, his arms folded tightly across his chest, Dick Smothers peered down through the shadows of the overhanging trees to study a string of race cars streaming through Elkhart Lake's Turn Five.

His dark mustache barely visible in the shadow of his cap, which was jammed down on top of his rectangular wire-framed sunglasses, he stood motionless in his blue-trimmed driving suit. A dishwater-blonde with broad hips stood beside him, a clipboard in her hand.

A dark-haired woman in plain blue slacks and flowered blouse, carrying a pen and a racing program, walked up to the blonde woman. "Excuse me, could I get his autograph for my little boy?" she said, motioning toward Smothers.

The woman with the clipboard turned to Smothers and passed along the request. "Just a minute, just a minute," the folk-singer-comic-turned-race-driver blurted, his hand flicking in the air.

"He says just a minute," the woman told the autograph seeker.

"One, two . . . three, four, five . . . six . . . seven, eight . . . NINE. George's ninth," Smothers counted, pinning down the position of his racing teammate, George Wintersteen, then he turned to the woman, who had the pen and program thrust toward him.

"This is for your little boy?" he smiled, "Isn't he here at the race?"

"No, he's at home with a broken arm," the woman answered.

"Oh." Smothers signed the program in a quick series of sweeping pen strokes, handed it back to the woman, and returned his gaze to the tree-shrouded track.

Two days later, the woman called her son over and proudly announced, "Here, look what I got for you at Elkhart Lake. It's Dick Smothers' autograph."

"Gee, that's swell, Mom," beamed the little boy, his left arm encased in a plaster cast turning gray with age and covered with childish scrawls. "Who's Dick Smothers?"

The old brown boards of the grandstand were wet and splintery. Anyone who came without a blanket or cushion would have a rough night of it.

One man, sitting on half of a folded plaid blanket, chatted with the woman who sat on the other half. Beside him, another man, seated on a green cushion, looked out at the track where race cars were being lined up methodically.

Every so often, each man—one white, one black—glanced at the other momentarily, quizzically examining the other's face.

They repeated the alternating glances three or four times before the dark-skinned, middle-aged man turned and spoke to his bushy-haired young neighbor.

"You're Jerry, aren't you? From the Marion paper?"

"Right. And you're . . . Dick, right?"

"Yeah, right. Haven't seen you for awhile."

"True, but I should have recognized you right away anyway."

"Me, too. I kinda thought that was you, but I wanted to be sure before I said anything. You know how things are these days."

"Yes . . . yes, I do know," the light-skinned man thought with a twinge of remorse.

The race burst into life, cars shooting past in an almost endless blur, engines snorting. Two men—one white, one black—sat and talked in the damp, ratty grandstand.

The blazing lights high above flooded the track like a Hollywood movie set, leaving the two men lost among the shadows reaching from the high-speed fantasy world where men still tilt at windmills to the slow-moving real world where things are as they are.

Pace car pulls onto pit road after pace lap
for Formula A race at Road America.

III PLACES AND RACES

26. Lake? . . . What Lake?

WHEN you drive through the gate into what clearly looks like a barnyard, you're tempted to think you have ended up at a rock festival instead of an auto race. At your immediate left stands a clean white farmhouse. Off to the right is a pleasant old barn with its sloping faded-gray roof. As your tires grind onto the gravel driveway, you almost expect to see Max Yasger or Chip Monck stroll out onto the porch of the farmhouse, lean over the porch railing, and shout enthusiastically at you: "Hi folks, welcome to Woodstock!" That doesn't happen, but you still believe it possible as you swing around the big barn and onto a narrow paved path.

To the west, on a wide grassy hill leaning back toward the Wisconsin skyline, a crowd of thousands is gathering in typical rock festival fashion. The hillside is peppered with clumps of people on blankets; thin lines of colorful clothing stream up one side of the hill and meld into a milling mass at the crest.

You swing to the right on the one-lane roadway and head toward a gray covered bridge. Pairs of young people, long-haired and barefooted, tramp along both sides of the road.

As you approach an old wooden bridge, you become aware of a sound. You don't hear it at first; you only feel it, a gentle kind of rumbling that seems to be getting nearer.

Suddenly, a little car, low-slung and delicate, shoots out from beneath the bridge. Its motor growling, the car darts straight off to your left on a thin strip of concrete. The motor crackles briefly as the car snaps through a right-hand turn, then resumes its muscular drone as it speeds straight up the far side of the sprawling hill. The car disappears as you drive through the covered bridge. When you emerge into the sunlight and slant off toward the base of the hill, two more little cars rumble from beneath the bridge, slip around the turn, and race on up the hillside.

Now you know. You're at Elkhart Lake, not Woodstock.

When you park your car and walk into that restless mob of people you saw from a distance earlier, you still find much of what you might expect at a rock festival: Girls looking very much like girls, boys looking roughly like boys, girls and boys looking like something in-between, and all of them doing the things they generally do together. Older couples sitting peacefully on the side of the hill, all ages eating, drinking, smoking, and buying souvenirs, children skipping along beside their hand-holding parents.

It may have many of the trappings of a modern rock concert, but the music here is in the throaty harmonies of auto racing. The melodies that draw people here are not the ones groaned through amplifiers by Ten Years After and Country Joe McDonald, but those pumped through racing engines by George Follmer and Lothar Motschenbacher.

Three times each summer, the lovers of such music converge on the shady soundstage that Clif Tufte, the man who runs the place, calls Road America. They pour in from Milwaukee, Madison, Sheboygan, Fond du Lac, Racine, Chicago, and all over the Midwest. They ramble into Tufte's Road America layout for two weekends of big-time road racing, the Trans-Am in July and the Can-Am in August, and one of frenetic amateur racing, the Sprints in June.

The June Sprints is an exclusive phenomenon of Elkhart Lake. College kids, fleeing the campuses of the Midwest's many schools, rush to the rustic race course, located at the northern edge of the Kettle Moraine forest, to get away from their academic frustrations. The Sprints features only the army of SCCA amateur drivers and their pool of second-hand Corvettes, MGs, Austin-Healeys, and the like, but it still outdraws the international stars who bring their technical finesse to the late-summer Can-Am, a fact that is not repeated at any of the other stops across North America on the proud Can-Am circuit.

The June Sprints is what revived the Elkhart Lake area, once a prime summer retreat for the idle rich of Milwaukee and Chicago, that suffered a gradual decline in its appeal over the years. When the racing began, first through the streets of the town of Elkhart Lake itself and then around Tufte's four-mile roadway south of town, the racing crowd sent most of the remaining tourists looking for a new resort town.

The transformation was almost too much for the local populace. The cozy little village of Elkhart Lake was built on the edge
of a small blue lake, and most of its 250 permanent inhabitants
enjoyed the relaxed pace of a resort settlement that only those
rich enough to afford had ever heard about. Only movie actor

Race fan enjoying the 1970 Trans-Am
race at Elkhart Lake's Road America.

Forrest Tucker and his summer acting school brought any no-toriety to the lakeside community, and not enough to do much harm.

But Road America changed all that. At first, the race through the streets was only a rude and noisy interruption of their lives. When the race was pushed off the streets and onto the farm-lands south of town, that should have been the end of it. How-ever, no one counted on Road America becoming famous. But that's what it did, and it shattered the anonymity which had been Elkhart Lake's big drawing card with the affluent from the rigors of the big-city social registers.

The resort hotels suddenly were being filled with racing people, not rich old dowagers from Chicago. The sidewalks now featured hordes of scruffy college kids instead of bald-headed men with prosperous paunches.

A new language could be heard in the town, with strange words like "downshift," "oversteer," and "slipstreaming."

The resort hotels were still in business though. The monied interests in racing could meet the prices at Siebkin's, Schwartz', and the other resorts as well as the old clientele, although they admittedly were not much interested in the lake or the tradi-tional atmosphere. So the hotels sold their beaches—the only large stretch of sand left is the public Firemen's Beach—and geared their graciousnes to the simpler tastes of racing people three weeks out of the year. The other weeks of the resort season, the hotels could still draw some of their old customers, who found that once the races were over nobody paid any more atten-tion to Elkhart Lake than in the old pre-racing days.

The rest of the citizenry of Elkhart Lake, and Plymouth seven miles to the south, turned their aesthetic headaches into soothing monetary gains with inventories of novelties, souvenirs, trinkets, and momentos to sell to the new breed of tourists.

Of course, a town accustomed to a few hundred leisurely trav-elers did not adjust completely to the influx of some 50,000 bois-terous racegoers.

Those in the race crowd who miss out on reservations at the resort hotels by calling less than three months ahead of time, even at the antebellum Plymouth Motor Inn, have to make do with campers and trailers or tents and sleeping bags in the old cornfield directly across from the Road America entrance gate or at one of the many other camp sites around Elkhart Lake.

The inflexibilities of the outside world fade away, however, when the roving band moves onto Mr. Tufte's property. Once inside the Road America gates, the physical discomforts of the improvised accommodations are meaningless. The setting is too lush, the atmosphere too free-wheeling to worry about such things. While the face of the big green hill and its smaller wooded companion to the north are heavily splotched with people and spread blankets, the heaviest concentration forms on a flat area atop the larger of the two slopes. The buzzing crowd steadily thickens as you move toward the pit area to the south side of the hilltop. The border between the pits and the rest of the area is almost indistinguishable. Only the fence, without gates across its loosely-guarded openings, and the sight of the race cars under the rusting tin awning provide real evidence.

The texture of the flock changes little on that side of the fence, except for the presence of the drivers and mechanics clustered around the colorful cars. There is less congestion, but the quality of life conforms to that on the outside of the fence.

From a male standpoint, there is more female skin visible than in an X-rated movie. Bikinis, hot pants, bare-midriff blouses, lace see-through dresses, and the infinite variations of each are the dominant fashions for Elkhart Lake. The girls are college coeds just liberated from the dormitory regimen, office secretaries on a weekend excursion, wandering swingers on leave from the communes, and racing campfollowers on the prowl. They come to Road America to watch, to rub shoulders, or more, with the race drivers, to work on somebody's scoring crew, to compete with the touring pros.

The male contingent is best identified by its hair length, probably collectively the longest of any race course in the country, and its assortment of tye-dyed shirts, threadbare bluejeans, and sandaled feet. Bushy-haired photographers—who get suspicious looks at the USAC shows at the nearby Milwaukee oval—are the rule rather than the exception and almost every guy in the place, right down to the drivers, boasts at least a fairly healthy mane and the casual dress of the so-called Woodstock Nation.

The scene gets crazier when you move back outside the fence.

At least in the pits there is some semblance of single-mindedness, with race cars and such to concentrate on. Away from them a multifarious mardi gras is in progress.

The lazy lines of celebrants, having dutifully passed along the fence-line to view the racing people and their curious cars, make their way toward the white concession stands scattered around the landscape to partake of the culinary oddities, which Road America is better remembered for than any of its races. They clamor for bratwurst sandwiches, usually generously smothered with sauerkraut to subdue the acrid taste of that ugly black sausage. They consume huge quantities of slippery ears of roasted corn, dipped in vats of butter, the singed husks still attached. They stand in line for cups of the foamy beverage brought to Wisconsin decades ago by the Pabst, Schlitz, and Blatz families.

Loaded up with all this food, they retire to the hillside to eat, drink, and occasionally watch some of the race. Those particularly fond of Milwaukee's finest shuttle between the grassy slope and the beer stand; others, better prepared, take their drinks from the bottles, flasks, cans, and wineskins they brought with them. And when the call comes, as it frequently does, they trudge off to Road America's quaint restrooms, done in early Appalachia, and then hurry back to their drinking spots.

Those who tire of eating and drinking turn to chemistry. Sticking with their original mates or pairing off through natural selection, the males and females warm up to each other—propped up against a shady tree, squirming beneath blankets, or hidden in the shadowy secrecy of the thick woods conveniently left standing just behind the Road America paddock.

The deep woods is the closest thing to privacy around for those who require it. Young men, from race drivers to college sophomores, and young women, from placid tour regulars to bubbly secretarial rookies, slip unnoticed into the cover of the tall trees to commune with nature—the trees' and their own.

The tableau of bratwurst, corn, beer, and coexistence is found all around the inside of Clif Tufte's meandering race course. On his race course, another picture is painted.

It is a portrait that no one person on the inside can see, owing to various diversions and the sheer expanse of the course itself. The only person who sees all of the rambling track's four miles of intrigue is the man who drives it. For him, it is a four mile exercise in the physical proclivities of auto racing.

He begins simply enough at the starting line in front of the paddock, at the very top of the big hill. He roars headlong through the heart of the forest where, hours before, he may have applied his surging virility to one of the local groupies. As soon as he clears the woods, he must swing right through the first flat curve and the gradual sweep that leads into a fast downhill right-hander. He then accelerates down a long straight with a dogleg to the right they call "Moraine Sweep."

He will be going as fast as he will all day when he approaches the sharp drop down to the flat, tight left-hander. He then shoots up a steep hill, underneath a pedestrian bridge, and snaps through another ninety degree left-hand corner.

He weaves, first right and then left, down the long "Hurry Downs" section and whirls into the fast two hundred ten degree right-hand sweep called "Carousel." Out of "Carousel," he picks up speed again as he shoots through a dogleg to the right and onto the "Kettle Bottoms" straight, which bends slightly to the left.

At the end comes treacherous "Canada Corner," with its off-speed twist to the right. Then it's down through the dale named "Thunder Valley" at full speed.

When he clears the auto bridge, his echoes booming behind him, he breaks past the old gray-roofed barn with the slender electronic scoreboard on its side. Coming to the end of the gentle left-hand bend that carried him under the bridge, he cuts back to the right power sliding through a flat right-hander. He pushes the accelerator as far as it will go and storms noisily up the hill to the thin line in front of the paddock where he started. He has driven the four miles of the Road America course, probably in just over two minutes, and has worked for every inch of it.

While he works for each four miles after four miles, the festival crowd moves to the rhythm of his labor. A bare-chested lad on the green hillside lifts a wineskin and squirts a dark liquid into his mouth. A writhing plaid blanket lets out muffled laughs. A staggering youth trudges off toward a crude outhouse. The woods are filled with shafts of sunlight and soft whispers.

Two miles to the north, shining blue water laps quietly onto clean, unmarked sand. The old chairs on the porch of the resort hotel near the lake's edge sit empty and motionless.

A woman in a brown dress skims a broom across the floor of the porch, stops suddenly and looks back to the south as if she heard something, then starts sweeping again.

The new music of Elkhart Lake is too far away to hear.

27. *Ring Around the Bullrings*

PLACES like Indianapolis, Daytona, and Watkins Glen get all the headlines with their pomp, their prestige, and their long lists of celebrities and movie stars. But they don't really do much racing there.

Indianapolis puts on one race a year; Daytona goes race-crazy for two whole weeks in February then puts everything in mothballs until the Fourth of July; the Glen has the Grand Prix in October and throws in a sports car doubleheader in July as an afterthought. That is a grand total of 19 days of actual racing per annum at racing's big headliners.

The other 346 days of the year, most of the action shifts quietly to unglamorous little tracks the magazine writers call "the bullrings." Crude and colloquial, these unsavory little racing emporiums are in business in all fifty states, filling the air with the sounds of racing two or three times a week from April through October.

It is at the bullrings, places like Sun Valley and Eldora, where Americans see their first race and where they regularly go to see racing that is untainted by the gawdy hoopla of places like Indianapolis and Daytona and Watkins Glen.

If they are in the vicinity of Anderson, Indiana, they go to Sun Valley Speedway. A paved quarter-mile oval with wide sloping banks, Sun Valley sits in a sunken piece of grassless land across the street from the Guide Lamp factory on Anderson's south side.

Its seating arrangements are of typical bullring variety. Old wooden bleacher-style seats, their gray paint badly faded and their surfaces rotting and splintery, ring the perimeter of the track in rising tiers.

The black asphalt of the track is smooth and clean, with two straight sections of pavement crossing in the center of the infield. A crumbling white concrete wall rims the oval except for a gaping open section at the end of one straightaway.

It is not a fancy place, to be sure. But its lack of ornamentation bothers neither promoter Joe Helpling, a crusty old gas station operator, nor the fans who take their chances on the bleachers to see the stock cars, jalopies, sprint cars, or figure-eight racers Helpling brings in to entertain them. With weekly racing shows throughout the summer, he keeps them coming back. But one night each year, he packs the stands to their limits with a race unlike any other held at any track.

Since 1949, Sun Valley has been the setting for the most frightening, uncanny, and insane race ever devised by man. Run each May on the Saturday night before the Indy 500, the escapade is called, cleverly, the "Little 500" and its inherent lunacy is so extraordinary that the race receives national press coverage each year.

The format is delirious. Thirty-three sprint cars line up three abreast, Indy-style, and race for 500 laps around the Sun Valley asphalt bowl. While the thirty-three-car concept works with reasonable success at Indianapolis, it makes an entirely different race when you run it on a quarter-mile track instead of on that 2½-miler to the south.

When thirty-three sprint cars, mostly from the IMCA ranks, pour into that first turn at Sun Valley, fans have been known to cover their eyes and cross their fingers. How that sea of wall-to-wall race cars ever makes it through the turn, which they do about as often as they don't, is one of the great mysteries of auto racing.

For over two hours, cars whiz around and around the little track in a steady blur. By the time it's over, only twelve or thirteen cars may be left running, but the track still looks crowded. Too often, before the Little 500 is finished, someone is hurt or killed. The colossal high-speed traffic jam takes its inevitable toll;

Sun Valley's Little 500 has earned its reputation as a big killer of race drivers. The most recent one was no exception. A car smashed into the opening in the wall, left gaping as an emergency exit for ambulances and wreckers, and killed its driver instantly.

Many of the other small tracks like Sun Valley have similar reputations. Death is no stranger to any of America's ramshackle little bullrings.

Sun Valley Speedway in Anderson, Indiana.

It is not the names of the dead that are remembered at Sun Valley, though. It is the names of those who have somehow lived through the Little 500 and gone on to race in its fabled namesake at Indianapolis.

It is a list probably unequalled by any bullring in the country, with names like 1963 Indy winner Parnelli Jones, Jim McElreath, Arnie Knepper, Johnny White, Bud Tingelstad, and Ronnie Duman included.

Sixty miles straight east of Sun Valley across the Ohio border lies Eldora Speedway, cradled in the valley of what had probably been a cornfield at one time. Located about a mile north of the tiny crossroads town of Rossburg, Ohio, Eldora, like Sun Valley, is a bullring with some unique qualities.

It is about the only one with its own dance hall and an adjoining gravel-pit-turned-lake for drunks to fall into. It is also one of the few good dirt tracks left in a country where dirt-track racing was once a national phenomenon and one of the few remaining dirt tracks with steeply banked corners.

Eldora's deep-dish configuration is awesome; even the most sure-footed of men cannot climb its banks without slipping. The drastic slant of the half-mile oval brings speeds that are unthinkable on other, gentler-banked dirt tracks.

Sprint cars will turn laps at nearly 100 miles an hour at Eldora, while at most dirt tracks, they average 75 or 80.

Twenty or more race cars slicing across those imposing brown walls of dirt—that's Eldora's attraction. Race fans from all over Ohio, Indiana, Kentucky, and Michigan will motor to the secluded speedway just to sit in the roofed grandstand or on the side of the hill rising above the track to watch those side-winding cars.

The man who brings the racing to Eldora, Earl Baltes, knows he has a gold mine. He carefully avoids the pitfall which has ruined the other dirt tracks, poor maintenance. Baltes keeps Eldora's racing surface smooth, well-packed, and moist. Other tracks, where less care was taken, have seen their races turned into absurdities when the track became too slick, too dusty, or too rutted.

Baltes usually has his track announcer tease the Eldora audiences with an impromptu poll on the idea of having the track paved. Having promoted races at two paved tracks in Ohio, he may not have any intention of paving his high-banked beauty, but he likes to hear the fans bellow their disapproval of the suggestion that he might.

Dirt-track racing, as practiced at Eldora and a handful of dirt ovals across the country, still holds a deeply emotional appeal for a large cross-section of America's racing buffs. Those who were nurtured on them still love the dirt-track races, despite all the unkind remarks by their counterparts in road racing who see them as an outdated and dying art form.

"That's for crazy people," road racer Rick Muther once commented on dirt racing, before adding thoughtfully, "I might like to go out and try it, if there was nobody else around. I think it'd be good for your reactions."

It is good for other things, too, if Eldora is representative of the genre. It keeps the fans happy, not even to mention Earl Baltes and the other dirt track operators.

One thing Eldora does share with the other bullrings, dirt or paved, is the unpleasant facility for throwing drivers' lives away. The tally of drivers who found Eldora's blazing speeds, or the trees that stand just outside the south end of its course, too harsh to survive is at least as long as those of the other brutal tracks.

But the drivers keep coming, to Eldora and all the rest. They come because they must if they ever want to move up the line to places like Indianapolis or Daytona. They won't make headlines at Sun Valley or Eldora, but they can't make them anywhere else until they have served their apprenticeships on the bullring circuits.

And even though they recognize the lethal potentialities of such tracks, they enjoy it. "I've run the track quite a bit, and I've had my share of spills over there, too," supermodified driver Mark Caldwell said of Eldora one day. "But I still love the place; it's a thrilling track to run."

Those are the bullrings—thrilling tracks, deadly tracks, and the tracks where the real racing is.

28. *Forget the Lollipops*

THE DRIVER pulled his race car slowly into the pits. As he rolled down the pit lane, he jabbed the throttle twice, then shut the engine off.

It had been his first practice run of the year, and it was a good one. He knew that and when he pulled to a stop in the pits he turned anxiously to his crew to ask, "What was my time?" When somebody told him he had turned the fastest laps he had ever run on this track, he flashed a wide smile and pulled his helmet from his head to hear more about his fast laps.

The driver was not Mario Andretti or A. J. Foyt and he had not just toured the two-and-a-half miles of Indianapolis at 170 miles per hour. The driver was Randy Campbell, age twelve, and he had just toured a one-twentieth mile track in nine seconds flat.

The track, a flat little oval with a sturdy chain-link fence around its perimeter, sat tucked away in a rural corner east of Kokomo, Indiana. Laid in a roadside-park-like setting, tall shade trees stood spotted around the well-kept, grassy parking lot. An old railroad line ran along the north edge of the miniature raceway.

The usual props for a race track, large or small, were visible— light standards spaced around the outer rim of the track, hay bales lining the retaining fence, a combination concession stand and scoring tower along one straightaway, sets of bleachers wrapped around the turns and along the mainstretch.

This particular day in early May, the parking lot at the tiny oval was soaked with rain and the scheduled races, the first of the year for the track, had been ruled out. Still, Randy Campbell and his parents brought their little purple quarter-midget from nearby Greentown to shake the cobwebs loose after the long winter layoff.

Being May, the racing headlines were originating 50 miles south, in Indianapolis, but the roar of the turbo-charged Fords and Offys could not be heard here for the steady whine of the one-cycle garden-tractor engine in Randy Campbell's quarter-midget.

Modeled after the full-sized midgets of professional racing, except for the extra-high rollbar and the placement of the small engine behind the cockpit, the purple car hurtled down the short little straightaway on its tiny wheels, then swooped down into the turn, crossing the 180 degrees of the tight turn in one fluid motion.

Around and around went Randy in his racer, rhythmically whipping through the same steady pattern lap after lap, coming wide down the straight stretches and then diving across each turn, pushing as close as possible to the inner edge of the corners and jumping back on the throttle as soon as his arc brought him out into the straightaway again.

Seven or eight laps like that, then into the pits went Randy for a conference with his dad, who passed on some pointers on how to get into or out of the corners a little quicker, where to get on or off the throttle a little faster. Then out went Randy again for seven or eight laps more, nicking a few tenths of a second off his lap times after each huddle with his father until he had registered the fast nine second circuit.

With the nine second tour clicked off on his stopwatch, Gilbert Campbell waved his son into the pits to give him the good news. The bespectacled youngster broke into a smiling, hand-clapping shout when he heard the lap times, then, with the pride visible in his step, walked slowly around his car, looking it over with youthful appreciation.

The fast lap persuaded the young racer and his equally proud dad to call it a day. Obviously feeling they were ready to race once the quarter-midget club got its weekly races underway, the father-son team agreed to load up their car and wait until next weekend to show their stuff.

But then a strange thing happened. A station wagon pulled into the lane leading back to the little quarter-midget track. Stuffed in the back of the wagon was another small race car, a red and white one, hauled from Lafayette, fifty miles away, by another twelve-year-old, Lloyd Hartman, and his older brother, Larry, a cigar-chewing serviceman on leave for the weekend.

Pulling into the parking lot, Lloyd, dressed in a professional looking driver's suit with "Hartman Brothers Special" neatly stitched across its back, bounded out of the station wagon and walked crisply toward the track as his brother unloaded the lightweight race car.

There, the black-haired and also bespectacled youngster encountered the Campbells, their plans for packing up their car already forgotten. In the tradition of all race drivers, Lloyd and Randy stood at the pit entrance discussing their cars and the condition of the track.

As Larry primed the car for his younger brother's turn on the track, two more of the little cars were hauled into the parking lot, unloaded, and rolled toward the track. In a strange example of natural selection, two pre-teen female drivers joined the two young boys at trackside.

Tall and brown-haired Kim Hall, eleven, and petite Kim Riley, ten, both from Kokomo, strolled up to the track in advance of their race cars, carrying racing helmets by the straps like some kind of spherical plastic handbags.

Before long, the air was literally filled with the whines of not one, but four whistling garden-tractor motors.

Whizzing around the tiny track, the four racers sliced through the turns one after another, then darted to the inside or outside of the straightaway to try to pass one of their adversaries. The Sunday afternoon of racing that had been called off because of the earlier rain suddenly became just what it was supposed to be, a Sunday afternoon of racing.

The four little cars, Randy Campbell's setting the pace with those steady nine-second laps, whirled around and around the gray asphalt oval like four colorful knots on a western cowboy's spinning lasso. Their hands locked tight around the steering wheels, their eyes fixed on the track all the way around, the four young drivers drove on and on, seemingly content to continue their race forever.

As with most things, forever was not within reach. Steaming out of the turn, Lloyd Hartman tried harder than nature could stand and, tires screeching and smoking in protest, his little car swept sideways in a lazy arc, directly into the path of a rather startled Kim Riley. The resulting collision bent a few pieces of metal, and maybe a little youthful pride, bringing the informal competition to a close.

The air now stilled, the young drivers and their families began the systematic process of packing up, stowing driving gear in slick leather satchels, storing tools and spare parts in toolboxes. Before rolling the race cars back to the parking lot to be loaded up for the trip home, the racing "teams" stood in a cluster for a few minutes talking over the afternoon's highlights and all confidently predicting even more electrifying things for the next weekend's full racing program.

The parents in particular talked of the amazing ability of all the young racers, who had driven faster and better than anyone had a right to expect them to, and of the miraculous racing feats which might well sound impossible to anyone unfamiliar with the ways of quarter-midget racing. "You should have been here at one race last year," submitted Bob Hall, Kim's father. "One of these kids made a move I don't think even Foyt could have made. He started on the outside of the second row and on the first lap he jumped out and split the pole and outside man on the front row just as pretty as you please. By the end of the first lap, he had pulled out in the lead and started stretching it out. It really was something to see."

Bob Hall paused for a moment, glancing down at the shiny blue car of his daughter, then resumed his story of the young hero of a past day at the now sunset-shadowed little track. "He got a little overanxious later in the race—these are only kids, after all—and got tangled up with a slower car and spun out, but he really made a show of it for awhile.

"You know, I think I'd rather watch these kids race than some of the big boys," concluded the tall, crewcut Hall. "I mean it, these kids really do a marvelous job."

29. And in This Corner . . .

It was just like a heavyweight title fight. The two top contenders stepped into the ring for the showdown match, with winner taking all.

The fighters, though, weren't boxers; they were racing drivers. And the ring wasn't a four-cornered stretch of canvas. It was a twisting, turning 2.6 miles of race course called Riverside.

On the line was the United States Auto Club's national driving championship, racing's equivalent to the heavy golden belt symbolic of boxing supremacy.

In one corner was Bobby Unser, the tall, gaunt man from New Mexico who six months before had won the big one at Indy. In the other was little Mario Andretti, the Italy-to-Pennsylvania transplant who had already pulled down the USAC crown twice.

Physically, it was a mismatch. Unser was a wiry six-footer, Andretti a five-foot-five-inch flyweight.

But it was Andretti who held the advantage going into the final round of the title match. Unser, winner of four straight matches early in the year, faltered, and Andretti came on with a rush, sweeping past Unser to hold a 308 point edge heading into the decisive finale.

The mathematics of the situation were decidedly in Andretti's favor. He had only to finish in fifth place or better to guarantee his third national title and the proud "1" for the side of his car.

For Unser, the demands were more stringent. To win the championship and collect $500 for each 1969 race he appeared in as the defending titlist, he would have to finish at least fourth. That wasn't all that had to happen to get the job done, but it was the first priority for the thirty-two-year-old who had finished only two races since Indy. "The only strategy was to finish the race; that's the only hope I had."

Finishing was not enough, though. Andretti could finish within five or six spots of Unser and still come out on top, so Unser would need some help to kayo his challenger for the crown.

And help is exactly what he got.

Andretti's original car blew up. Then the turbine car he hurriedly jumped into, trying to get a slice of somebody's points, crashed. And finally, another borrowed car failed to capture second place, the slot which would have then paid off with enough points for the title.

Before the finish of the grueling 300-miler at Riverside—the second longest race on the circuit—the tide had turned in Unser's favor

Unser, second to Dan Gurney and more than five miles ahead of Andretti, had the championship within reach. All he had to do was finish, if his sometimes-fickle machine would let him. "I've never babied a race car like that in my life. I had nothing to lose by slowing down. I certainly wasn't interested in catching Gurney. I just had to keep the wheels turning."

The wheels kept turning and after the adding machines were done the tally was: Bobby Unser, 4,330 points; Mario Andretti, 4,319 points.

Eleven points, that was the margin, a none-too-comfortable one for the new champion. "About a thousand points, you know, would have been just a little better," Unser sighed.

Andretti, who had finally struggled in third at Riverside in Lloyd Ruby's car, was sighing too, but not from relief. A little arithmetic quickly told him he could have taken the championship if he had moved into Ruby's mount just four laps earlier. "At the time, I didn't know just exactly what I needed. So all I was trying to do was to go as fast as I could and maintain my position."

The capture of the national title brought Unser's season full circle. He had appeared invincible early in the year when he won four out of the first five races, and people were beginning to concede the championship crown to him. "Everybody started saying that," Unser confided at season's end. "I thought they should have known better."

After Indianapolis, the only thing Unser won was his race, the Pike's Peak Hillclimb. Normally an insignificant factor in the point standings with its twenty-five first-place points, the hillclimb ironically provided Unser with most of his final margin over Andretti. Andretti took a fourth at the Peak, worth fifteen points, just ten less than Unser.

Unser needed all ten of those points as his fortunes sank lower and lower, finishing only two races, winning none. The pattern was hauntingly reminiscent of the so-called jinx which supposedly befell past Indy winners.

But Unser refused to buy that story. "It was plain old bad luck. It wasn't the fault of the mechanics—they did a good job with the car. Things just kept breaking or I'd be the victim of circumstances."

Despite that, Unser bagged the two biggest trophies of U. S. racing—the Indianapolis 500 and the USAC crown, with the first only slightly more shiny than the second to Unser's way of thinking. "I think Indianapolis is the thing. I feel Indianapolis is about the best a person can accomplish, but the next closest thing is to win the national championship."

Andretti, meanwhile, was pondering that very same championship that had slipped from his fingertips. The closeness of the final outcome made it an even more bitter pill to swallow. "It's hard to explain a disappointment like that. If I had lost by a couple of hundred points, I wouldn't have thought so much about it. The way it happened, it was a bit of a slap."

The sting was made more severe by the thought that a few extra laps somewhere along the line earlier in the season could have salvaged the title for Andretti, who had lost it by only eighty points the year before. "For instance, I dropped out of a couple races early in the season where you really don't think much about it. All I had to do was jump in a car for a couple laps and I'd have made enough points to win. Not getting any points at Indianapolis, of course, hurt me badly and perhaps lost me the championship the past two years."

The desperate push for more points by Andretti and by Unser led both drivers to engage in a practice peculiar to close pointstanding finishes. The practice, racing's rendition of hopscotch, sent the two scrambling for another car to drive whenever their own machine proved incapable of going the distance in a given race.

The strange brand of car-hopping was the direct result of a USAC policy that permitted relief drivers to share in the points a car collected in a race, a policy both Unser and Andretti found fault with at the close of the 1968 season. "I think they should do away with it and I think they probably will," Unser said bluntly.

At the heart of the car-hopping question, at least for the two men who had been most directly affected, was the advisibility of a driver jumping into a car set up for someone else's particular tastes and abilities. "I think it's a very unsafe thing when you jump into a strange car in the middle of a race," Andretti charged. "Especially in my case," the diminutive driver added. "You don't always fit in a car. Sometimes you can't even reach the pedals."

Andretti didn't have to look far for an example of what he was talking about. When he hopped into the turbine car at Riverside, a car prepared for the physical stature of brawny Joe Leonard and already dangerously low on brakes, Andretti went less than two laps before crashing the car on one of the corners. "However safe I tried to be, I certainly wasn't prepared for any circumstance I might run into. Only the system drives you to do such things," Andretti hastened to add.

Touching on another evil of the system, Unser commented, "Besides, it really isn't fair to take a driver and yank his car out from under him. Whoever starts the race in a car should get all the points," suggested the man who had replaced teammate Mike Mosley twice in his frantic pursuit of the crown.

In a rare piece of legislative wisdom, USAC officials listened to Unser and Andretti and voted out the points-for-relief-drivers system before the 1969 season got underway. Strangely enough, the elimination of the car-hopping policy would not have had any effect on the results of Unser and Andretti's boxing match for the 1968 title. Throwing out the points each collected by taking over someone else's machine, the two still would have been in practically the same tense position they were when the Riverside race started.

In the end, the "heavyweight" title still would have gone to Unser on what might be called a split decision, though both battlers would have had a little more room to breathe in the clinches.

As it was, both were on the ropes when the final round began and determined to make the finish of the title bout a rousing go-for-broke slugfest, which is exactly what it was.

30. The Persecution and Annihilation of the Indiana State Fairgrounds

PRECISION is auto racing's trump card. Beneath all the speed, spectacle, and hoopla, it is precision—the taut-muscle control of the drivers as they snake their way around a crowded race track, the rhythmic churning of crankshafts and pistons, the quiet beauty of finely engineered chassis—that provides the basic fascination for the thousands who stream into the grandstands for a big race.

They come, as much as for any other reason, to be awed by the seemingly flawless performances of steel-nerved men and their chrome-crusted machines.

If you are involved in racing, the premium is on precision and you come to expect perfection from everything connected with the sport. But every so often, the clay feet of your idols will suddenly give you a swift one in the seat of the pants.

One such occasion, when racing sank into the class of those frustrating "easy-to-assemble" Christmas toys and infuriating folding lawn chairs of the everyday man, came in June of 1969.

The race was the "Indiana Classic" at the venerable Indiana State Fairgrounds on the northeast edge of Indianapolis. The race, in theory, is a fairly straightforward one; thirty USAC stock cars race 100 miles around the fairgrounds track, starting at 8:00 P.M. and finishing up around 9:20 P.M.

Likewise, the track is not very complicated. A one-mile flat dirt oval, the Hoosier fairgrounds layout has traditionally been one of the better dirt tracks in the Midwest, with its "Hoosier Hundred" for USAC's championship cars the second biggest date of the year for Indiana racing followers.

But this particular night in June, very little was straightforward or uncomplicated. By the time the night was over, at 11:10 P.M. instead of 9:20 P.M., the revered old fairgrounds looked more like an urban renewal site before renewal than a race track.

Things went wrong that just shouldn't go wrong in a sport of precision, and the record of the night's events read like something out of Daniel Defoe's *Journal of the Plague Year.*

Item 1: The demolition derby began when the cars tried to qualify for the race. First Les Heikkila, then Al Straub, skimmed the top of the guardrail and gouged gaping holes in the wooden outer fence at opposite ends of the track. The time taken to clear the wrecked cars and pieces of the splintered fence from the track pushed the starting time of the race back half an hour.

Item 2: As the cars were being pushed onto the track for the race, the concrete under four rows of spectators at the northwest end of the massive fairgrounds' grandstand groaned, then cracked and began sinking. With its occupants scurrying for safety, the section of the opulent but old grandstand kept sagging until the rows of seats resembled a grotesque sway-backed cement horse. The bewildered fans in the section were moved down to the box seat sections for the night.

Item 3: The race finally got underway, but it lasted only three laps before Whitey Gerkin's Chevelle spun in the third turn and ripped out a healthy chunk of the inner guardrail. The race was stopped and another forty minutes lost while workmen pieced the rail back together and welded it up again.

Item 4: The guardrail restored, USAC officials attempted to restart the race, a simple procedure normally. But when some of the leading cars decided to fulfill the mandatory pit stop rule by ducking into the pits during the lineup laps, things became more and more confused, even for the officials. Assistant starter Shim Malone ran along the front straightaway pointing and yelling at cars and drivers in the single-file parade who weren't where they should have been. Several laps went by before the cars could be lined up to the satisfaction of the starters, and then the increasingly tedious race resumed.

Item 5: After a handful of suspiciously trouble-free laps, Bill Puterbaugh's car expired in the second turn and the yellow flag was displayed to get a wrecker to him. During that so-called lull, Billy Nelson proceeded to hang his car on the outer rail in the third turn, which shouldn't happen when slowed under the caution flag, getting another wrecker into the act.

Item 6: The green flag flying again, Jack Bowsher, A. J. Foyt's car owner and driving teammate, got his blue and white Ford into the guardrail coming out of the second turn while trying to pass his employee for third place, became airborne, punched yet another hole in the outside fence, then went pinwheeling through the air like a majorette's baton. Verlin Eaker's Dodge also caught up in the melee; a six-foot-long splinter from the blasted fence hung on the side of his car when he came around to the pits.

Item 7: With the yellow flag waving again while the debris from Bowsher's spectacular but ouchless spill was cleaned up, pudgy Butch Hartman, the race leader, blew the engine in his Dodge, something else that's not supposed to happen during a slowdown, and coasted to a stop in his pit. Half of the dizzied crowd did not even realize the lead had changed hands until the cars lined up for the resumption of the race. Little wonder, since besides watching the cleanup of Bowsher's wreck and waiting to see the stunned but unhurt driver emerge from the ambulance, they were kept busy looking for any other weird little happenings that might spring up on this night of surrealistic racing. They weren't disappointed, as Woody Walcher obliged by attempting to exit the pits in reverse gear. That particular maneuver prompted every woman in the crowd to turn to her man and exclaim "See, I'm not the only one who does that."

Item 8: Three hours and ten minutes after the scheduled starting time of the race, the checkered flag fell. It went to Norm Nelson, a forty-seven-year-old, white-haired, once-retired racer who was driving the Plymouth normally driven by the defending USAC car champion, Roger McCluskey. McCluskey was a spectator for the fairgrounds farce, a distinct benefit this particular night. Injured the weekend before in a mass pileup at Syracuse, New York, his injured eye was covered by a bandage.

The fans, a little hesitant even to get to their feet, finally managed to do so and began filing out of the fairgrounds. The fallibility of man and his machines was in evidence everywhere they looked.

The grandstands, guardrails, and fences looked like they had been used for artillery practice, bringing to mind all those old war movies on *The Late Show* with scenes in London immediately after a Blitzkrieg. It was not a night for the timid or the faint of heart.

31. Jungle

JUNGLE PARK was no race track. It was a green-eyed monster, a bad dream, a live grenade, a hangman's noose.

They called it a race track, and races were run there. For nearly forty years, men raced at Jungle. They didn't race to win; they raced to stay alive.

Just how many died on that infamous piece of racing real estate, no one knows for sure. All anyone familiar with the place can remember is that it sure seemed like a lot.

Jungle Park came into existence in the 1920s, as one of the primitive little dirt tracks in the Midwest. It was the idea of the late Earl Padgett, who decided a race track would be a nice addition to the gas station-restaurant complex he owned in western Indiana.

It would not be accurate to say Jungle Park was built. It was simply gouged out of a hilly tract of farmland along what is now Highway 41, some seven miles north of Rockville, Indiana.

Whoever laid out the track originally was either a comedian or a sadist. Just looking at the oblong half-mile of hard brown dirt convinced you it was the devil's work. Every foot of the track was bad, first twisting up, then down, then to one side, with uneven, pinched turns at each end.

The front straightaway slanted downhill into an irregular curve, not banked nearly enough to handle the momentum built up on the sloping frontstretch. The first two turns joined together in a lopsided V-shape and emptied onto the back straightaway,

The remains of the old Jungle Park race track in Bloomingdale, Indiana.

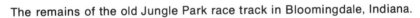

which tilted sharply uphill. The third turn was banked only slightly, like the first two, but listed menacingly as it connected with the fourth turn, which was cut out of the side of a hill.

After managing to navigate that half-mile of bad road without mishap, the drivers then had the privilege of going through the whole nightmare again and again until the race was finally over. That never came soon enough to suit them; they held onto the steering wheels of the race cars for dear life.

One man who knows the terrors of Jungle Park as well as any-one—anyone still alive, that is—is Bob Stroud, who tackled its deadly hazards in the late twenties and early thirties. The pudgy-faced and congenial Stroud is now a top USAC race official. It has been some forty years since he raced at Jungle, but it's not the kind of track that is easily forgotten. "It had kind of an egg shape to it—it wasn't an oval—and it was a dusty, dirty place. I first raced at Jungle in 1928. At that time, all the cars were basically what we call sprint cars now. This was before the midgets came along."

It was also before such lifesavers as guardrails had come to racing. At Jungle Park, a driver whose car soared off the track had to make his own peace with the neighboring landscape of trees, poles, and that unyielding Indiana ground. "A lot of people were hurt, many were killed there," Stroud relates. "Two that I remember were George Axe and a young fellow by the name of Tiny Jenkinson. Tiny drove one of my cars back then and was killed in it at Jungle."

Stroud himself felt the sting of the treacherous Jungle Park course. "I got hurt there myself," he explains. "I don't remember exactly what year it was, but I broke both my legs in a crash there. A spindle broke on my car and I flipped right in front of the grandstand. I spent six months in the hospital. It was a sport back then, you know. There was no hospital fund. If you got hurt, you paid your own hospital bills," he adds, a smile crossing his face.

Stroud and all the others who raced there knew the physical and financial risks they were taking. They knew Jungle Park was a monster. "It sure was that," Stroud confirms. "But it was a sport, almost a hobby, in those days and nobody backed away from Jungle. At that time, there just weren't too many tracks around. A lot of fellows who later raced at Indianapolis, like Mauri Rose, Louis Schneider, Jackie Holmes, and Spider Webb, all ran it at one time or another."

The terrors of Jungle Park did not go unnoticed by the rest of the population, either. Many of those who filled the long wooden grandstand at Jungle, like some of those who clamor to today's modern speedways, were attracted by the likely prospect of spectacular and violent crashes. "It drew a lot of people," Stroud admits, "They really packed them in."

As if it wasn't bad enough in its all-dirt form, the gruesome legend of Jungle Park includes constant recollections of the time the killer track was half-asphalt and half-dirt.

Stroud, whose acquaintance with the track stretches from 1928 to the present, isn't sure whether that part of the Jungle Park story is true or just a romantic illusion.

"I understand that at one time it was half and half, but I don't remember any half-pavement on it. There used to be a track like that over in Illinois, but I don't think Jungle was ever like that. There were times that it felt like pavement, though, I'll tell you that."

Cliff Chapman, who now runs the Jungle Park gas station-restaurant complex and owns the old race track site, explains that they used to coat the track surface with heavy oil to cut down the clouds of dust kicked up by the race cars, giving it the appearance, and the feel, of pavement.

"They put this oil on the track, about an inch or two thick," Chapman relates. "A lot of times, it would have little rocks in it and when they packed it down hard it looked like asphalt."

Half-dirt, half-pavement, or all-dirt, Jungle Park remained a tormenting fixture on the calendars of AAA and America's other top racing organizations. But time overcame Jungle. As better and safer tracks were built, the racing groups began to bypass that particular snake pit for more attractive tracks. "A track like that wouldn't be running today," Stroud asserts, with an eye to contemporary race-track safety standards. "Different outfits tried to run it—it still didn't have guardrails or anything—but finally they gave up trying a few years ago."

The last group to try was the Car Owners' Racing Association, an Indiana-based midget group. Herb Berry, CORA president at

The old grandstand at Jungle Park race track.

the time, recounts what happened: "We tried to run a couple of programs there in 1962 or 1963, but a spectator got killed and we didn't run it again. A car went into the infield and killed a woman spectator, her relatives filed a $100,000 lawsuit against us and the track, and the track closed down right after that."

Jungle Park had not mellowed much in forty years. Though the lawsuit was eventually settled out of court, Jungle Park was beyond saving. "It never was the best in the world," Berry notes. "But by then, it really was terrible. It was so dusty you could hardly run on it. The grandstand was all rotten and everything."

Jungle Park, racing's recurring nightmare, was put to rest without so much as a decent burial. Tall grass, woods, and brush now cover the hilly plot along Highway 41. But Jungle Park is still there. Beneath the tangles of Indiana vegetation, the ugly old track is still discernible. The old grandstand, sagging with decay, still stands.

Someday, someone may decide to revive the slumbering monster called Jungle Park. Somebody could bring the murderous track back to life.

Chapman, who says he wants to plow the whole thing under and turn it into a campground, admits that periodically someone comes around and talks of putting the track back in business. But the men who knew it before, men like Bob Stroud and Herb Berry, secretly hope no one ever does.

32. Fast Company

THE GATE in the chain-link fence almost seemed to be opening into a foreign land. As we passed through it into the garage compound, we felt a little uneasy, to be truthful, as if we were wandering into an unfamiliar and possibly unfriendly country or onto a restricted military base.

After all, NASCAR racing has been a southern phenomenon— its big tracks are down there, most of its drivers live there, and only a handful of people up north ever had an opportunity to witness America's top late-model stock car circuit in action before.

But a Detroit businessman, Larry LoPatin, changed all that. A dealer in everything from apartment complexes to amusement parks, LoPatin had decided to have a whirl at auto racing. In 1967, he barged into the speed sport like a Las Vegas novice intent on breaking the bank his first night. Moving with all the finesse of a runaway bulldozer, he shoveled dollars, millions of them, into race tracks.

LoPatin started construction of two new superspeedways—one in Michigan, the other in Texas. At the same time, he began grabbing up stock in two existing racing plants, Riverside and Atlanta. The new speedway near his home base in Detroit, dubbed Michigan International Speedway, was the cornerstone of what LoPatin envisioned as his personal racing empire. Erected in the

scenic Irish Hills area west of Detroit, the $4 million racing lay-
out was to bring top-notch auto racing back to America's automotive womb. And, on an early-summer day in 1970, there it
stood, this speedway Larry LoPatin built, punctuating the green
Michigan landscape with splashes of concrete, asphalt, and glass.
It was, as LoPatin had often promised, everything a superspeedway was supposed to be.

Its mammoth gray bank swept smoothly toward the sky—at
eighteen degrees, twice as steep as the turns at Indianapolis—and
curved evenly around each end of the two-mile-long track. Its
lanes marked off with broken white lines, the wide ribbon of
asphalt resembled a stretch of expressway tilted on edge. Along
the west straightaway rose rows of metallic benches, glittering
silver. Above the tiers of spotless aluminum seats and concrete
slabs, stubby pillars supported a massive glass-encased press box.
From inside the elevated suite of observation booths, the floors
covered with plush carpeting, newsmen, race officials, scorers,
and corporate executives looked out across the luxurious racing
facility. Directly across from them, the fenced-in garage area,

Lee Roy Yarbrough

Bob Allison (12) and Richard Petty (43) at
NASCAR's Atlanta 500. Bob Allison won.

with its gleaming metal buildings, throbbed with activity. Immediately below the high-rise observers, racing fans from Michigan,
Ohio, and Indiana squirmed on their narrow aluminum benches
in anticipation of the "Good Ol' Boys" of NASCAR taking to the
track to show their stuff to a Yankee audience.

So, not surprisingly, the chain-link fence at this sparkling,
streamlined superspeedway represented the border between two
separate worlds—the southern racing legions on the inside of the
fence and midwestern racing fans on the outside, filling the grandstands and the infield. For this one midwesterner, who crossed
over nervously into the southern stockade, there was some reason
to wonder if he might not be in a certain amount of personal
jeopardy. Those fellows from such backwoods-sounding places
as Hueytown, Alabama, and Timmonsville, South Carolina, might
not take too kindly to an intruder whose hair wasn't exactly crewcut and whose boots were more the kind you wear to a rock
festival than the kind you wear out in a cow pasture.

There they were, as big as life, around the corner of the garage building. That, in itself, was a giant-sized shock.

For one who has spent the bulk of his time around the jockey-sized drivers of the Midwest's predominant circuit, USAC, the sight of a six-foot, five-inch Buddy Baker, a six-foot, two-inch Richard Petty, and several other six-footers can momentarily boggle the mind. It doesn't do much for the confidence either. At least with the more diminutive USACers there is a slight psychological edge.

As had been suspected, their haircuts were fairly conventional, maybe just a little longer. There was an abundance of long sideburns, but, then, they had those years before there was anything called hip. Their boots bore no traces of having stepped in anything in the cow pasture.

Just then through the garage gate came Fred Lorenzen, the former NASCAR superstar who was in the process of making a comeback. "Fearless Fred" wore brightly-colored bell-bottoms and his hair fell down around his neck. Well, he had been away for three years and he was a northerner to begin with, so maybe that was to be expected.

Then from the other direction came Cale Yarborough, all five-feet, six-inches of him, his blond hair draped over his ears and cut off in a page-boy effect low on his neck. Hardly the spitting image of a dirt farmer from the deep South.

There they stood, in an uneven circle—the burly Buddy Baker, flashy Fred Lorenzen, toothy Richard Petty, pixish Cale Yarborough, balding Dave Marcis, pensive Wendell Scott (the only black in big-time racing), and boyish Pete Hamilton.

They didn't exactly look like the cast of *Hair* at intermission, but they were a long way from resembling an Army inspection line.

The scene led one to suspect these big dudes might not be much different from northern racers, allowing for their unusual size and distinctive drawls. The next question raised then was: "How about on the race track?"

Well, as W. C. Fields once observed about sex, "There may be some things better and there may be some things worse, but there's nothing quite like it."

Richard Petty

Round and round they went at 180 miles an hour, the leaders bunched up like a sack of Georgia cotton, with seemingly endless dashes into the pits for fuel and new tires. The drone of the forty screaming engines easily explained the preponderance of ear plugs around the pit area.

When it was all over, Cale Yarborough and Pete Hamilton had staged one of the most exciting race-ending duels ever seen on either side of the Mason-Dixon Line. It was only on the final lap that the seasoned Yarborough, his blond locks flapping in the breeze, edged in front of the youngster from Massachusetts.

As the Michigan sun slowly set behind the penthouse on stilts above the main grandstand, long after the speedway queen kissed Yarborough's grease-streaked face, the NASCAR boys did what most racers do at that point.

They began loading their cars and equipment for the long trips back to Hueytown, Timmonsville, Catawba, Spartansburg, Charlotte, and Randleman. By this time, it had become perfectly clear that those places weren't really any farther away than Indianapolis or Elkhart Lake or Mid-Ohio. No farther at all.

33. No Winners, Please

IF THE FIRST California 500 proved nothing else, it proved that nobody loves a winner. That observation comes not from viewing the inaugural California 500 from the plush, presumably air-conditioned press box at the Ontario Motor Speedway, but from watching it instead from the dusty, stuffy floor of the Indiana State Fairgrounds Coliseum.

Air travel being what it is in the era of the heroic sky pirate, the closed-circuit telecast of the initial California 500 became the most prudent and practical method of covering the West Coast carbon-copy of the Indianapolis 500 for a midwestern racing writer.

I had misgivings, to be sure, but one needs steady work to eat regularly so those longings to jump the first freight to California had to be sternly repressed. Only on the morning of that Sunday before Labor Day was I forced to admit to myself that now that the day of the race had come, I was in no mood to eat anyway.

Be that as it may, I took a seat in the darkened and terribly warm fairgrounds coliseum. Sitting there, squashed together in a line of hard wooden chairs, the smell was not of exotic racing fuels and scorched tires but of that pungent, persistent odor common to all fairgrounds at fair time.

Up on the screen, our eyes were being tormented as painfully by the cameramen as our noses and glands were by the surroundings. For the first half of the race at least, the herky-jerky camera work on the telecast was only slightly better than home movies of a fishing trip, minus the strings of slimy trout.

But once the camera quit jumping around and somebody finally realized there was more to a race than following the lead car all the way around the track lap after lap, things got considerably more interesting.

Al Unser, naturally, was so far in front of everyone that they could have switched to a baseball game for a little excitement. They didn't though, and as it turned out they didn't need to.

"Albuquerque Al's" last real challenger was disposed of when young Peter Revson, who should have won the crazy race, got stuck in the pits for seven and a half minutes more than he had planned after his electrical system short-circuited.

Then all of a sudden there was Al back in the pits one more time than he was supposed to be, pointing frantically back to his engine compartment. His crew pointed just as frantically at the track and persuaded him to get back on it, for what it was worth —which turned out to be not much. He never got back up to a racing speed and parked the car in the infield.

That development turned the coliseum crowd, apparently tired of watching Unser win by a country mile all year, into a hysterical bunch of shouting, cheering, foot-stomping fanatics, first screaming with delight then breaking into a ragged chant of "Come on, Lee Roy."

Lee Roy Yarbrough, the southern boy who insists stock car drivers can win in those little Indy cars, was suddenly, dramatically leading. He had it right in the palm of his hand then, but that, too, passed away in a puff of white smoke from his engine as the television cameras zeroed in on him, less than ten laps from the end.

Then the frenzied crowd looked hurriedly for another hero, and found two of them. Art Pollard and Jim McElreath, both over forty and only sometime-winners, incredibly were dicing for the lead only five miles from the finish of the three-hour race.

Just who won made little difference. Just so it wasn't a regular winner, like Al Unser, or like Mario Andretti, who got a similar blast of unsympathetic cheers when his car expired late in the race, a legacy no doubt from his 1969 successes and the accompanying shenanigans of Andy Granatelli.

They settled for Jimmy McElreath, a burly Texan who got bumped at Indy and finally started dead-last at the Brickyard a few months earlier. He hadn't won a big race for several seasons, so he was perfect for the hero role.

But even as the ecstatic, bleary-eyed, sweaty customers filed out of the Indiana coliseum, the message was clear. Enjoy yourself, Jim McElreath, while you can. Next year, when these people come back to watch the second California 500, they'll cheer when you lose. You're a winner now, Jimmy. And nobody loves a winner.

IV INDIANAPOLIS

34. Hookers, Hangers-on, and Warren G. Hardings

As YOU DRIVE west along 16th Street, there is little to indicate you're going anywhere important. Clusters of gas stations, crowded used car lots, endless strings of drive-in restaurants and car washes—all the things you expect in a town that's too large to be quaint and too small to be exciting. Only the small sign that said "Speedway" and pointed you westward when you turned onto 16th Street hinted at where you were headed.

As you swing through the lazy curve past the baseball stadium, where the minor-league Indianapolis Indians play, you might easily imagine the sign had pointed in the other direction. You hit the Lafayette Road intersection and another of the "Speedway" signs convinces you the first sign was interpreted correctly. The traffic begins to slow, pressing together in the three westbound lanes as you move past Michelle's Massage Parlor, then the awning-shrouded Columbia Fish and Oyster Co. and, across the street, the Big Donut Shop with the giant plastic donut rising twenty feet in the air.

A block or so down the street, St. Stephen's Eastern Orthodox Church slides by on the left, followed by a Rix Roast Beef drive-in and the squat brick Romanian Orthodox Church building.

To the right, the Rainbow post office branch passes, then a MacDonald's hamburger stand, the hacienda-style Taco Bell, a Chicken Delight, and the Speedway Pet Shop.

The traffic slows even more as you crawl between the Taco House and Boll's Furnace Co. and down a decline toward the New York Central Railroad underpass. Rolling beneath the underpass, a faded white building comes into view standing on the knoll at the right-hand side of the street. Dark red letters spell out "Firestone Racing Division" on the side of the white structure. Beyond it, the plush—by Indiana standards—Speedway Motel appears, with a foursome of middle-aged men in Bermuda shorts strolling toward a golf green just yards from the edge of the street.

The traffic creeping now, you edge past the checkered sign in front of the motel. At the western border of the motel, a towering steel-and-concrete grandstand rises, empty and cold under the pale early-May sun.

You reach the entrance gate where two guards in dark blue shirts and gold pith helmets process the lines of cars like custom agents at a border checkpoint. They check your tickets or credentials quickly, then motion you toward a narrow aisle that disappears below a thin strip of white concrete. Driving down into a tunnel, you drive cautiously between the pillared divider and the pedestrian walkway until your car hits sunlight again and noses up a steep grade toward another of the gold-helmeted guards.

The burst of sunlight glazes your eyes momentarily and you only vaguely catch the guard's signal to steer to the left. As your vision clears, you finally see what you struggled through the blocks of curious landmarks to see.

Fans stay at the Indianapolis race track even when it rains.

Spreading out before you is a flat expanse of grass, dotted with spindly trees, golf greens, and sand traps. At the rim of the green carpet, a thin ribbon of asphalt bends around behind you. Stark grandstands filled with black shadows block the horizon.

A rocket-shaped little car grumbles into the curve of dark asphalt, slips behind you, then whistles through a second turn and out of sight behind a row of top-heavy trees.

In the distance, between you and the glass-encased scoring tower, a fenced compound juts out into the grassy landscape. Even from the bumpy parking lot you can see bright-colored racing cars sitting inside the tall fence, with steady columns of men weaving around the three rows of green-roofed garage buildings.

Walking up to the fence, you can see the cars more distinctly, their complicated engines seemingly too large for their bodies. Men in white trousers kneel beside them, working with wrenches.

Men in yellowish one-piece uniforms lean against the open garage doors. Striped with red or blue up the sides, their glossy jump-suits are decorated with sponsors' names, miscellaneous patches, and American flags clustered together like military medals.

Semi-circles of men in sports shirts hover around the cars, watching, taking pictures, pointing toward the machinery.

Along the outside of the fence, men, women, and children press against the chain-link. Some people hold cheap cameras to their squinting eyes. Kids and middle-aged, blue-rinsed women scream for autographs whenever a race driver, any race driver, wanders within range. Younger, sleeker women stand quietly at the fence and watch the drivers with the eyes of the hunter.

These are the fans of Indianapolis. They come here every May. They come to watch a race in the making. They don't really understand why the cars go so fast; they just know they do. They are most likely to believe the television or newspaper commercials that say someone won a race because he had STP in his engine or wore a Bellstar crash helmet on his head.

The men huddled in the garages have little time to worry about what products the commercials say they use. They use them because the companies pay them to do so. They know the real secret of winning is in setting up the suspension properly, tuning the engine precisely, and getting a driver brave enough and talented enough to do the job.

Drivers are plentiful, to be sure. Besides those who already have cars to drive, dozens of others mill around the garages in search of their chance to get into the big race. Young drivers looking for their first break, old drivers still holding onto their dream of making it—they stand around in groups and keep their eyes open for an opportunity that, for most of them, doesn't come.

Also filtering through the garage area is an assortment of old grisled men everyone seems to know, but nobody knows exactly who they are or where they came from. Pot-bellied, in stretched T-shirts, work shirts with the tails hanging out, engineer's hats or battered caps, movie cameras dangling by their sides, they have been described as the Warren G. Hardings of racing. They are here every year but no one knows why. A few have some tenuous connection with the cars or the track, but most are simply part of the tribe of hangers-on that always shows up at race tracks.

Past the garage area gate, beneath the cloth banner that reads "Gasoline Alley," you squeeze through the crowd of spectators to get to the pit area, where the cars and drivers that were in the garages earlier have moved. For nearly a month, the cars, their mechanics, and their drivers slip back and forth from the garages to the pits, running a few laps on the track, returning to the garages to work on the machinery, then heading back for the pits again.

When the first weekend of time trials approaches, and traffic on 16th Street begins backing up to the Chicken Delight, the pace steadily quickens. More cars run more laps trying to put everything together in time to qualify on the first Saturday of time trials for the big race.

On that particular Saturday, the traffic backs up to Lafayette Road and 200,000 people jam into the grandstands and infield to see the cars, one at a time, take their four laps around the mammoth two-and-a-half-mile oval. It is a race unto itself, as the best drivers in the best cars battle each other and the clock to squeeze their ten-mile runs into the shortest amount of time.

The one who manages to do it with the most precision, the most speed, wins something tradition has labeled the "pole" position for the start of the Memorial Day weekend race. The pole, the inside spot on the front row of the three-abreast and eleven-deep lineup, doesn't really pay that much, about $20,000, and is of questionable value in terms of winning the actual race; only one out of seven who have started first have finished first, but everyone who can tries to get it.

It makes little sense except as just another competition to be won or lost, but the fans and the newspapers make a big deal out of it. The contest for the pole draws almost as many spectators as the race—many of whom wouldn't walk across the street to see the race but think the first day of time trials is the greatest—and the drivers make a go of it, and maybe break a few track records in the process.

The pole scramble occurs only on that first Saturday of time trials since, under Indy rules, second-day qualifiers must line up behind the first-day qualifiers, regardless of their comparative speeds; the third-day qualifiers fall in behind the second, and the fourth behind the third.

That fourth day of time trials, the Sunday before the race itself, provides another phenomenon peculiar to Indianapolis. As the clock rolls around to the 6:00 P.M. cutoff time, people concern themselves with a curious thing called the "bubble."

When the thirty-three-car lineup is filled, which it generally is by Sunday afternoon, the slowest qualifier is placed on the bubble—that is, he is in the unenviable position of being eliminated from the starting field by anyone who can outqualify him.

Unlike the pole, the day a contestant qualified doesn't enter into the question of the bubble. It is predicated solely on speed—whoever is the slowest qualifier left in the field automatically inherits the bubble, whether he qualified on the first day or the last.

In the late hours of that final Sunday of time trials, the emotions get pretty ragged. Those who aren't qualified get desperate as the clock marches toward 6:00 P.M.; the slower qualifiers get very nervous.

Indianapolis 1969—Dan Gurney car in the pits.

When the "bumping"—that's what they call it when the man on the bubble loses out to a faster qualifier—begins, drivers start shuffling in and out of race cars like men trying on suits in a bargain basement. The fits usually aren't snug enough to do any good, but every now and then the right driver jumps into the right car and sends some other driver hunting for a chance to do the same thing.

When the gun cracks ominously at 6:00 P.M., there is usually a car circling the track in a last-ditch effort to get into the lineup, with a string of would-be qualifiers left stranded in the pit lane.

As that last car swings around the track, the driver on the bubble listens intently to the announcements of its speeds. If they are faster than his own, the color drains from his face, his eyes close heavily, and he wrestles with the realization that there will be no second chance for him this year. If the speeds are too slow to remove him from the race field, the bubble man and his crew dance around joyfully, as if they had won the race itself.

Most of those involved in the final-hour drama are Indy's hardship cases, those with less money, less experience, older equipment, and fewer frills than the top-line entries. The big-money outfits clean the table on opening day, when as many as twenty or twenty-five qualify, leaving only scraps for the underprivileged.

Through it all, from the day the gates open the first of May to that final Sunday of time trials, the horde of Indy fans, that strange collection of hookers, hangers-on, and Warren G. Hardings, keeps a constant watch, milling in a steady stream from the Gasoline Alley gate to the fence behind the pits and on into the grandstands.

Even on the very first day of practice, when only three or four cars go onto the track all day, they are here, a few hundred of them, patiently overseeing the activities. Each of these early-bird spectators is an expert on the track, the cars, and the drivers. Each once shook hands with Bobby Unser or Mario Andretti and subsequently built a repertoire of significant facts to back up the argument that his particular favorite is the greatest driver alive or, in the case of the oldtimers, each once saw Wilbur Shaw drive at Indy and is convinced that none of the current crop of drivers can hold a candle to him.

Those self-ordained high priests form the nucleus of a congregation whose number multiplies rapidly as May moves along. By the end of the first week, its size has increased to a couple of thousand. Two or three days before the first Saturday of time trials, the crowd has almost doubled.

The fence-line experts are joined by the young women looking for a score, and the middle-aged ones just looking, the austere businessmen having their one afternoon of smug reacquaintance, the kids clutching their autograph books, the drunks aching for a fight, the Warren G. Hardings searching for their identities.

They are all here to be a part of the racing carnival, and they all have done their homework. They have methodically studied the historical statistics, the legends of the sixty-year-old race course they always refer to as "The Speedway," never "Indianapolis" or even "Indy." They know the names of the men who have won the race, the ones who have won the pole, and even the ones who have died since 1911.

They can talk confidently of the legendary winners of the 500—Ralph DePalma, Tommy Milton, Pete DePaolo, Louis Meyer, Wilbur Shaw, Mauri Rose, Rodger Ward, A. J. Foyt.

They can get a genuine thrill recalling the special men who, unlike some of the other winners, solved the mysteries of the giant speedway almost as soon as they drove it and dominated the races they ran without the usual long apprenticeship—Frank Lockhart, Bill Vukovich, Parnelli Jones, Jimmy Clark, Mario Andretti, Al Unser.

They remember, with solemn faces, the men they think should have won the big race but never did, many of whom died trying—Rex Mays, Ted Horn, Tony Bettenhausen, Jack McGrath, Pat O'Conner, Johnny Thomson, Freddie Agabashian, Don Branson, Eddie Sachs, Dan Gurney, Lloyd Ruby.

On and on, they can talk of names, years, numbers, speeds, wins, losses, deaths, close calls. They have boiled the sixty long years of history into a neat package of facts and statistics ready to be recited at a moment's notice.

The epitome of this worship of statistical details has to be the yellow-haired British lad, Donald Davidson, whose enchantment with the famous race in Indiana led him to compensate for his inability to actually see the race—he could only listen to it on radio as a youngster in England—by committing to memory the complete finishing order of each and every 500 in the history of the Indianapolis speedway.

He memorized the names of the drivers, the relief drivers, the names of their cars, the names of their sponsors, how many laps they completed in each race, and the reasons for their departures from the race. When he finally came to Indianapolis to witness the race in the mid-1960s, he was an immediate sensation.

Davidson outdid the regular Indy fact-fondlers. With total and instant recall, the slender young Briton dazzled the racing fraternity in general and USAC officials in particular. USAC promptly put him on the payroll as a race statistician.

Davidson's reverence for the famed American race, however, is not typical of how Europeans who come to see it view Indianapolis. Many of the foreign drivers and fans who journey to the speedway on West 16th Street speak with considerable disdain for the U. S.'s mightiest racing event.

They charge the five-hundred-mile race around the two-and-one-half-mile oval demands no real skill of a driver and requires only super-human stamina on the part of those who sit through the three-hour event. They reinforce their claim that grand prix racing, performed on long and twisting European road circuits, is the true test of men and machines by citing the relative ease with which grand prix champions like Jimmy Clark, Graham Hill, Jack Brabham, and Denis Hulme have mastered the Indianapolis course.

Conveniently overlooking the apparent inability of such grand prix headliners as Pedro Rodriguez, Richie Ginther, Lorenzo Bandini, and Chris Amon to cope with the box-shaped Indy oval, the Europeans say Indianapolis is a five-hundred-mile roller derby where speed and endurance, not driving talent and courage, count for everything. Their argument is an artistic one, similar to the one Indy buffs offer against figure-eight or jalopy racing.

Yet, even the European drivers will admit that, while they prefer the rigors of grand prix racing, Indianapolis is not as simple as it looks. It's no cakewalk, they have discovered, and it does require a particular, if somewhat more subtle degree of skill from a driver.

While it is true the long straightaways are little more than glorified dragstrips and the two sets of turns merely excuses for connecting the straightaways, the sad old course does have its complexities. Any driver who has tried it, even the grand prix campaigners, will tell you the turns at each end of the Indy oval, with a little straight section stuck in the middle of each pair, are

Crewman sits with numbers, letters, and signs to be used on his pit board during the running of the race.

Denis Hulme tests tractor used to push race cars from Gasoline Alley.

as difficult as any in the world. Not that the four turns at Indy are wild, wheel-wrenching terrors—they're not. They are gentle, nearly-flat things, and although all four of them look identical, each one is really quite different from the others. Each has its own idiosyncracies, and any driver who wants to do well at Indy must solve the individual problems of each turn. It is the four corners of the big oval that hold the secret to the eternal quest for greater speed around a race track originally built to handle seventy-five-miles-per-hour laps. A driver must find precisely the right line to follow through each of the turns and his mechanics must set the suspension of his machine with equal precision to accommodate that line.

It is no simple task. Even the most talented and perceptive drivers and mechanics spend hours, days, weeks, even years exploring the hidden mysteries of those four deceptive turns. Those who find the answers succeed at Indy. Those who don't are sure to fail.

The European drivers who succeed at Indianapolis do so because they are able to deal with its intricacies. They are the best drivers with the best cars. Those who fare less well are less well-equipped, less able to adapt. It is not, as suggested, a question of the artistry of one group of men over another, but of the substance of individual men. It is the perpetual story of auto racing.

If its curious turns are difficult to fathom, Indy's attraction to men who race is not. The legend and the challenge are part of it, certainly, but the underlying reason drivers, mechanics, and car owners pour in from all over America and Europe has a dollar sign in front of it. Any race that offers over a million dollars in prize money can't be all bad. And for the one of the seventy original entries who wins the race, a first prize of nearly a quarter of a million dollars is impossible to resist.

Yet it is a race you have to win. Second place won't pay all the bills if you're running a top Indy team. Anything below third won't even pay for the spare parts and a month's stay at the Speedway Motel or Holiday Inn Northwest. You can lead one-hundred-ninety-nine of the two-hundred laps at $150 a lap but still not have enough to pay for your car when you wreck it on the last lap. You literally can't afford to lose this race. There have been some who found out they couldn't even afford to win it.

Only one man makes money every year, and he does it with the least risk of anybody. He's Tony Hulman, the man who quietly reaps the May harvest of gold that flows through the speedway gates, concession stands, novelty shops, and so forth. Hulman is one of those men who just naturally attracts money. He owns Clabber Girl Baking Powder, the Speedway Motel, and half of Terre Haute, Indiana. His wife's family controls the LaFendrich cigar empire. He didn't need the Indianapolis Motor Speedway when he bought it right after World War II, but it just seemed like a good idea at the time.

It was, of course, a very good idea. Even with the layoff for the war, the Indianapolis track retained its magic. Millions of people have come through the gates in Hulman's twenty-five years as speedway owner, paying enough admission fees, eating enough hot dogs, drinking enough beer, and buying enough cheap souvenirs to pad his already-bulging bank account. The 300,000 or so race-day spectators—Tony never does report exactly how many attend his shindig—pay a minimum of five dollars a head, and that's enough in itself to cover the race purse with at least a few dollars left over for miscellaneous expenses. Any of those 300,000 who expect to sit down on anything other than what Mother Nature provides also put up to thirty dollars apiece into the kitty.

All that beautiful money rolls in without the least bit of persuasion from Tony. He doesn't spend even one nickel on newspaper ads, television commercials, or radio spots. He doesn't have to. The seats will be filled and the infield covered with people even if they scheduled an H-bomb test at the place five minutes before race time. The people come almost compulsively. It is an instinctive thing, like an animal drive, that convinces them they cannot survive unless they are there. They are driven to the massive race track like salmon struggling upstream to their spawning ground.

With that kind of biology going for you, there is no real need for any kind of an advertising campaign. The speedway publicity department spends its time handling ticket orders, issuing press credentials, and publishing the speedway's souvenir program. And when all the preparation, the drama, the madness of the month jells on race day, the scene is enough to take your breath away, put a lump in your throat, and harden your arteries.

The cars on 16th Street back up past the Indianapolis Indians' stadium. Some of them were lined up the night before, their occupants getting a head start on their consumption of American racing's official beverage, beer, and getting the annual party off to a rousing start.

Bleary-eyed drivers now squint over the tops of steering wheels as each tries to balance a freshly-opened can of beer on the dashboard. Every hundred yards, the hood of an overheating car flips up in a cloud of steam.

Pedestrians are packed together inside the speedway complex as tightly as the cars outside. Engulfed in an endless ocean of bobbing heads, men and women with picnic baskets and beer coolers inch toward their assigned seats. As each new arrival reaches his place, the party grows. The baskets and coolers open and fried chicken, beer, binoculars, and suntan lotion fly out.

On the track, the thirty-three shining cars are being rolled into their proper starting positions. Hundreds of men with cameras surround the racing machines.

Somewhere in the mob is Tony Hulman, his face glowing like that of a child with a new toy. He may just be looking at those wonderful ticket-buying customers in the stands and calculating his profits, but there is something in his face that says he is as caught up in the spirit of the day as everyone else. Tony Hulman really seems to love it all, and the emotion almost overcomes him as he gives the order to fire up the race cars.

At his command, the sound of high-powered engines fills the air and the party comes to a momentary halt. The participants in America's biggest beer bash pause just long enough to get the Indianapolis 500 on its way.

For that one moment when the pole-sitter and his thirty-two-piece accompaniment sweep past the green flag, the crowd stands in silent, though brief, awe. It is that one instant when all five human senses are saturated with the sight, sound, smell, taste, and feel of thirty-three racing cars rushing headlong into their individual destinies, that they paid up to thirty dollars a seat to experience. From then on, however, the race will become mostly a curious distraction for the gathering of beer-slurping, chicken-gobbling, girl-watching, sunburning onlookers numbing their

Indianapolis 1972 — Bobby Unser in the cockpit of Dan Gurney's Olsonite Eagle. In this car Unser set new speed records while qualifying for the 1972 Indy 500: Single lap speed of 196.678 miles per hour and fastest all-over qualifying speed of 195.940 miles per hour.

rumps on the ingeniously uncomfortable grandstand seats that surround the mammoth speedway or on the hard ground graciously left for the poorer relatives.

As the audience eats, drinks, and argues about a race held ten years ago, soothes its reddening skin with suntan oil and its aching hindside with four-letter oaths, and keeps asking when the race will be over, the thirty-three steely-eyed men in their thundering cars race for their slices of the million-dollar melon dangled so temptingly in front of them by Tony Hulman.

Over three hours pass before the spectators—those who have not staggered along the infield and passed out from sunstroke, intoxication, or just plain boredom—give their undivided attention back to Mr. Hulman's race.

Only when one of the thirty-three cars flashes past the checkered flag ahead of the others remaining in the once-bulging field does the throng get interested again. Then, the fairly unsophisticated assemblage rises as it did at the outset and cheers the man who wearily unstraps himself from his grimy race car, gets kissed by the race queen, and maybe by his car owner, and mumbles something over the speedway loudspeakers.

Its beer drunk, its fried chicken devoured, its arguments either settled or forgotten, and its girls out of view, the population of this once-a-year city of 300,000 strains to get a glimpse of the winner. Then, each swaggers unsteadily home to tell his friends and neighbors all about the big race, almost as if he had seen it happen.

Why they all do it, year after year, is a question which is never answered. In fact, it's never even asked. They do it, put up with the hideous traffic, the rib-crushing crowding, the loud and annoying drunks, because they are somehow expected to do it. They do it to be present at what is admittedly not a very good race. The race is long, often boring and its outcome is usually predictable—the winner almost always is someone starting in the first two or three rows—and the winner is so far ahead at the finish that usually nobody's really sure who is second. The only time the lead changes in the last half of the race is when a frontrunner makes a pit stop, his car gives out on him, or he crashes.

The shorter Indy-car races are closer, have more exciting finishes. And any guy in the stands can tell you a sprint car race at New Bremen or Terre Haute is more fun to watch.

But Indianapolis is something special, like the World Series, the Super Bowl, or the Kentucky Derby. It doesn't have to be good. It's just special and that makes all the difference. It is Indianapolis. That's all there is to it. And, somehow, that's enough.

35. One Man's Family

WHEN YOUR name is Bettenhausen, you have your own special reasons for racing at Indianapolis. The reasons go unspoken for the most part, some probably couldn't be put into words anyway, but they are there, anchored in the back of your mind as a legacy of your name, your heritage, your destiny.

When your name is Bettenhausen, you come to Indianapolis because tough, leathery-faced Tony Bettenhausen, your father, came for fifteen years without winning. You come because the last time your father came here he lost everything to this brutal devil of a speedway. So when, in 1970, you are Gary Bettenhausen, Tony's strapping, no-nonsense son, you head back for Indianapolis full of purpose and determination. You raced here last year, and the year before, and you know what you are searching for is within reach.

You come to race, not to talk about the historical significance of your presence here. As the first of Tony's sons to follow the same road he did, you've been toughened by the ordeal of bringing the name of Bettenhausen back into racing and being expected to walk on water right from the start. "If you want to do something bad enough, it doesn't matter who you are or what your name is," you say now, recognizing that you have made it to where you are as much in spite of your name as because of it.

When you are Merle Bettenhausen, the next in line, you come

Gary Bettenhausen (right) assists younger brother Merle
(in car) at Indianapolis in 1972. Merle failed to qualify.

to Indianapolis this time to watch, to wait. Already in your fourth
season as a racer, your timetable for competing here makes this
your final visit as a spectator. "When I started in 1967, I told
myself in five years I should be at the Speedway," you say. "That's
next year."

To get here next year, or even the year after that, you will race
the smaller, less-glamorous midget and sprint cars this summer
and, like your older brother, you will speak less of the destiny
that drives you toward the giant speedway that engulfed your
illustrious father.

But when you are Tony Bettenhausen, Jr., you do not, in 1970,
come to Indianapolis. You stay away, for the most basic of reasons—you are too busy laying the groundwork for the day when
you, too, head for this fabled race track.

The youngest of Tony's tough sons and in the final year of
high school, your time is spent on the dusty rough-and-tumble
tracks of Texas, learning how to be a race driver. The training

you get there will lead most immediately to the super-fast super-speedways of stock car racing and eventually will buy you your coveted ticket to Indianapolis. "I'd like to be at Indy in 1973, depending on how I do on the superspeedways," you say now, your sights already set.

Unlike your older brothers, you are still able to talk of the past and how your arrival at Indianapolis will bring the legend of the racing Bettenhausens full circle. "It's not so much racing against my brothers. It's more like the goal is having all three of us in one race at Indianapolis. I'd just like to see one of us win it, to have a Bettenhausen in Victory Lane."

This thought of a family goal, once formulated by all three brothers, now becomes yours to dwell upon until, as your brothers did, you absorb it as an ingrained and unspoken personal ambition. "Gary and Merle have mentioned this to me, although they haven't said anything about it lately, but all three of us have said at one time or another that we wanted to get a Bettenhausen in Victory Lane; this is something I'd like to see us achieve."

When you do come to Indianapolis, you won't express the dream with words. The closer a dream comes, the more the work of fulfilling it preempts the need to voice it. Now though, you can

Gary Bettenhausen readying himself for a practice run at Indianapolis.

still talk with conviction of destiny and even pattern a fanciful dialogue to occasionally remind your brothers that, at one time, they spoke almost the same words. Brothers Gary and Merle are familiar with your routine. "He'll count on his fingers, figuring out when he'll be at the Speedway, and then he'll say, 'Just think, I'll be on the pole—you guys can fight it out for the other two spots,' " Merle tells. "The first turn oughta be somethin' else," you chime in.

And when, in 1973 or so, the third Bettenhausen brother comes to Indianapolis, the mural will be complete. But it all will melt into a continuing collage of anguish and hope for yet another member of this racing family.

When Tony, Sr., came here in 1946, you were here. When he left here lifeless in 1961, you were still here. And you, Mrs. Valerie Bettenhausen, will be here with your three sons as they follow their father, each in his own shoes.

Through two generations, you have endured the emotional strains that are the lot of a racing wife and racing mother. Your personal ordeal watching your sons race today has little difference from the feelings you had watching their father chase his dream twenty years ago. "Of course, I worry about them as I did for twenty years with Tony, but I know they wouldn't be happy otherwise. I don't think a mother ever does get used to it. I'm not that brave. When they get in a tight squeeze, I hide."

As difficult as it is, you have become resigned to watching your men risk their lives on race tracks. For as long as you can remember, you've known this was your likely fate. "I didn't want them to race, but I think I knew all along. It's always been such a part of their lives, I really couldn't expect anything else. And I think they've done beautifully."

So you, too, come to Indianapolis for your own special reasons. Like your late husband and your three thriving sons, you come because it is part of your nature and you would feel strangely empty if you weren't here.

Despite the tragedies of the past, you must come to this terrifying speedway, whether you're a wife, mother, or son, because it still holds the same promise now as it did for a tough old man named Tony Bettenhausen. When your name is Bettenhausen, you come to find the end of the rainbow.

36. *The Elementary Watson*

SOME MEN work all their lives trying to win the Indianapolis 500 and never do it even once.

A. J. Watson has won it, directly or indirectly, eight times and has several years left to do it again. But even he admits it may be harder to win the next one than it was to win the first eight.

Watson, a lean six-footer whose sloping shoulders give his chest a concave appearance, was a phenomenon of Indy's roadster period which began in the early fifties and ended abruptly in 1965. First as a mechanic, then as a car designer and builder, Watson mastered the roadster art-form as no one had done before with any type of car. He demonstrated a natural genius for those streamlined missiles that exiled the old high-riding speedway cars to the dirt tracks.

In a ten-year span of the roadster reign, cars either built, designed, or maintained by A. J. Watson won eight times at Indianapolis. The peak years of that era consistently saw at least one-third of the thirty-three cars in the Memorial Day lineup carrying the "Made by Watson" label. It was an awesome one-man display of mechanical skill and vision unequalled in the history of Indianapolis racing.

Watson, who had grown up in Mansfield, Ohio, first tested his mechanical talents in Glendale, California, where he settled in 1946 after a stint in the military. He and a fellow student at Glendale State College spent their free time building a "hot rod" to race on weekends at small tracks around Glendale. From that meager beginning, Watson quickly cultivated his gift, building more and more cars, becoming more proficient with each one.

Just three years after that first hot rod had been built, he was at Indianapolis. He came as chief mechanic for a crude little car with a Mercury engine owned by a boisterous Italian from Chicago named Andy Granatelli and driven by a sallow-faced Irishman named Pat Flaherty. The trio, all unknowns then but each destined to show up in Victory Lane eventually, worked enthusiastically and confidently, but when race day came they watched from the sidelines.

The next year, Watson came to Indianapolis with his own car, and driver Dick Rathman qualified it well, but it was the second machine to drop out of the race.

Watson then underwent a five-year apprenticeship with the Bob Estes Indy team, working on the chassis of the cars piloted by such seasoned drivers as Don Freeland and Joey James. In 1955, Watson made the move that was to make all the difference. He was hired by Oklahoma industrialist John Zink to serve as chief mechanic on the shocking-pink roadster built by Frank Kurtis, the venerable car builder who had given birth to the roadster era with the startling bullet-shaped bodies he built for the early Novis. Applying his own ideas of proper weight distribution in a racing chassis, Watson set up the car perfectly, and steady Bob Sweikert won the 1955 race with it.

Several racing drivers, Sweikert among them, have won the 500 prior to their thirtieth birthdays—that is not particularly unusual—but few chief mechanics made it that soon. It normally takes many years to nurture the precision required to conquer Indy. Most of the mechanics who make it have been trying for at least a decade or two. A. J. Watson, at Indy for only six years, was thirty years old when he trotted into Victory Lane in 1955.

That one success taught Watson what he needed to know about putting a winning roadster together. Frank Kurtis' successful designs, which had been viewed as the ultimate in roadsters, were about to become obsolete.

In 1956, Watson built a new roadster for the Zink stable, just a little lighter, a little lower, a little sleeker than the Kurtis car. That same Irishman who had driven for Andy Granatelli, Pat Flaherty, put the Watson machine on the pole and won the 500 going away.

With two consecutive victories, Watson was beginning to look invincible. Many car owners started ordering new roadsters from A. J.'s Indianapolis workshop. But no man is completely unbeatable as Lady Luck, and something called a horizontal-engine roadster, were soon to demonstrate.

For 1957, Watson built a new roadster for the Zink operation which 1952 Indy winner Troy Ruttman promptly put on the front row of the starting grid. Ruttman jumped into the lead quickly in the race but retired early with a sick engine.

In 1958, Watson seemed to have it in the bag once again. Three of his cars, two built for the Zink team and one sold to another owner, occupied the front row, and when the trio of Watson roadsters hit the starting line it seemed inevitable one of them would be the winner. Three-quarters of a lap later, Watson was an also-ran, as two of the cars were demolished in an insane pileup in the third turn and the third machine was crippled sufficiently to keep it out of operation.

For the second year in a row the race was won by a gleaming yellow car built by mechanic George Salih. The car had its engine tilted to one side to give the body a lower profile, and many of the Indy regulars were beginning to think this concept would outmode Watson's roadsters just as his had mothballed Frank Kurtis'.

Watson didn't agree, however. Sticking with the upright engine and careful weight distribution, he built two new roadsters for the 1959 five hundred miler. One went to his new boss, Milwaukee playing card manufacturer Bob Wilke, for an unspectacular—at the time—driver named Rodger Ward. The other went to veteran car owner Lindsey Hopkins for 1957 runnerup Jim Rathmann, Dick's brother. Those two combinations sent George Salih and his horizontal-engine creations to the showers. The Watson cars finished one-two in both 1959 and 1960, Ward edging Rathmann the first time and Jim returning the favor a year later.

By the time 1961 rolled around, no one questioned the invincibility of the Watson roadster. When qualifying was over, eleven roadsters built by A. J. or copied from his blueprints were in the lineup.

Watson's own Leader Card machine, driven again by Ward, finished third, but a Watson-inspired model prepared by George Bignotti was wheeled to victory by A. J. Foyt.

The next May, with twelve cars of his design in the field, Watson watched as his Leader Card creations finished one-two, Ward first and Len Sutton second.

In 1963, the year Lotus' Colin Chapman introduced his flashy rear-engines to the Indy fraternity, there were fourteen Watson-style roadsters taking the green flag. One of them, sold to J. C. Agajanian and driven by Parnelli Jones, won it, pursued closely by Scotland's Jim Clark in one of the pesky Lotus entries. Ward drove the Leader Card car home in fourth.

The rear-engine revolution had taken hold in 1964, but there were still twelve Watson roadsters in the lineup on Memorial Day. There were also two new rear-engine cars built by A. J. for the Leader Card stable. The race, marred by the fiery crash that snuffed out the lives of drivers Eddie Sachs and Dave MacDonald, went to Foyt and Bignotti in another carbon-copy Watson roadster. Ward was second in one of the new rear-engines, followed by two old Watson roadsters.

That was the end of the roadsters, though, as even their staunchest defenders, like Foyt and Jones, switched to rear-engine machines for 1965. The changeover did not appear to pose much of a problem for Watson since his first try in 1964 at building a rear-engine had proved relatively successful. But some seven years later, that original effort still stood as his most-productive venture with a rear-engine car.

The fall from the top was a brutally rapid one. In 1967, just three years after his creations took the top four spots at Indy, a Memorial Day field roared away without a Watson-built entry for the first time in twelve years. Cars built by men with previous experience in the preparation of the intricate European grand prix cars—Chapman's Lotus, Dan Gurney's Eagle, Eric Broadley's Lola—were now in the most demand by Indy car owners, and A. J. Watson simply couldn't unravel the secrets of the low-slung machines.

Even Bob Wilke changed, putting his primary efforts into a Gurney Eagle driven by Bobby Unser and tooled by Jud Phillips, who had worked with Watson on the Bob Estes Indy team. Unser and Phillips went to Victory Lane in 1968 while Watson, relegated to second-team status in the Leader Card operation, watched quiet Mike Mosley bring his unsophisticated car across the line eighth.

In the years that followed, Watson's cars improved little by little each year, and so did Mosley's confidence behind the wheel.

They ran a little better each year, but not well enough to win.

Today, he comes back to Indianapolis in May with a new car he hopes will bring him closer to solving the rear-engine mystique. Admittedly, he is using the ideas of the other, more-proficient designers rather than setting the trend himself as he had in the roadster days. He readily admits the rear-engines are still an unsolved riddle for him. "It sure looks like it—yes, I have had a couple of problems with them. Of course, they're really not that much of a problem. If you can build things, you can build them rear-engine or front-engine. It's just that the suspensions on the rear-engines are a little more critical."

Watson, his silver hair cut in a precise flat-top, now works on

A. J. Watson

his car with much of the casualness of the scores of other mechanics who are not under the pressure of the established front-runners. His philosophy of car-building remains much the same as it was in his days of glory with the roadsters, however. "The main thing I've always worked on is dependability. You know, I try to make it sturdy so it will last."

His view of the future is pretty bedrock, too. "I just figure to run the circuit and go from there. I don't have any super-plans for the future."

Watson clearly has mellowed somewhat from his younger days and has now closed down his California workshop to remain in Indianapolis year-round, allowing his daughters to finish their schooling there. There still are some signs of the old Watson spark, though. In his Indianapolis garage, he keeps a sprint car which he tinkers with when time allows, alternately dropping a racing Ford or Offy into the engine compartment "just to be different." While he races it infrequently, the sprint car has shown amazing prowess against its Chevy-powered contemporaries. "If I really campaigned the sprint circuit like some guys do I think I could really get it running good," he relates with a flash of the old confidence

Confidence is also evident in Watson's evaluation of Mosley, whose off-the-track shyness is both uncommon and misleading. "I think he's going to be a great little driver. He's improved with every race he's run."

Still, it is the past of which Watson can speak with the most verve, even back to the hot-rodding days at Glendale when he made his first and only try at being a racing driver. "I was going to be the driver for that first car I built, but I was retired in a hurry," he reveals with an embarrassed grin. "I hot-lapped it a few times and thought there was nothing to it. Then, when I went to qualify, I spun it two or three times in the first turn. So I quit. I guess I was too much of a coward to be a driver. I've been building cars ever since."

The great days of his roadster triumphs are still fresh in his memory, too. Typically, when he singles out the car he feels was his best, he points to one that didn't win at Indy, one that, in fact, ran only thirteen laps. "I think the best roadster I ever had was the one I came out with in 1957. That's the one Troy Ruttman drove at the Speedway. He was leading it until the engine started to overheat and he dropped out after about thirteen laps," Watson recalls as he stands in front of the garage where his latest rear-engine model sits idly. "I think we had it over the field that year. Even with the Novis, Ruttman was really flying that year."

As he talks of those days when his cars were always the ones to be beaten, A J. Watson, who has watched other men beat him for so many years since, shoves his hands under the waistband of his pants and glances down briefly at the ground, where his foot kicks restlessly at a small smooth stone.

After a few moments, he kicks the pebble away, rubs his hands together, and walks back into his garage and the glaring realities of a new order.

37. *Herkules*

THE WHITE car with the long snout rolls through the sliding, rattling gate. Its front wheels snap to the left, and the car turns obediently onto the gray pit apron.

As the tuberous car, resembling a giant metal cucumber with wheels, moves down the pit lane, cheers burst out from the scattered clumps of spectators in the tier of bleacher seats behind the pits.

A man with a crewcut, pushing the car along with one hand and steering it with the other, lifts his hand from the steering wheel momentarily to acknowledge the cheers, then he and the two men who are pushing at the rear corners of the car continue on down the pit lane.

That sequence has been repeated twenty or thirty times each May for the past five years. The cheers are as loud and enthusiastic the thirtieth time as they are the first. The man steering the car smiles as broadly when the crowd first cheers as he did five years ago or, for that matter, ten years ago.

Jim Hurtubise has been turning on Indianapolis fans for ten years, and he probably couldn't turn them off if he wanted to. The legend of "Herk," as his fans call him, began in 1960 when, as a brash young rookie, he qualified for his first Indy race just a tick of the watch under 150 miles an hour. It was the closest anyone had come to what was then the magical figure of 150 mph, and it was the last time Jim Hurtubise surprised any of the thousands of Indy onlookers. The fans expected spectacular things of Jim from then on. He drove spectacular cars like the Novis and drove them spectacularly until they cracked under the strain.

In 1965, another element was added to the legend that forever cemented the emotional bond between the Indy crowd and the short, stubby man from North Tonawanda, New York. Horribly burned in a racing wreck at Milwaukee less than a year before, Hurtubise came back to Indianapolis with his future as a racing driver seriously in doubt. After the Milwaukee crash the doctors told him he would never drive again, but when they told Jim they would have to set his badly-burned hands in a fixed position, he insisted they be shaped to fit the contours of a steering wheel.

His raw, gnarled arms were still painful and weak when Jim returned to Indianapolis the following May, but he was determined to climb right back on the fiery stallion that had thrown him so viciously. Most of the car owners were skeptical, but finally Andy Granatelli let Jim try one of the backup Novis. He promptly qualified it for the race, although near the rear of the field.

On race day, "Herk" proved his point in one lap, passing half the field with gusto on the backstretch in the first lap. That was the extent of his glory, though, as the burst of power and sheer guts shattered the Novi's transmission, ending his race after one lap.

Jim's courtship of the Indy crowd was not over, however. After a brief affair with a rear-engine machine, he stubbornly set out on a one-man crusade to defend the tried-and-true front-engined roadster. Building his own streamlined roadster, which he dubbed "Mallard," he attempted to demonstrate that the front-

At Indy in 1969 is Jim Hurtubise with his front-engine Mallard.

engine concept was not dead in racing. In large measure, he was motivated by a feeling that the flimsy rear-engines were not as safe as the solid-axle roadsters and a realization that the owners of the really good cars—whether front or rear-engine —had begun to shy away from him after his Milwaukee crash.

Jim, unfortunately, had picked up a reputation as a wall-crasher. A daring driver from the earliest days, he seemed to have more than his share of scrapes with the cold gray Indy wall. In fact, the first rear-engine car he had driven there painted a mural of ugly black smudges on the south wall when it smashed against the concrete during practice.

Some car owners had come to suspect Jim's arms no longer were strong enough to cope with a race car even though he competed in eight 500s—five before his accident, and three after— without a serious mishap. "Hurtubise always did take that little extra chance," said one car owner, shortly after Jim clipped the wall with his Mallard on a 1968 qualifying run. "It just seems to get him in more trouble now than it used to."

His attachment to the front-engine Mallard added to his troubles, too. Introduced in 1967, the car missed the race that year, made it in 1968 but ran only nine laps before giving out, and missed again in 1969, 1970, and 1971. Championing the cause of the front-engine was costing Jim the one thing he wanted most, the opportunity to charge around the old Indy oval with a chance of winning the classic 500 race. That would prove to be the one day when all the courage and cheering really would mean something to him. Still, his obstinate devotion to the front-engine car was one of great proportions in the eyes of the Indy fans, who rewarded him with their undying affection and loyalty. Even so, that devotion did weaken somewhat in 1972, as Jim landed an Indy ride in a rear-engine car for the first time since 1966. But he still brought along the old roadster and defended its virtues. "I'm sure the car's capable of running over qualifying speed."

Back at his garage on a May afternoon, Jim Hurtubise leans against the rear wheel of his car and chats with the constant stream of well-wishers who search him out in Indy's Gasoline Alley. He sits relaxed, his face in an almost perpetual grin, his driving uniform peeled down to his waist. From his T-shirt sleeves extend his scarred arms with their stiffly curled hands.

One side of his face is scarred too, but it's not as noticeable as his grimly deformed hands. Photographers, however, still detect a self-conscious shift of Jim's eyes whenever they aim their cameras at him.

Jim talks good-naturedly of his persistent but frustrating efforts to make his front-engine Mallard competitive with the low-slung rear-engine cars that now dominate Indy racing. He remains sure his sturdy, solid-axle roadster is superior to those fragile newcomers with their delicate suspension systems. "I like

Hurtubise, waiting to make qualifying run the last day of time trials at Indianapolis in 1971.

it better than having all those little shafts you have on the rear-engines, and I feel safer in it. I really didn't mind the rear-engines, but I decided I wanted to build something better. If I didn't think it could win, I wouldn't monkey with it. I've proved the car will go fast, but I've just had trouble with my engines. I've had a lot of bad luck with the car. I never have had any good luck in racing, when you get right down to it."

He talks also of his racing at other tracks in NASCAR's Grand National headliners and in smaller sportsman stock events. After

his Milwaukee crash, he gradually moved to the stock car circuits from the more demanding Indy-car and sprint car programs. "There's a lot of good Grand National racing and these
sportsmans, well I enjoy running them," relates the man who,
before his bad crash, won four USAC big-car races and eighteen
USAC sprint car features. "I always enjoyed the sprint cars and
other open-cockpit racing. It's just that one day I decided I
wanted to go this way."

The exceptions to that decision have been, naturally enough,
the glorious five hundred miler at Indianapolis and later, the
similar contests at Ontario and Pocono. It was a simple matter
of keeping the legends alive, both Indy's and Jim Hurtubise's. "I
guess it's because I have something different and have always
had something a little different at the Speedway," he says of his
Indy appeal, coyly shifting the focus from himself to the machines he's driven. But he does admit to an awareness of the fans'
feeling for Jim Hurtubise, the man, beyond any considerations
of his cars. He recognizes the cheers from the stands are as much
for his courage and determination as anything else. "It just
makes me want to try harder," he concedes in acknowledging his
public's sentiments.

Later that afternoon, Jim Hurtubise will zip up his driving
uniform and push his balky roadster out toward the pit lane,
turning left just beyond the sliding gate. As the cheers swell up
once more, he will wave quickly at the stands and amid shouts
of "Go get'em Herk" will move on down the lane, determined
once again to try as hard as he knows how.

38. When They're Good . . .

STOCK CAR drivers at Indy—one of the strangest enigmas in auto
racing. Stock car drivers have been migrating from the big superspeedways of the South to the flatter Indianapolis oval for years,

and their record has been one of marked extremes. When they're good, they're very good, but when they're bad, they don't come back. More have spun or crashed, then packed up and gone home, than have done well. And none of them has ever won the classic open-cockpit 500-miller.

Such stock car stalwarts as Fred Lorenzen, Curtis Turner, Cale Yarborough, and Junior Johnson have journeyed to Indy over the years, and each has left with a rather glum feeling towards Indy racing after turning in a less-than-spectacular performance.

In comparison, though, is Paul Goldsmith, a slender dark-haired Hoosier who was a motorcycle champion before becoming a top stocker. He ran exceptionally well in the 500 in the early sixties, posting a third and a fifth on his Indy record. And Marshall Teague, one of southern stock car racing's finest during the fifties, was a consistent challenger in his Indianapolis appearances.

Yet, with their successes, those two stock car standouts were touched by even greater controversy and tragedy than their less successful colleagues. Goldsmith was suspended from open-cockpit racing in 1963 for competing in a non-USAC race and never raced in the 500 again, and Teague met death during practice for an Indy-car race at Daytona, one of the stock car world's most famous tracks.

More recently, in 1970, three of the country's top stock car drivers came to Indianapolis to race the fragile open-wheeled Indy cars. Their efforts that May again reflected the differences in those of their predecessors, but with one major difference. Charlie Glotzbach, the soft-spoken racer from southern Indiana who had practiced at Indy the year before, spun twice in the same day early in May. Next Donnie Allison, another of NASCAR's big-name competitors, spun and hit the wall during the Indy practice period—though he later qualified for, and finished, the race itself. But the unofficial leader of the southern stock car delegation, 31-year-old Lee Roy Yarbrough from Columbia, South Carolina, practiced diligently and without embarrassment. He seemed ready to make the big breakthrough by extending the hottest winning streak in stock car history into the Indy-car arena.

The previous season had been a record-smashing success for

Yarbrough. He had won seven big superspeedway races on the NASCAR circuit, an unprecedented feat. In the process, he had become the first man ever to complete a stock car "Grand Slam" —winning at each of the South's five original supertracks—in a single season. At the wheel of Junior Johnson's factory-backed Ford Torino, he had completely dominated the 1969 Grand National action with two big wins at Daytona, two at Darlington, and single triumphs at Charlotte, Atlanta, and Rockingham. For his efforts, Lee Roy pocketed some $187,000, $50,000 more than any NASCAR driver had ever won in a season. The spectacular victory skein also brought Yarbrough Ford Motor Company's "Man of the Year" award and "Driver of the Year" honors from four racing organizations. On top of all his stock car achievements, Lee Roy was the eighth fastest qualifier for the Indy 500 and ran a strong race until turbocharger failure sidelined him.

So, when Lee Roy Yarbrough came to Indianapolis the next May, he was not just another stock car jockey trying his hand at open-cockpit racing. He was clearly a man who could do something about the image of stockers at Indy. And, in his off-track conversations, he confidently predicted the lot of stock car drivers was going to improve dramatically.

"This year, I just expect to see all that change," Yarbrough said, regarding the stockers' generally undistinguished past history at Indy.

Yarbrough, who himself had spun twice during the 1967 Indy race, underscored the basic natural ability of stock car racers as their ticket to eventual success in other forms of racing, like Indianapolis.

"All the drivers I've met around the world—they are race car drivers," Lee Roy elaborated in his smooth Carolina drawl. "They're not just road race drivers or oval drivers or stock car drivers; they can adjust to what they're doing. If he's got a natural ability—true, he may be better at a certain kind of racing— he'll make himself adapt to whatever he is doing. And I think this year you'll see more stock car drivers branching out into other kinds of racing."

Lee Roy quickly discounted the idea that the adjustment from the more secure closed cockpits of the heavy iron stocks to the open cockpits of the Indy cars was a serious handicap for himself and his NASCAR comrades. "By the same token, the open-wheel car is so much easier to drive than a stock car, physically," he noted.

Yarbrough also dismissed the fact that some stock car drivers came to Indy and then decided it wasn't for them. "So what? A lot of other people crawled into one of the cars and didn't like it either. A stock car driver is a racer, just like any other."

One had only to watch Lee Roy Yarbrough in 1970 to see what he meant. In addition to his plans to race the Indianapolis

Lee Roy Yarbrough (98) and Charlie Glotzbach (99).

and California 500-milers that year, Lee Roy was laying the groundwork for branching out even further, into the world of the sophisticated Can-Am cars. Even as he prepared for his third Indy race, Yarbrough was embroiled in arranging for himself to race in one of the powerful Can-Am cars on the tricky road courses unknown to most NASCAR pilots.

"I've entertained this thought for a couple of years now," he noted, "I know you can't jump in there and blow those guys off right away, but I have an offer to drive a good car and I thought I would get in and give it a try. I think it will take a lot of thought on my behalf, but I'm certainly prepared to do this. I know I'm not known as a road racer, but I'm certainly going at it with an open mind."

His ventures into new areas of racing had been prompted, at least partially, by Ford's withdrawal of financial backing from its Grand National teams. That action helped turn Yarbrough toward Indy and road racing and made running the full NASCAR schedule impractical.

"We're being very selective on the races we run," he related on the outlook he and Johnson were adopting for 1970. "Right now, we're just playing this thing race-by-race," he added. "The main thing we're doing is looking for a sponsor who can put the kind of money into this that Ford Motor Compnay did."

Until such a sponsor could be found, Yarbrough conveniently had more free time available to develop his Indy-car and Can-Am skills. With both those enterprises going for him, Yarbrough appeared to be the very man to dispel the tarnished image of the stock car fraternity in other racing circles. His hard work and hard driving at Indianapolis convinced even the most skeptical observers of that. His Indianapolis experiences had shown, too, that he was not going to settle for anything less than winning. Yarbrough, the master of the southern superspeedways, had made it clear in 1969, when he passed up a suggestion that his malfunctioning turbocharger could be fixed to keep him running near the rear of the pack, that he was shooting for only one place—first.

"That's the reason for coming here," he observed a year later as he stood along the Indy pit wall. "That's my prime reason anyway."

39. *Of Wheelchairs and Cantaloupes*

THE WHEELCHAIR, its metal frame glistening in the sun, rolled steadily down the pit lane. The young man in it rhythmically whipped the chair along in powerful spurts, his sun-burned, tightly-muscled arms expertly pushing down on the spoked wheels as they turned. Pressed against the side of the wheelchair seat was a red, white, and black decal that read: "USAC Chief Mechanic."

Beside the man in the wheelchair walked a tall man with a hard, chiseled face. He wore the rumpled suit of shiny fire-resisting cloth that race drivers wear. Across the left breast of the suit, stitched in red script, was written: "Darrell Dockery."

The pair moved down the pit row, passing the three or four racing machines sitting quietly along the pit wall just north of the gate into the Indy garage area. They moved on past the cars to the very end of the pit lane, where the concrete inner track wall opens to let the cars off the track. There they stopped beside a low-slung red race car. Its paint slightly faded, the car bore a ragged scar across its nose, a jagged mesh of fiberglass resembling a nervous surgeon's incision.

The car, flashing less chrome than the others passed earlier, obviously was one that had more sweat than money in it. Its body was clean and solid but with few frills, and its engine bore the big dull-gray exhaust pipes that identified it as the power-plant of Indy's less-affluent set, the stock-block Chevy.

Dockery walked over to the two officials standing by the small wooden scoring table on the inside of the track wall where rookie tests are administered. The man in the wheelchair rolled up beside the red car, reached into the engine with a small silver wrench, and made a few quick twists with his hand.

Beside his left shoulder as he leaned into the engine compartment, written in white paint on the side of the car, were the words: "Chief Mechanic—Larry Burton."

Larry Burton (right) and Darrell Dockery.

Larry Burton began tinkering with fast cars as a teenager. In the early 1950s, he served his apprenticeship in the Muncie, Indiana, speed shop of Tom Cherry, a legendary figure in Midwest racing circles.

His legs worked then. His teenage years and a tour in the Air Force behind him, he set out on a career as a racing driver in the summer of 1959. Just turned twenty-one, he wheeled old jalopies and motorcycles around countless dusty race tracks with the typical blind desperation of a young man pursuing the glitter and glory of racing success.

But before that summer was over, Larry Burton was wheeling a totally different vehicle, a slow and balky wheelchair. Cut down by crippling polio, he filed away his ambitions as a race driver and concentrated on what seemed to him the next-best thing under the circumstances, becoming a racing mechanic.

He went full speed after his new avocation. "Three weeks after I had polio," Larry recalled with a measure of pride, "I was out of the hospital and working on a guy's drag car."

He kept right on working, pouring his growing mechanical know-how into a variety of cars until news of the remarkable mechanic who could make engines hum from a wheelchair reached the men who operate racing's top teams. It reached Mickey Thompson, the sportsman whose racing ventures spanned the speed spectrum from Indianapolis to the Bonneville salt flats. Thompson put Larry on the payroll and put him to work on his eccentric Indy cars. He also took Larry to the Bonneville flats where Thompson launched his many assaults upon various land-speed records.

It was in the endless expanses of the Utah speed range that Larry discovered one particular handicap he had to concede to his more able-bodied counterparts. "The salt ate my wheelchair up. It was pretty grim."

Sports car racer Charlie Hayes also learned of Larry's unusual talents and gave him the task of preparing his McLaren-Chevy for the demanding Can-Am circuit.

In the winter of 1969, road racer Bill Simpson utilized Larry's abilities by signing him on to handle the mechanical chores on his formula car in the Tasman Series at courses in Australia and New Zealand.

On his return from the Tasman expedition, Larry became involved in the venture that brought him to Indianapolis in May 1970. Darrell Dockery, a West Coast sprint car driver who worked with Larry on the Mickey Thompson operation a few years before, was ready to tackle Indy. He spent the past few months packing cantaloupes in California and saved enough cash to buy an old Indy car.

After buying the car, Dockery turned to Larry Burton to put it in shape for an Indianapolis try. "Darrell just called me up and said, 'We're going to do it.' And here we are."

Larry Burton sat in front of his garage on the south side of Gasoline Alley. Beside him stood Darrel Dockery. Behind him, inside the narrow cubicle cut out of the long white speedway garage building, sat their race car.

The skies over the Indianapolis speedway layout were dark with rain clouds; drops of moisture splattered spasmodically on the pavement along the rows of garages. But the rain made little difference to Larry Burton and Darrell Dockery. They weren't going to race today, the first day of time trials for the Memorial Day 500.

While others were roaring around the track qualifying their cars for the race, the two men stationed in front of their quiet garage chatted casually, waiting for the day's activities to cease, waiting to go shopping for a new engine. Like a half-dozen others who tried to get by with a stock-block engine, Burton and Dockery didn't make it. Like the others, they learned the hard truth—that the stock-block powerplants would not get them over the 160 mile per hour mark at Indy, would not put them in the race.

So now they waited out the qualifying, and the rain, to start again on their almost hopeless search for a better engine, one of the double-overhead-cam racing Fords or maybe an Offy.

While he waited there in the stony silence of the garage area, Larry Burton talked of the particular problems faced by a wheelchair-bound racing mechanic. "I seem to get things done. I just have to do it a little differently. I haven't found anything I couldn't do, though. It's really no problem, just sometimes I have to figure out weird ways to do things. I get a lot of burns because when the car comes in I have to lean on something, so I end up leaning on the hot headers. Of course, with these low rear-engine cars, I do have an advantage." Larry went on, his face suddenly beaming devilishly, "The other guys stand up and bend over these things and their backs kill them. I don't have that problem. Actually, the only problem I have at this place is out there," he commented, becoming serious and pointing westward toward the parking lot behind the garage area. "They might pave the parking lot for me. Sometimes I get bogged down in the gravel."

Just then, the pace of the rain quickened, dancing across the asphalt walkway in front of the garages. The pavement darkened all the way across in a few minutes. Cars and crews that had been on the other side of the concrete grandstands between the garages and the pits began to filter back into the three rows of garage buildings. The yellow light had been turned on. Qualifying was done for the day.

With life returning to the garage area, Larry Burton looked up at Dockery, who was standing beside him. He shot a quizzical look his way, thought for a moment, then said, "How about it? Let's go see if we can drum up an engine."

Whipping his wheelchair around at a right angle, Burton darted off down the wide walkway, Dockery quickly falling into an easy stride beside him. They disappeared around the corner of the garage building, their eyes fixed in a determined forward stare.

40. A Sudden Storm

LIKE A TORNADO from the dark Indiana sky, Johnny Rutherford came out of nowhere and spun the Indianapolis Motor Speedway on its ear. With the suddenness of a thunderclap, Rutherford lashed the nerves and necks of the totally unprepared speedway crowd that had gathered to watch the first day of time trials for the 1970 Indianapolis 500. The 200,000 or so assembled fans thought they read all the storm warnings for the Saturday qualifying session, but racing, like the weather, is sometimes unpredictable.

The fried-chicken-eating, beer-drinking fans already saw what they thought would be the day's highlight: A. J. Foyt made a run for the pole position, and Al Unser had taken it away from him. All that was left to do, reasoned the complacent fans, was eat more chicken, drink more beer, and wait for Mario Andretti to join Foyt and Unser on the front row of three. Nobody really paid much attention when Rutherford moved onto the track for an apparently routine qualifying run.

There was no obvious reason to watch Johnny Rutherford. He was a good driver but rather unimpressive since his arms were smashed in a 1966 sprint car crash and his hands roasted in a 1968 fire at Phoenix. Never had so many people been so wrong about anyone.

When the speed for Rutherford's first lap was announced by

the astonished track announcer, the crowd was shocked out of their revels. His speed was 171.135 miles per hour, faster than either Unser or Foyt managed. Startled, stunned, and suddenly reminded of Rutherford's past misfortunes, most of the bewildered crowd jumped to their feet shouting encouragement for the driver and his four-year-old car that had drawn almost no notice when they rolled onto the track only moments before.

With each lap Rutherford drove, he lost just a little speed from that first mind-blowing lap. But when the checkered flag fell, he still had a chance to edge out Unser for the pole spot in the thirty-three-car race field. The crowd, wildly cheering seconds before, now waited breathlessly for the announcement.

It came, and Rutherford missed getting the pole. The crowd cheered anyway. After putting up a fantastic challenge, he missed ripping the pole from Unser's grasp by a tick of the watch—one 100th of a second, to be exact—but that didn't even matter. Johnny Rutherford whipped Indy into a frenzy, and gave it a severe case of whiplash in the process.

"Just beautiful," Johnny shouted to his young crew chief, Mike Devin, as he rolled to a stop along the pit lane. Devin and his crew could hardly contain their joy over the fast run, a run three miles an hour faster than Rutherford ever had turned in during the two weeks of practice prior to Saturday's time trials. "I finally got the feel of it this morning. We did some things to the car and went over 170 this morning—that's the first time I'd ever gone that fast. I guess we just got it dialed in and working right," the elated Texan said, referring to his car, a remodeled 1966 Eagle.

Asked if he was surprised he had run that fast Rutherford answered directly, "No, I kind of anticipated it. I knew if we only ran 167 or 168 we were in trouble. When I came by the first time, I knew we were on the way."

With his run completed and all the photographs and television interviews done, Rutherford, who never before started better than the fourth row at Indianapolis and never finished the 500-mile distance in six tries, walked back to the garage area with his crew, musing over how very close he had come in the chase for the pole spot. "If I just hadn't bobbled in the fourth turn, I might have blown Al off the pole," he exclaimed, eyes flashing, as well-wishers began to congregate around the yellow number eighteen car in the garage area.

The congratulations continued even as raindrops began to drip down from the blackening Indiana sky. It would rain on many men's parades this day, but not Johnny Rutherford's. Even though he had missed the pole, he was still the happiest man at the speedway. He had taken the staid old track and its crowd of 200,000 through the eye of a tornado.

41. Tomorrow Is Next Year

THE LITTLE BOY in an orange shirt was crying uncontrollably. His father bent down and jostled him playfully. "Hey, come on, it's alright," the stocky, balding man pleaded.

The boy kept on crying. As his father stood erect again, his colorless face clearly showed he too was on the verge of crying. His wife, a red racing jacket draped over her shoulders, clutched her husband's arm in her struggle to hold back tears.

Her husband, still wearing a wrinkled racing suit, knelt down to the little boy again and tried to coax him with a forced smile but the boy cried on.

His mouth drawn tight, trembling at the corners, Dick Simon led his wife and son away from the area in front of Gasoline Alley, disappearing around the corner of the fence enclosing the garage compound. If ever a man wanted to cry, he did.

Dick Simon was an insurance executive from Utah. Before taking up racing he had been a champion parachutist. After working hard all month, he had qualified for the race early—and very securely, it seemed at the time.

He was ready, he thought, to start the 1971 Indianapolis 500, his second 500. He was so confident of his position he turned his reserve car over to a talented rookie, John Mahler, and worked hard for another week to put that car into the race as well. But on Sunday, the last day for qualification, Simon's cushion of slower qualifiers was slowly eaten away, and late in the cloudy afternoon his own car no longer was listed on the electronic scoring pole located near the end of the Indy pit lane.

Desperately he had tried to qualify again, first in one car, then in another. But when the gun fired at 6:00 P.M., the only thing Dick Simon, his wife, and his son could do was get away from the crowd and try not to cry.

Jim Hurtubise didn't cry. He had been at the game too long, had been denied too many times in the past. As he rode through the pits in an ambulance, he smiled and waved to the crowd, which gave him a standing ovation. Hurtubise leaned over to the ambulance driver and whispered, "Step on it, fella. There's still some time left."

There wasn't really, and Hurtubise knew it. By the time he got to the track hospital for a routine check, there would be no time left. But Jim Hurtubise had not received a standing ovation today or other days because he conceded defeat easily.

There had been an anticipatory air to the moment. As Hurtubise lapped the big oval at speeds closer and closer to that needed to get into the race, firemen in the trucks stationed around the track started their motors and nervously slipped their trucks into gear. Seconds later, Hurtubise's awkward old roadster swerved headlong into the wall. The fire trucks were ripping onto the track before the crumpled race car rolled to a stop at the north end of the pits.

Bob Harkey could neither cry nor smile. He was the man in the position the Indy crowd calls the "bubble"—the one Hurtubise and all the others who took to the track in the final minutes before 6:00 P.M. were trying to replace in the race-day lineup.

Harkey, a journeyman driver, hadn't started in the 500 since 1964. He sat on the pit wall, still wearing his driving suit, staring down at the pavement. His crash helmet rested against his left leg. He sat motionless for several moments before moving out to a group of men standing near the yellow line down the middle of the pit lane.

Members of his crew smiled silently at him as he joined the little group. The drivers there, ones who were safely qualified, needled him, telling him the car due to go out next had turned fantastic speeds just a few minutes earlier. They said it for each car that moved past them on its way to the track's surface.

Harkey smiled each time they said it. After the jokes, his eyes gazed unblinkingly at the track and his ears listened for the reports on the speeds of the cars circling the giant oval.

He knew most of the cars left couldn't go fast enough. But he also knew that magic sometimes happens in those final minutes of Indy qualifying. And he suspected Dick Simon, the racing latecomer who seemed to improve with every race he drove, was the man he had to worry about.

Simon pulled out of the pits in one car, but its engine was sputtering so badly he didn't even try to qualify it. Later, he roared onto the track in another car, one he had never even sat in before.

As Simon moved by the cluster of men in which Harkey stood, young Billy Vukovich said he didn't think Simon could do it. George Follmer, who had raced against Simon back in their roadracing days, disagreed and snapped up Vukovich's offer for a two-dollar wager. But Simon could not master the unfamiliar car in three short laps, and his speeds fell well below those posted by Harkey earlier in the day. Follmer surrendered his two dollars to a smug Vukovich.

When Simon failed, Harkey looked relieved. Even though a car was on the track when the gun finally sounded, he knew it was one that had no magic left in it and his face broke into a broad smile.

Somewhere else, a little boy in an orange shirt began crying. In the infield hospital, Jim Hurtubise was telling a doctor to hurry up with his examination.

The fans began filtering slowly from the bleachers behind the pits. The first act of the drama was over. Nearly a week later, the curtain would go up again. The play would resume. The actors would be different, but the ending would be very much the same. Men would fight back tears. Others would smile. And tomorrow would be a full year away.

42. Gennnttlllemmmmen . . .

AT PRECISELY 10:53 A.M. race day morning, speedway owner Tony Hulman delivers those electrifying words, "Gennnttlllemmmmen . . . start your engines."

Thirty-three whirring electric starters crank life into a like number of exotic, powerful racing engines. With their eager drivers pumping blasts of fuel into their spasmodically scream-ing motors, the thirty-three fragile cars roll away from the crowded starting line to fall in behind the pace car like three strings of brightly-colored, booming Chinese firecrackers.

For five minutes, two slow laps around the two and one-half mile track, the thirty-three men and their machines prance be-fore the mammoth crowd of people lining the fences around the charcoal colored oval with the ghost-white concrete wall at its rim. Steeling themselves for the coming ordeal, the men with masks and spaceman-like helmets wring their gloved hands ner-vously on the quaking steering wheels of their cars.

Then as the clock hands edge toward eleven o'clock, the pace car and its eleven-row flock pour out of the fourth turn and rush headlong toward the starting line. The pace car slips away to the inside of the track and heads for cover in the pit lane, leaving the thirty and three to bear down on starter Pat Vidan, a gray-haired man, poised like a statue, standing at the starting line with the green flag raised over his head.

The hundreds of thousands who have come to see, hear, and smell this, the moment of all moments in racing, rise and press against one another to watch Vidan whip the green flag down across his body and dangle it in front of the freckled cloud of motion sweeping toward him. The flag dances around in the air and the thirty-three cars fly past it, their engines now whining like fighter planes on a strafing mission.

All in the crowd snap around to watch the thirty-three dive into the first turn and, in the moments of silence which follow before the sounds and sights and smells flash by again, stand spellbound in the wake of this almost mystical experience.

By the time the cars come around again, the thirty-three men are settling back in their cockpits to spend the afternoon racing for the biggest prize in sports. The hundreds of thousands of men, women, and children, already turning lobster-red in the hot May sun, are settling back into their seats, dragging out the sandwiches and beer they lugged across the infield hours before.

For some three hours this day, they remain like that, isolated from the world outside, locked together in the seance of speed, spectacle, and survival—the Indianapolis 500.

43. Race Day Morning

CLINT BRAWNER just didn't look comfortable, moving around the pit area in spotless blue trousers with white stripes and stovepipe cuffs and a white turtleneck sweater.

The sponsor put Clint and the rest of his crew in the modern-fashion outfits, but on the leather-faced old craftsman it just didn't look right. He still had his old straw hat though, which probably had come all the way from Phoenix to ward off the Indiana sun, but even it looked out of place with the outfit, especially without the red bandana that was usually stuck out of Clint's pocket or wrapped around his head.

He would have looked more comfortable in his white denim trousers with an occasional grease spot and his old white T-shirt. He had worn them most of the thirty-five years he worked on race cars, and he wore them last year when he came to Victory Lane. Clint Brawner had looked natural in that outfit, in that place, a year ago, but this year his sponsor dressed him in stovepipe pants and turtleneck sweater, and his red-splotched old face was the only natural-looking thing about the man.

Beside him stood his young protege, Jim McGee. Slim, dark-haired, with a boyish face, his clothes fit him well. They were the clothes of a young, modern man.

The two, the old master mechanic and his youthful partner, stood there in a contrast it was hard not to notice.

Politics crept into the Indianapolis Motor Speedway, not on little cat feet but on big kangaroo feet, pouncing down once, hard, then springing away.

Birch Bayh, the young and handsome senator from Indiana, the man who from time to time gets mentioned as potential presidential timber, had just been introduced to the crowd. And the crowd, in uncharacteristic bad humor, booed him.

The Hoosier crowd, which cheered television stars earlier and would cheer for race drivers later, let something get in the way of its holiday spirit when the youthful and sometimes controversial senator flashed by on the rear deck of the pace car convertible. Perhaps some political disagreement somehow clouded their vision for just a moment, for the crowd booed him in much the same way they would have booed a baseball umpire who called a player for the home team out at the plate.

Later, Edgar Whitcomb, the gray-haired war-hero governor of the state, strode down the pit lane with radio announcer Sid Collins. Photographers and newsmen shadowed the tall, sun-tanned pair as they exchanged small talk about the race, the weather.

A short distance away, behind the Tower Terrace section of grandstands, Dr. Otis Bowen stood with his wife and family. He was casually dressed, wearing a brightly colored plaid sport shirt and no tie. Bowen, who challenged Whitcomb for the governorship two years ago and could well be the next man to sit in the governor's chair, chatted with his family as they waited for one of their members to emerge from a restroom. They were undisturbed by reporters or photographers as they stood there. Then Bowen and his family, carrying boxes of sandwiches as many speedway spectators do, moved on, disappearing into the sea of people shuffling along behind the grandstands.

The two men walked through the gate into the pits. Both carried racing helmets and wore driver's suits, but neither had a car in the race.

Bob Veith, his thick hair gray for some years now, and Al Miller, without much hair for as long, stood in the middle of the

Denis Hulme checks the engine in his Team McLaren car.

pit lane and scanned the scene for a moment. The men, both a little paunchy now, were taking on the roles of relief drivers for this special auto race.

They both had driven in this race many times before, and both had come fairly close to winning it. But that was many years ago and they no longer come to the speedway with a car of their own. They must wait until there are almost no cars left and time has just about run out before they can have their chance to qualify. And when they again are unable to start the race, the two aging drivers get into their driving suits on race day just in case relief drivers are needed.

A relief driver has won this rich race only twice in fifty-four races, and none has done it since 1941. Relief drivers seldom are needed anymore unless the weather is monstrously hot and humid.

This particular day, the skies are overcast with dark rain clouds and the temperature is only moderately warm. Still, Bob Veith and Al Miller put on their driving suits and carry their helmets with them. Miller moves down the pit lane, saying hello to the crewmen and car owners of the cars in the race, letting them know he is available just in case. Veith stands at the edge of the track, looking over the quiet cars as they sit, ready to race without him.

Both seem to be holding onto the dream of winning this great race, but the faces of these two old warriors hint that they know they never will now. But they are here anyway. There is no other place for them to go.

44. The Kiss

IT TOOK Andy Granatelli three years to go twenty-five miles, the last twenty-five miles, at Indianapolis, but he finally made it in 1969.

Granatelli, whose turbine-powered cars almost won the race twice, found himself in the same agonizingly familiar position on Memorial Day 1969 that he had been in the two years previous. Nearing the end of the 500 miles, Andy had a car in first place.

This time, he had a piston-engined car, with Mario Andretti at the wheel, leading the way toward Victory Lane. But, for Andy, there was no premature celebrating. He had seen almost certain 500 victories end less than ten laps from the finish in 1967 and 1968 and now he stood, stationed along the wall at the Andretti pit, nervously watching his dream come closer and closer.

Flanked by his brother Vince, mechanic Grant King, and driver Art Pollard, who already retired from the race in another Granatelli car, Andy watched Mario in the red number two flash by with less than forty laps to go.

After Mario disappeared into the first turn, Andy glanced first at the scoring tower on the inside of the track and then at the stopwatches in his hand.

The pit board to Andretti read: "E-Z."

Another fifteen laps later, Pollard and King wandered down the pit lane, leaving only Andy and brother Vince to find out if they would be victorious.

With the ominous 190-lap mark drawing near, Andy takes time to gulp down two cups of water on this sizzling hot day.

The pit board held by the Granatelli crew now reads: "Gurney Sour." This tells Andretti that second place Dan Gurney is now too busy nursing a sick engine home to try to challenge Mario. But there is no indication of relief or confidence in the dark face of Andy Granatelli. Staring blankly at the track, his thoughts undoubtedly are on the final ten laps, twenty-five miles, that have robbed him of victory the last two years.

And then there are just ten laps to go. An interviewer from television's "Wide World of Sports" steps into the pit to ask Andy what he is thinking about. "What do you think?" says Andy, neither smiling nor frowning.

Nine laps to go. A quick drink of water and then Granatelli moves back to the pit wall to hand his stopwatches over to members of his STP crew. Last year, a "flame-out" in Joe Leonard's turbine crushed Andy's hopes at this same point in the race.

Eight laps to go. Andy, his hands on his hips, gazes momentarily at a helicopter hovering over the front straightaway. Some crewmen on the STP team begin tapping their feet nervously, the rhythm quickening as the laps roll by.

Seven laps to go. Andretti flashes by and Granatelli eases the mounting tension by following a late-developing duel for third place between Bobby Unser and Mel Kenyon.

Six laps to go. Very slight smiles creep onto the faces of the crew members, but Andy remains expressionless. He continues to stare out across the steaming race track.

Five laps to go. The "LAP–195" sign is flashed to Andretti. Andy and Vince exchange a brief comment, then return their attention to the track.

Four laps to go. With Andretti already by, a slight, almost imperceptible smile begins to appear on Andy's still-cautious face. Two years ago, the bubble burst at this moment when a six dollar part broke in Parnelli Jones' turbine car while leading by a full lap.

Three laps to go. The crewmen can no longer control themselves and begin clapping each other on the back. Andy waits.

Two laps to go. With newsmen and photographers beginning to gather around the Granatelli pit, Andy and Vince lean over the pit wall to see Andretti speed by and intently watch as starter Pat Vidan picks up the white flag to wave at Mario the next time around.

One lap to go. Almost as if in disbelief, Andy lowers his head and nods slowly. Hurriedly, his crewmen help him into his fire-red sportcoat for the trip to Victory Lane. Yet a small hint of uncertainty still haunts Andy's face.

And now Andretti is coming toward the finish line. An eternity passes, but finally the checkered flag waves for his roaring race car.

The dam bursts. All 275 pounds of Andy Granatelli are vaulting over the pit wall, his hands clasped over his head in a victory sign. He brought cars to this race for over twenty years, came close to winning twice, and now was a winner.

The kiss in Victory Lane.

Mario Andretti moves out of the pits on his way to victory at Indy in 1969.

The STP crew, with chief mechanics Clint Brawner and Jim McGee leading the charge, surround Andy and smother him with hugs of congratulations. The mass bedlam, moving as a single entity, edges toward Victory Lane—that little corner of this giant speedway that only a few men reach.

There, Andy will embrace Mario as if they were meeting for the first time on a busy Italian street. And then Andy will vigorously kiss the man who has made a twenty-year-old dream come true. On occasions such as this, grown men are allowed to embrace and kiss one another.

45. Victory Lane 1970

THE FACES in Victory Lane were all old ones. Most of them had been there before, but they all had their reasons for needing to be there again.

First there was Al Unser. He finished second at Indianapolis three years ago, then crashed the next year and he watched his big brother, Bobby, make the trip to Victory Lane.

Last year, while Andy Granatelli was delivering his famous kiss to Mario Andretti on this very spot, Al was back home in

Albuquerque nursing a broken leg suffered unnecessarily when his motorcycle flipped over on top of him during some horseplay in early May.

Al Unser was on the outer fringe of the small knot of people in Victory Lane before, but never there in the center, his head popping out of the middle of the red, white, and green victory wreath. Never there laughing and celebrating with the men—and one woman—who were making return trips to this roped-off island of grass at the far end of the pits.

There was Parnelli Jones, the still-youthful but balding driving great, who was co-owner of Al's car. He had been there in 1963 after dominating the long race in much the same fashion Unser had this day. But that triumph was marred by a controversy over an oil leak on Jones' car and the ensuing storm over the issue took much of the sweetness out of the victory.

In 1967, Jones had fallen four laps short of returning to Victory Lane when his turbine car coasted to a stop while leading by a country mile. Al Unser finished second that year, the last time Parnelli Jones drove in the 500.

There was George Bignotti, the veteran mechanic who put the car together and kept it like that for 500 miles. He had made the trip to Victory Lane three other times but never with the supremacy of his mechanical creation so clearly demonstrated.

In 1961, A. J. Foyt won with a Bignotti car only when Eddie Sachs made a controversial pit stop a few laps from the finish. Three years later, Foyt again won for Bignotti, but that race claimed the lives of Sachs and another driver, and the other frontrunners were eliminated with a variety of bizarre mechanical failures.

Two years after that, another Bignotti car won, with Graham Hill driving, but during that race eleven cars were eliminated in a first-lap pileup on the mainstretch; most of the ones who survived that melee never made it to the 500-mile mark.

Though a three-time winner, George Bignotti needed to win decisively, as he had, in fact, done this day with the smiling Al Unser behind the wheel of his gun-metal blue racer.

Unser, Jones, Bignotti—they all needed this trip to Victory Lane to even the score with this unsympathetic old race track. Mercilessly, the three men showed their joy at conquering the track, shouting and slapping each other on the back.

They did not, however, kiss each other. This was a different day, a different year, and different people—if a car owner had ever tried to kiss Parnelli Jones, Parnelli probably would have pushed his face in—and the joy was handled differently.

Yet emotion was there again in Victory Lane, in a quieter, more solemn vein. Standing silently just to the left of the three men was Unser's mother, known as "Mom Unser" by those who know better than to call her Mrs. Unser.

She had been there before, too. Another of her sons had brought her there to Victory Lane two years ago. But even years before that, another son, Jerry, her eldest, died at this track without ever completing a lap in competition in the race, without ever getting a chance to go to Victory Lane, that grassy spot where another son now stood. That day, some ten years ago, gave Mom Unser more than enough reason to want to be there in Victory Lane again. The same need would be there should her sons win at Indianapolis a hundred times. For her, the mother of three racing sons, not just two, the score can never be evened. This is as close as she can come.

46. The Shape of Things to Come

THE TWO MEN met at the gate leading to the garage area. They were undoubtedly happy, but they limited their outward signs of celebration to two broad smiles. The man in the race car had just run a long, fast race with apparent little difficulty. The other man, waiting for him at the garage gate, had kept things going smoothly and efficiently in the pits.

Not far away, Al Unser was being slapped on the back by his delirious crew as newsmen shoved microphones into his face and screamed questions at him. But here in the relative quiet of the garage entrance, this young man stepped from his race car, pulled

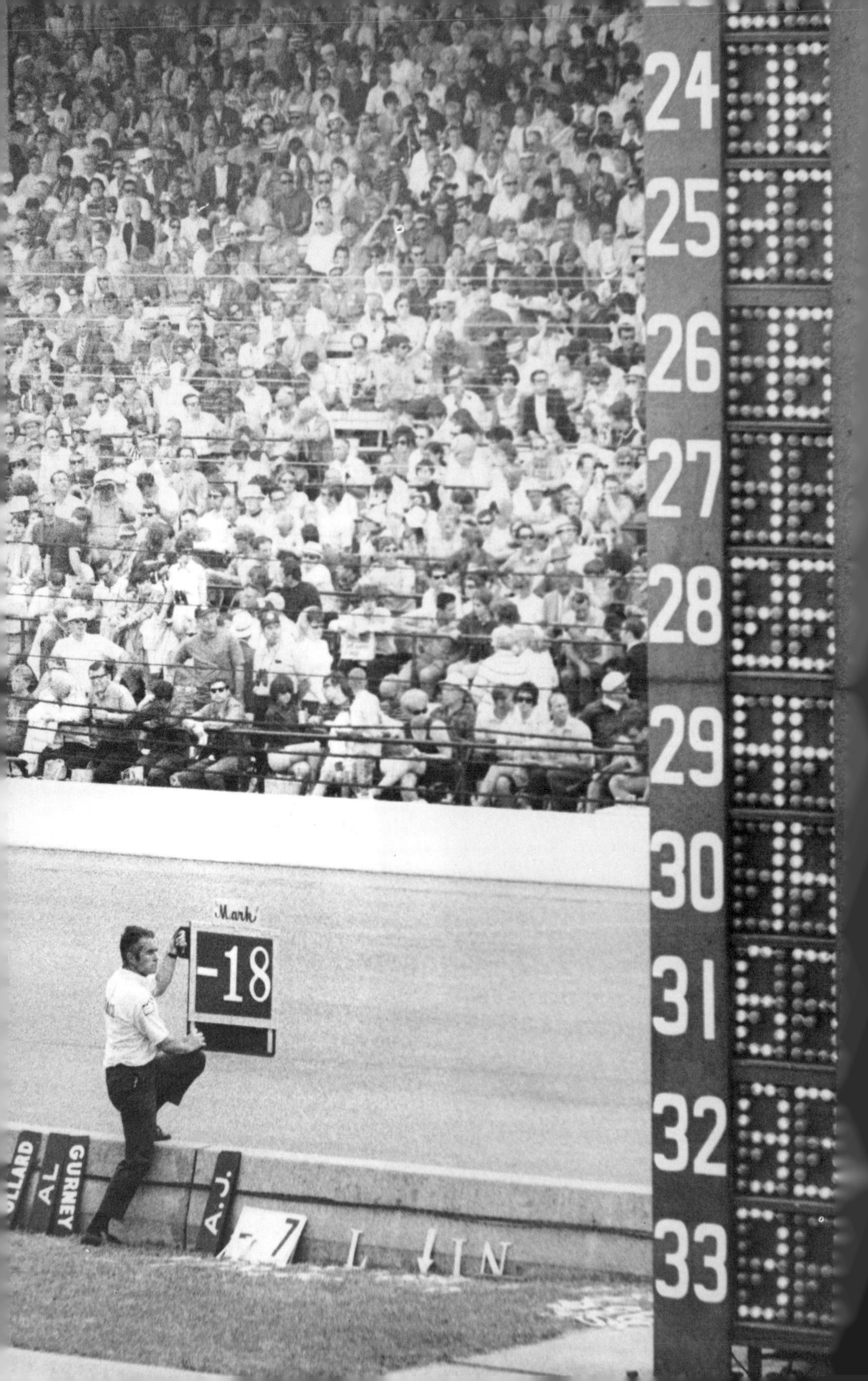

24
25
26
27
28
29
30
31
32
33
Mark
-18
AL
GURNEY
A.J.
7

his helmet from his head, and reached out to shake the hand of the tanned man standing beside the car.

The firm handshake was followed by light conversation that broke the day-long tension of running a race the magnitude of Indianapolis. Then the two, Mark Donohue and Roger Penske, rolled their deep-blue race car back toward the garage area.

The scene lacked the normal exuberance that even a second place finisher can draw at Indianapolis, but the two men, who had worked with such precision and professionalism all month, handled the elation of their near-triumph in much the same manner. It almost seemed reasonable to foresee the same controlled emotions when, some year soon, Donohue, the graduate engineer from Brown University, and Penske, the former race driver, would meet not at the garage gate but in chaotic Victory Lane.

The two Philadelphians exemplified the new breed of racing professionals infiltrating the sport peopled for so long by equally talented but often less disciplined speed devotees. Everything about their approach to Indianapolis this month of May 1970 reflected the premium they placed on efficiency. Their car was simple, clean, and direct. They ran it as much as necessary to get the speed they wanted, but not so much that they wore it out. They performed their mechanical chores matter-of-factly, with little wasted motion.

On race day, Donohue's pit stops literally ran like clockwork. While the car was on the track, Penske, from his post along the inside track wall, flashed precise, no-nonsense signals to his driver every lap of the race. The drivers of the other thirty-two cars had their signals flashed by pit crew members, but here Penske himself took on the job of keeping his driver informed of the ever-changing race situation on each of the 200 laps around the 2½-mile course. When the race ended, Penske calmly collected all the paraphernalia for his pit board and loaded it neatly on the cart to be towed back to the garages by his crew.

Precision, efficiency, professionalism—all had been obvious in the Penske-Donohue operation in its two-year stand at the

Indianapolis 1970—Roger Penske along inner track wall with pit board for Mark Donohue.

Roger Penske with Gary Bettenhausen
before the start of the 1972 Indy 500.

speedway, a consistency that brought them short of victory this
time, but not by very much. "I know it helps to finish the race;
I don't know if it helps to win the race," a weary Donohue says
of this consistency later that same day. "Of course, you come
here to find out what works and what doesn't. If you don't win
it, you always want to try again, so we'll be back next year."

In May 1971, Donohue and Penske were back at Indy for the
third time. But Donohue, who was the favorite choice to win the
500, was forced to drop out of the race on lap sixty-seven with a
gearbox failure. So ended that year's race to fame.

In 1972, however, the Penske- Donohue dream of a trip to Victory Lane was finally realized. In one of the most spectacular
Indianapolis 500 finishes of all times, Mark Donohue roared
across the finish line and right into Victory Lane.

The 1972 race had been led up until the last laps by Gary Bettenhausen, Donohue's teammate from the Roger Penske racing
stable, driving the blue number seven Sunoco-McLaren Special.
When Bettenhausen was forced out in those last laps with engine
trouble, the lead was quickly taken over by Jerry Grant, Bobby
Unser's teammate from the Dan Gurney All American Racers
team. Mark Donohue was only seconds away in second place. On
lap 188, Grant was forced into his pit with tire problems, and
Donohue took over the lead by one full lap. Grant was never able

to overtake Donohue, and in fact, lost his second place finishing position and was dropped down to number twelve by USAC officials, who ruled in favor of a protest by George Bignotti (chief mechanic for Al Unser) that Grant's car was filled with fuel from the pit tank of Bobby Unser. USAC officials declared Grant's attempt ended on lap 188, when the fuel incident occurred. Al Unser, trying for his third straight Indy victory, captured second place, with teammate Joe Leonard finishing third.

With that 1972 Indy victory, the youthful Donohue moves onto the famous list of Indianapolis 500 victors, a living example of that old saying, "if at first you don't succeed, try, try, again."

Penske (left) discusses racing with Mark Donohue (seated in car) at Indianapolis Motor Speedway in 1972.

47. The Last Time I Saw Indy

HOURS BEFORE the Indianapolis crowd pushed and shoved itself into place, the pit crews for the thirty-three starting entries in the 1971 race had filed out from the garage area and put their own particular pits in order.

In each pit, roped off at the rear with plastic apron-strings decorated with checkered flags and sponsor decals, the crewmen carefully arranged the assortment of tools, spare parts, fireproof wearing apparel, and food that would be needed to get them through the day. All brought more things than they could possibly need in a normal three-hour race, as most were familiar with this race's history of abnormal occurrences.

All the pits had endless stacks of red tool trays on rollers, standing ready immediately behind the low wall from which the crews would spring onto the pit apron to service their race cars at least three times today. Stacks of a dozen or more tires, most of which would not be needed, filled one corner at the rear of each pit, next to the brightly-painted fuel tank and its drooping gray hoses. A tall red fire extinguisher stood to one side of each pit. A chalkboard with a name stenciled at the top leaned against either the low wall or the fuel tank in most of the roped-off sections.

All the pits had their similarities, and each, too, had its individual touches. Near the south end of the pit lane, opposite the towering scoring pillar, the pit area prepared by Dan Gurney's blue-shirted crewmen for the entries piloted by 1968 winner Bobby Unser and Jim Malloy featured a portable pantry topped with a glass water cooler. As the race cars were pushed out to the track in the hour before the race, Swede Savage, who would have driven in this race but for a brain-jarring crash in March, and a crew worker munched on bologna-and-cheese sandwiches. To one side of the squat cupboard sat a jar of instant coffee and a box of teabags. Beside them was a sparkling red crash helmet, a spare for Unser or Malloy.

Mark Donohue voodoo doll hanging outside the Indianapolis
garage area of Johnny Rutherford during May 1971.

Moving north, past the opening in the pit wall that led back to
the garages, the Team McLaren pits were spread out with typical
efficiency and order. Enough orange body segments to outfit a
whole new car were strategically placed around the two-car pit
compound. A whitewashed scoring stand rose near the back of
the McLaren pit, with two men in bright-orange shirts already
neatly stacking the papers they would use to keep track of the
cars driven by pole-sitter Peter Revson and team leader Denny
Hulme.

Next to the McLaren layout, the pits for 1970 Indy winner Al
Unser and teammate Joe Leonard were tidy, though somewhat
plain. Only a box lunch tucked beneath one of the fuel tanks and

Drivers meet along the track wall during practice runs
before attempting to qualify for the Indianapolis 500.

another protruding from the top of a stack of tires broke the
sterile appearance of the pit.

The next in the line, that of the Roger Penske-directed crew,
revolved around a dark-blue scoring stand. From there, men in
yellow shirts would follow Mark Donohue, the driver who had
turned laps around the amazing 180-mph mark day after day in
practice and was expected to win this race, and his teammate,
British road racer David Hobbs. Plastic numbers arranged sys-
tematically in a blue box rested in a larger box filled with fresh
pears and oranges, two large cartons of milk, and a supply of
chocolate bars.

North of the Penske section, that of three-time Indy winner
A. J. Foyt and his running mate, NASCAR stalwart Donnie Allison, reflected the same simplicity of organization found in the
Unser-Leonard pit. Only a stack of box lunches and a brand-new
pair of white-and-black driving shoes interrupted the landscape
of tools, tires, and fuel tanks behind the pit wall.

Adjacent to the Foyt pit, those for the team of old favorite
Lloyd Ruby and Cale Yarborough, another NASCAR star, continued the pattern. Eight plastic tubes with red caps, each con-
taining a spotless spark plug, laid beside each of the two fuel

tanks. One of the marchers from the Purdue University band sat on the wall at the Ruby-Yarborough pit with his head in his hands, a victim of the dizzying combination of hot sun and locked knees.

On up the line of pits, the array was generally the same—tools that wouldn't be used, tires that wouldn't be worn, spare parts that wouldn't be installed, food that there wouldn't be time to eat. It was all there, just in case. And the men who put it there knew better than anyone that if they used the tools or the spare parts or ate much of the food it would mean they weren't winning the race.

Charles Darwin was right. Only the fittest survive. The high-speed aboriginal jungle war in deepest, darkest Indianapolis proves that, and even the very fittest are bruised and breathing hard at the finish. The casualties in the annual struggle that shoves aside thirty-two of the tribe and leaves one unconquered chieftain, began early and continued throughout.

Even as the herd of thirty-three race cars safely manuevered through the first turn, those who were not even prepared to be a part of the battle were struck down. The pace car, sprinting muscularly down the pit lane, plowed into a stand full of photographers and littered the battlefield with twenty-four bodies. As the wounded photographers were loaded onto ambulances one by one to head for the sick bay, the ranks of the original combatants were already being thinned out.

As early as the fourth lap, race cars were sending up smoke signals which could only be translated as big trouble. Mario Andretti, the big survivor two years ago, was the first. The officials waved the black flag at him, but he refused to surrender. George Snider and Rick Muther were next to weaken. Snider's machinery was not strong enough to continue; Muther's was mended and fought on.

As Mark Donohue, the sleekest and fittest warrior from the beginning, lapped his first victims, others slipped away from the action long enough to adjust their slipping armament. A. J. Foyt, Jim Malloy, Cale Yarborough, and Bobby Unser fled to the pits to try to adapt to racing's own process of natural selection.

Andretti, whose car had been given an engineering award earlier in the month, found the one flaw in that engineering—the car could not march through another car's oil. Neither could those of his teammate Steve Krisiloff, Mel Kenyon, and Gordon Johncock, and all four were suddenly out of the fray.

They started falling like flies then. Larry Dickson, Art Pollard, Mark Donohue, Wally Dallenbach, Bob Harkey, Bentley Warren, and Sam Sessions all parked their war horses before the fight was half over. Muther and David Hobbs, the British enlistee, came together on the front straightaway and the explosive crash left both running for cover. Pieces of race cars flew like spears, one ricocheting off the helmet of a startled Al Unser as he skirted the skirmish.

The list of non-survivors grew. Joe Leonard, Denis Hulme, Yarborough, George Follmer, and Lloyd Ruby were added when their engines broke under the strain.

Bobby Unser and Mike Mosley, among others, were ducking in and out of the pits with wounds difficult to heal. The two met a little later along the wall at the end of the fourth turn, Unser walking away from the flame-throwing conflict with only a headache and Mosley carried away to a hospital as the most-seriously injured casualty of the day.

That left only a dozen of the fittest to carry on the battle. Some of those—like Johnny Rutherford, Roger McCluskey, Gary Bettenhausen, Dick Simon, and Denny Zimmerman—were only hanging on for what they could, after innumerable furloughs in the pits.

And through the jungle brush rustled Al Unser, the fittest for the second straight year. There had been chinks in his armor, too —his right rear tire needed changing three times more than it should have—but none was fatal.

The only other survivor who might have pulled Unser down, Peter Revson in one of the fearsome McLaren battlewagons, was burdened with a car that "didn't feel right" and a reluctance to move in for the kill on the last yellow-flag moratorium.

And so Al Unser led the other stragglers—Revson, Foyt, Malloy, Billy Vukovich, Donnie Allison, Bud Tingelstad, Zimmerman, McCluskey, Bettenhausen, Simon, and Rutherford—to the golden spoils that belong to the victorious.

Unser's tribe signaled him at the close of the battle with a chalked message that read: "You're the greatest."

To which Darwin would surely have added: "You're the fittest. You survived."

The line of red wreckers rolled solemnly down the pit lane like a procession of misshapen funeral caissons. Suspended grotesquely behind them, the remains of once-graceful race cars swayed in awkward unison. The track still, the race over, the wreckers bore the mechanical corpses in silent cadence to their garage area catafalques.

The red tumbrels shuffled past the emptying pits, past the crush of people encircling a wreathed and smiling Al Unser, and cautiously through the gate to the garage area.

First came the olive-green car of Mel Kenyon, its nose pushed back in hideous accordion-like pleats between its front wheels. Spinning in another car's oil on the eleventh lap, Kenyon's car had nosed into the third-turn wall and was hit by another machine that flew across its cockpit. Kenyon, crouched tight in the cockpit when the other car skimmed over him, escaped with an ugly gash on his leg and the clear imprint of a tire tread on his helmet.

Next came the swaying hulk of the deep-blue Penske McLaren of Mark Donohue. Sleek and magnificent when it leaped into the lead at the very beginning of the race, its side was now ripped wide open, its skin thinly coated with the white residue from fire extinguishers. Donohue, who pulled away easily from the field before his gearbox failed on the sixty seventh lap, was nowhere near his car when it was decimated. He had been back in his pits for over an hour when another car careened into the parked Mc-Laren, smashing it against the inner retaining wall.

The pimiento-red machine of Mario Andretti drifted by next, its nose twisted to one side and covered with the same white fire-extinguisher coating. It skated through the same oil Kenyon had, hit another car, and spun to a halt in the infield.

Another glowing red car followed Andretti's, its front wheels cocked unnaturally to the right. This one, nearly identical to the one dangling from the wrecker ahead, was driven by Andretti's young teammate, Steve Krisiloff. It had been Krisiloff's mount, its engine exploding, that laid down the oil slick Andretti and Kenyon had swirled through. He spun through the infield grass with Andretti, bringing Andy Granatelli's lofty aspirations to a swift conclusion before his two cars had gone thirty miles.

Next came the midnight-blue and white Eagle of Bobby Unser, the car ex-racer Dan Gurney had hoped would finally make him a winner at Indianapolis. It was no winner now, its body bent out of shape, its rear corner torn away. The car had pranged the wall when Unser, as he closed in on second-place runner Peter Revson, swerved to avoid a crashing machine in front of him exiting turn four on the 165th lap. The jarring crash had given Unser a nagging headache to share with the disheartened Gurney.

The next wrecker carried the orange machine of Gordon Johncock, its wheels askew, its nose missing. It had been Johncock who had collided with Andretti, then pounded into and over Kenyon's car in that early-race melee.

At the rear of the procession came the mangled, unrecognizable carcass of the car driven by young Mike Mosley. Its white skin turned ghostly by the powdery residue from the fire extinguishers, the car was only a battered, wheel-less shell. Mosley had cracked into the outer wall, then shot across in front of Bobby Unser and piled into Donohue's parked machine, exploding in a ball of flame against the inside wall at the head of the front straightaway. Pulled from the fiery wreckage by speedway workers and fellow driver Gary Bettenhausen, Mosley left the speedway grounds in a screaming ambulance with a broken leg, broken foot, broken elbow, and burns on his hands and face.

Though Mosley's smashed machine was the last to be hauled through the garage area gate, two others had also made the slow, grim trip. They had begun the grisly procession some ninety minutes before. The dark-blue car of David Hobbs and the white-and-orange machine of Rick Muther traveled the same route after banging together along the main straightaway on lap 112.

The Hobbs car, the second of the proud Penske stable entries, hung clumsily from the wrecker, its nose ripped off and its front wheels bent at a bizarre angle. Muther's machine, a snub-nosed racer to start with, was sliced off at the front firewall, wheels absent and silvery rods hanging loose. Muther had swerved to miss the slowing Hobbs and clipped the inside wall with his rear

Bob Harkey, the man on the "bubble," during the
last minutes of qualifying for the 1971 Indy 500.

wheel. His car darted across the track and rammed the unsuspecting Englishman, with both cars smashing against the outer
wall.

Muther's whirling car then tilted up on two wheels as it slithered down the track, teetered for a long moment, and dropped back down onto the track. Spinning to a stop in the middle of the track, Hobbs jumped from the cockpit of his car and dashed to the safety of the pit area as unblemished cars bore down on him. Muther followed a few seconds later, hobbling to the inner wall on a badly bruised foot.

The nine cars, immaculate and beautiful when the race began, passed before speechless spectators as they were borne indelicately to the dark coffins of their garages.

Nine cars, maimed and mutilated even more than their drivers in the inevitable carnage which accompanies the discovery of greater speed on the unchanging Indianapolis course—the funereal parade of their destroyed bodies offered stark testimony of the violence the quest for greater speed visits upon machines . . . and upon the men who drive them.

Lines of people shuffled along the rows of grandstand seats toward the jammed aisles. Like slow, bulging rivers, the columns drained down from the stands and curled around through the exit corridors. The crowd, weary and crushed uncomfortably together, made only a weak murmur, punctuated with an occasional intoxicated laugh.

The rows of seats, their dark green boards numbered with white paint, were almost deserted. Two men with cans of beer in their hands, a woman tossing left-over food into a picnic basket, a young boy tossing an empty beer can in the air, interrupted the landscape of green boards and stenciled white numbers.

A young man in a college sweatshirt and battered tan hat reared up from his seat and crowed loudly, flapping his arms like a giant, unsteady pelican. He collapsed back onto the seat, belched, and jerked a cup of beer to his mouth.

The jostling streams of people poured from the exits, feeding the larger sea that pressed toward the outside gates of the speedway.

Beer coolers, carried high and dry earlier in the day, sagged near the ground, dripping water along the paved walkways.

A bare-chested man rose up from the infield grass and, rubbing his eyes, asked those passing by, "Who won?"

One column of people flooded through the garage area gate. They walked lazily along the rows of garages, examining race cars and taking pictures.

Inside the garages, men in grease-stained trousers drank beer and talked. Those who had finished the race showed their satisfaction with smiles. Those who had not showed their resignation the same way. Those who had not raced at all talked easily as they walked along. They talked of how Al Unser had won at Indy again, how Mark Donohue could have won if he'd finished, how they had seen Bill Vukovich win two 500s in a row fifteen years ago, how a television star had waved at them during the pre-race parade.

They talked on as they plodded out through the infield, the speedway gates, the parking lots. They kept on talking as they climbed into their dust-coated cars and drove them into the creeping lines of traffic edging toward the streets outside the speedway.

As the sun dropped behind the empty grandstands along the front straightaway, they were beginning to arrive home. They were telling their friends about the race—the parts of it they saw —and turning on their television sets to watch the parts they missed.

By the next morning, they had begun talking of going back next year to see it all over again.

For the Indy crowd, as always, there was a whole year to remember the thrill of "The 500," to talk about it with friends from time to time, and to look forward to being a part of it again next time.

Gasoline Alley, Indianapolis Motor Speedway 1971.

GLOSSARY

AAA—American Automobile Association, chief sanctioning body for oval-track races in U. S. until 1955.

accessory company—Manufacturer of auto parts, such as tires, spark plugs, etc., who produces special racing version of its product.

ACCUS—Automobile Competition Committee for the U. S., made up of officials from top national sanctioning bodies who represent U. S. interests in Federation Internationale de l'Automobile activities.

aerodynamic styling—Aircraft-like styling techniques that utilize wings, airfoils, spoilers, and other devices to reduce wind resistance and exert downward forces on vehicle.

AHRA—American Hot Rod Association, sanctioning body for drag-racing events.

amateur—Racing participant who competes primarily for personal pleasure, rather than for profit.

ARCA—Automobile Racing Club of America, sanctioning body for late-model stock car races.

axle—Solid horizontal shaft on which road wheels rotate.

back marker—Car running near rear of race field.

back off—To let up on accelerator, reduce speed.

backstretch—On oval track, straightaway opposite starting line.

backup car—Car held in reserve by race team in case primary car malfunctions or is wrecked.

bank—Tilted section of race track, usually a turn, where outer edge is elevated higher than inner edge.

black flag—Signals car into pits for consultation because of apparent mechanical malfunction or infraction of race rules.

blower—Supercharger or turbocharger.

blown engine—Major engine failure.

bore—Diameter of engine cylinder.

brake fade—Loss of braking ability in car due to brakes overheating under constant use.

BRM—British Racing Motors, British auto factory which builds Grand Prix and Can-Am racing cars.

bubble—Status of slowest qualifier for race field, who remains "on the bubble" until faster qualifier bumps him from field or qualifications end.

bullring—Any small, crude race track.

buy the farm—Die in a racing crash.

Can-Am—Canadian-American Challenge Cup series, races for unlimited sports racing cars staged at road race courses in U. S. and Canada by Sports Car Club of America.

championship cars—Open-wheel, open-cockpit cars raced in Indianapolis 500 and other oval-track races on United States Auto Club's "Championship Trail."

chassis—Basic structural unit of race car, including frame, axles and suspension components.

checkered flag—Signals end of race.

chicane—Small S-turn on race course.

chief steward—Race official who supervises rules enforcement, track workers and conduct of race.

Christmas Tree—Electronically-controlled lights used to start drag races, consists of red, yellow, and green lights on pole at starting line.

chute—Any straight section of race track, particularly short sections between the turns at each end of Indianapolis Motor Speedway and similar tracks.

cockpit—Driver's compartment in racing car.

compound—Mixture of rubber and chemicals used in racing tire.

CSI—Commission Sportive Internationale, rules-making arm of Federation Internationale de l'Automobile.

cubic inches—Unit of measure for size of automotive engine, determined by multiplying square of cylinder bore times piston stroke times number of cylinders times .785. Outside U. S., measured in cubic centimeters or liters (1,000 c.c.).

Daytona—Daytona International Speedway, built in 1959 at Daytona Beach, Florida, 2.5-mile tri-oval with 3.8-mile road race course through infield, oval turns banked at thirty-one degrees.

downshift—Changing from higher gear to lower one while racing, an important technique in road racing.

drafting—Following another car very closely at high speed to take advantage of decreased wind resistance. Also known as *slipstreaming.*

dragster—Specially-built drag-racing car on long rail-type chassis, with one or two engines of unlimited size.

drift—Controlled four-wheel slide through a turn.

elapsed time—In drag-racing, time recorded by car from starting line to finish line. Abbreviated *e.t.*

eliminated—Defeated in drag race.

esses—Series of S-turns on road race course.

EZ—Common pit-board message advising driver to slow his pace when advantage over trailing cars appears secure.

Ferrari—Italian auto factory, builds Grand Prix, Can-Am, and sports racing cars.

FIA—Federation Internationale de l'Automobile, governing body for international racing events.

figure-8—Form of racing where cars compete on 8-shaped track.

fishtail—When rear end of car whips from side to side; usually indicates driver has lost control.

flat-out—Racing at maximum speed. Also called *full bore* or *full tilt.*

flying start—Racing procedure where race field approaches starting line in two or three-abreast formation, gradually reaching racing speed by the time cars hit the starting line.

footprint—Surface area of racing tire which actually makes contact with ground.

formula car—Any of several types of single-seat, open-cockpit, open-wheel racing cars, most familiar of which are Grand

Prix (formula one) machines in Europe and Formula 5000 in U. S.

four-wheel drive—Mechanical system in which engine power is transmitted directly to four wheels instead of two.

fuel injection—Metered system which feeds fuel directly into cylinders of engine rather than through a carburetor.

Funny Car—Lightweight drag-racing car with supercharged engine and fiberglass body. (Also slang name given to rear-engine Indianapolis-type cars when they replaced front-engine roadsters in mid-1960s.)

garage area—Area at race track where race cars are repaired and stored prior to the race.

Grand American—Series of races for American sports sedans sanctioned by NASCAR, primarily at southern race tracks.

Grand National—Series of late-model stock car races sanctioned by NASCAR, primarily at southern oval tracks.

Grand Prix—Any of the races counting toward World Driving Championship, held at tracks in various countries in Europe, North America, South America, and Africa. Also known as *formula one.*

Grand Slam—Victories by same driver in NASCAR Grand National races at five original superspeedways in the South—Daytona, Darlington, Atlanta, Charlotte, and Rockingham.

green flag—Signals start of race and remains displayed during race when track is clear for full-speed racing.

grid—Alignment of cars in starting field for race.

groove—On oval tracks, fastest route around track, usually recognizable by heavy layer of rubber laid down by tires of cars following that route.

Group 7—Sports racing cars which compete in Canadian-American Challenge Cup series, large two-seaters with unlimited engine size and minimum of restrictions in body and chassis design.

guardrail—Metal barrier erected along edge of race track to prevent cars from skidding into trees, spectator areas, or other hazards.

gymkhana—Competitive event where entrants race against the clock by driving through twisting course defined by rubber pylons. Also called *autocross* or *slalom*.

hairpin—Extremely sharp turn on road racing course.

half-shaft—Short shaft which replaces solid axle in transmitting power to rear wheels in rear-engine racing cars.

heel and toe—Driving technique where one foot, usually the right, is used to operate both accelerator and brake pedals.

hemi—Auto engine with hemispherical combustion chambers.

hobby stock—Stock racing car with very few modifications.

homologation—Procedure by which auto manufacturers verify that necessary number of model of car has been produced to meet standards set for racing events.

IMCA—International Motor Contest Association, sanctioning body for stock car, sprint car, and midget races.

IMSA—International Motor Sports Association, sanctioning body for sports car, formula car, and small sedan races.

Indianapolis—Indianapolis Motor Speedway, built in 1909 in Indianapolis, Indiana, 2.5-mile oval with turns banked at nine degrees.

Indy-car—Open-wheel, open-cockpit cars with special racing engines raced in Indianapolis 500. Also called *championship cars*.

infield—Area enclosed by race track, excluding pits and garage areas.

inverted start—Racing start where fastest cars are placed at rear of field.

lap—One complete trip around race track.

lapping—Process where leading cars pass cars which are one or more laps behind.

LeMans—Road race course at LeMans, France, 8.36-mile circuit made up primarily of public roads.

letting it all hang out—Driving at, or beyond, limits of car and-or track.

line—In road racing, route used by particular driver or drivers to go through turn.

Lola—British auto factory, builds formula, Can-Am, and sports racing cars.

lose it—Lose control of race car at high speed.

Lotus—British auto factory, builds Grand Prix, Indianapolis, and sports racing cars.

magneto—Alternator which produces electric current for ignition system of race car.

mainstretch—On oval track, straightaway directly in front of main grandstand. Also known as *frontstretch* or *main straightaway*.

marshal—Flagman, communication worker, or other official at road race.

McLaren—British race car factory, founded by late Bruce McLaren, builds Grand Prix, Indianapolis, and formula cars.

methanol—Alcohol-based fuel ingredient used in Indy-cars and some drag-racing cars.

midget—Small upright racing car with wheelbase of roughly six feet, open-wheel and open-cockpit, raced by USAC and several smaller sanctioning bodies.

Mid-Ohio—Mid-Ohio Sports Car Course, 2.4-mile road race course located near Lexington, Ohio.

monocoque—Race car chassis designed without frame, with body and chassis unitized into one structure.

Mosport—Mosport Park, 2.459-mile road race course located near Bowmanville, Ontario.

move-over flag—Blue flag with diagonal orange stripe, signals slower cars to move aside to let leading cars pass them.

NASCAR—National Association for Stock Car Auto Racing, sanctioning body for late-model stock, sports sedan, and modified stock car races, mostly at oval tracks in the South.

NHRA—National Hot Rod Association, sanctioning body for drag-racing events.

nitromethane—Special fuel blend used in Indy-cars and some drag-racing cars for temporary horsepower increase.

Nomex—One of fire-resistant fabrics used in racing driving suits.

Novi—Indianapolis-type car introduced in 1946 by Ed and Bud Winfield, featured powerful custom-built V-8 engine and front-wheel drive, never won at Indy.

Nurburgring—Road race course near Cologne, West Germany, 14.2-mile circuit built in mid-1930s under auspices of Adolf Hitler.

Offy—Four-cylinder racing engine designed by Fred Offenhauser and Harry Miller, used in many Indy-cars, sprint cars, and midgets.

oil cooler—Small radiator-like unit used to cool oil in racing car.

on his head—Upside-down in racing crash.

Ontario—Ontario Motor Speedway, 2.5-mile oval (nearly identical to Indianapolis track) with 3.194-mile road race course through infield, built in 1970 near Ontario, California.

open-cockpit—Car without cab or roof around driver's compartment.

open-wheel—Car without fenders around wheels.

out of shape—Losing control of race car, as evidenced by skidding, wiggling, spinning, etc.

oval track—Race track with elliptical shape, usually symmetrical with four similar turns and two long straightaways.

oversteer—Steering condition in which front wheels turn too quickly, causing rear of car to slide. Also called *pinch*.

pace car—Passenger car used to lead race field around track on one or more laps prior to start of race and on yellow-flag laps during race.

pace lap—Non-racing trip around track by race field immediately before flying start.

paddock—At road race course, infield area set aside as combination work and parking area for race teams. Also section of seats atop main grandstand at Indianapolis.

parade lap—Non-racing lap where race field tours track slowly in formation for viewing by spectators, precedes pace lap.

PDA—Professional Drivers Association, quasi-union formed by NASCAR Grand National drivers.

pieces—Slang term for components or parts of race car or engine.

pit—Stall or space, usually alongside main straightaway, where cars stop for fuel, tires, or repairs during race. Long row of such spaces referred to as *pits* or *pit area.*

pit board—Chalkboard held by crew of race car to give signals and pass messages to driver during race.

pit popsy—Attractive young lady in pit area, presence generally is more decorative than functional.

pit road—Road leading into, past, and out of pit area. Also called *pit lane.*

pit stop—Stop made by competing car at pit during race.

Pocono—Pocono International Speedway, 2.5-mile tri-oval built in 1971 at Mount Pocono, Pennsylvania.

pole—First starting position in race field, usually inside position on front row, outside of front row at some superspeedways.

pony car—Small U. S. sports sedan, such as Ford Mustang, Chevrolet Camaro, Plymouth Barracuda, American Motors Javelin, etc., raced in Trans-Am and Grand American series.

pop—Slang for nitromethane.

Porsche—German auto factory, builds Can-Am and sports racing cars.

production—Model of car produced for general highway use.

promoter—Individual who organizes and finances racing event.

Pro Stock—Class in drag racing for highly-modified late-model U. S. production cars.

prototype—Sports car that does not conform to usual homologation production figures, normally built specifically for racing.

purse—Total amount of prize money awarded to race entrants.

push-rod engine—Auto engine with overhead valves but no overhead camshaft, with metal rods transmitting motion of camshaft to valves.

qualifying—Determination of race field alignment by timed laps, either one or more laps on clear track (in oval racing) or laps run during practice period with other cars on track (in road racing).

rain tire—Racing tire specially designed for use on wet track.

rally—Competitive event where entrants attempt to maintain pre-determined average speed over each of several segments of prescribed course, often conducted on public roads and highways.

red flag—Signals stoppage of race.

relief driver—Driver who takes place of starting driver during race.

retaining wall—Concrete barrier around edge of race track.

revs—Engine revolutions per minute. Abbreviated *r.p.m.*

ride—Assignment to drive certain car in race or series of races.

road course—Race course with irregular shape, usually with several right and left-hand turns of different sizes and shapes, often consists of public roads or facsimiles thereof.

roadster—Indy-car design of 1950s and early 1960s, front-engine car with solid axles and engine offset to the left.

rollbar—Loop of tubular steel projecting above the cockpit of a race car to protect the driver if the car overturns.

roll-cage—Box-shaped structure of tubular steel inside a stock car cockpit or above a sprint or midget car cockpit to protect the driver if the car overturns.

rookie—Driver competing in a race for the first time.

sanctioning body—An organization which governs series of races, licenses competitors, sets rules and regulations for entrants, and negotiates race purses.

sandbagging—Driving below maximum speeds in pre-race practice to conceal the potential of the entry.

sanitary—Extremely clean or efficient, applied to race cars, racing teams, pit crews, or races.

scattershield—Protective steel housing around clutch and flywheel assembly.

SCCA—Sports Car Club of America, sanctioning body for Can-Am, Trans-Am, Formula 5000 (A), and amateur road races.

scrutineer—Road race official who inspects entered cars to verify that they comply with race rules.

Sebring—Road race course near Sebring, Florida, 5.2-mile circuit laid out on abandoned airfield, will be moved to a new course nearby in 1973.

shoes—Slang for tires.

shut the gate—To block the path of a car which is attempting to pass.

shut-off—Point on track at which driver, approaching a turn, lets up on accelerator and reduces speed.

slicks—Wide, flat-surface tires used on rear wheels of drag-racing cars.

slide—To skid sideways.

slingshot—Dragster design where driver sits behind rear wheels.

slingshotting—Driving technique in stock car racing where one car, drafting another, darts to one side and whips past other car in a sudden burst of reserve power.

sorting out—Lengthy series of test runs to discover engine, suspension, or handling problems in race car.

soup—Rain or standing water on the race track.

spin—To lose control of race car and revolve in circular motion.

spoiler—Air deflector mounted to front or rear edge of the car to combat lift tendencies at high speeds.

sponsor—Company or individual who finances a race car or team for advertising purposes.

sports car—Small, agile passenger car, designed for highway driving but easily adapted for racing.

sports racing car—Sports car built specifically for racing.

sprint car—Open-cockpit, open-wheel racing car, similar to the midgets but with a longer wheelbase and larger engine, raced by USAC, IMCA, and several smaller sanctioning bodies.

squirrelly—Slang for erratic or incompetent driving.

stock—Unmodified production car or component.

stockblock—Racing engine with cylinder block from production car, usually a push-rod engine.

stock car—Racing car which resembles a production car but may be extensively modified for racing.

straightaway—Any long, straight section of race track where high speeds are attained. Also called *straight*.

stroke—Distance piston travels inside engine cylinder.

stroking—Driving slower than possible to minimize chances of mechanical failure.

supercharger—Mechanical device which forces air into engine for greater horsepower.

supermodified—Racing car similar to sprint car, but often with a home-made body or a large wing above cockpit.

superspeedway—High-banked, high-speed oval or tri-oval race track of one mile or more, such as Daytona or Talladega.

suspension—Assembly of springs, shock absorbers, torsion bars, etc., which cushions road shocks and keeps wheels in constant contact with track surface.

swallow a valve—When a valve breaks and falls into the engine cylinder.

tachometer—Instrument panel guage which measures the speed of the engine in revolutions per minute.

Talladega—Alabama International Speedway, 2.6-mile tri-oval built in 1969 at Talladega, Alabama, turns banked at thirty-three degrees.

time trials—Qualifying runs against clock to determine starting lineup for race.

torque—Twisting force produced by rotating shaft or engine, measured in foot-pounds.

torsion bar—Metal bar in suspension system that functions as a spring.

Trans-Am—Trans-American Championship for pony cars and small sports sedans, staged by SCCA at road race courses in U. S. and Canada.

trap—Section of race track monitored by electric-eye timers to record speeds of cars on that portion of track.

tread—The pattern cut into surface of tire.

tri-oval—Triangular-shaped race track (such as Daytona or Pocono).

turbocharger—Supercharger powered by exhaust gases instead of engine itself.

understeer—Steering condition in which front wheels turn slowly, allowing car body to shift into proper attitude for drifting through turn (unless understeer is excessive). Also called *push*.

USAC—United States Auto Club, sanctioning body for Indy-car, sprint car, midget, and stock car races, replaced AAA in 1955.

USRRC—United States Road Racing Championship, series of races for sports racing cars begun in 1963 by SCCA, discontinued after 1968 season. (Not to be confused with American Road Race of Champions, final national road racing meet of SCCA amateur race calendar.)

Victory Lane—Area where post-race ceremonies are conducted with race winner, most commonly associated with Indianapolis 500.

wastegate—Turbocharger component that permits exhausting of air.

Watkins Glen—Road race course near Watkins Glen, New York, 2.4-mile circuit, site of U. S. Grand Prix.

wheelbase—Distance between center of front wheel and center of rear wheel of car.

white flag—Signals one lap remaining in race.

wing—Airfoil mounted above front and-or rear of race car to induce downward thrust on car, thus improving traction and stability at speed.

yellow flag (or light)—Signals wreck or other hazard on race track; drivers are required to reduce speed and refrain from passing other competitors.